Broadway Musical

Andrew Parry

Published by Andrew Parry, 2024.

While every precaution has been taken in the preparation of this book, the publisher assumes no responsibility for errors or omissions, or for damages resulting from the use of the information contained herein.

BROADWAY MUSICAL

First edition. October 17, 2024.

Copyright © 2024 Andrew Parry.

ISBN: 979-8227509673

Written by Andrew Parry.

Table of Contents

The Golden Age: A History of the Broadway Musical

Broadway musicals have long held a central place in American culture, representing not just a form of entertainment but a reflection of societal values, creativity, and ambition. The Golden Age of Broadway, typically considered the period from the 1940s to the early 1960s, is often seen as the pinnacle of musical theater, producing some of the most iconic and enduring shows ever staged. It was during this time that the art form truly came into its own, blending story, music, and dance into a seamless theatrical experience that captivated audiences and set the standard for what a Broadway musical could be.

The birth of the Broadway musical as we know it can be traced back to the late 19th and early 20th centuries when operettas, vaudeville, and variety shows dominated the stage. While these earlier forms laid the foundation, it wasn't until the emergence of the fully integrated musical that Broadway began to take on the shape it holds today. A fully integrated musical is one where the songs, dances, and storylines are interwoven so that each element serves to advance the plot and develop the characters. This revolutionary approach became a hallmark of the Golden Age.

One of the first musicals to embody this fully integrated approach was *Oklahoma!*, which premiered in 1943. Written by Richard Rodgers and Oscar Hammerstein II, *Oklahoma!* was groundbreaking because its songs were not merely musical interludes but integral to the storytelling. Characters expressed their deepest emotions through song, and the choreography, led by the legendary Agnes de Mille, served to illustrate and heighten the emotional stakes of the narrative. The success of *Oklahoma!* marked the beginning of the Golden Age, setting a new standard for what Broadway musicals could achieve artistically and commercially.

The 1940s, 1950s, and early 1960s saw the emergence of some of Broadway's most celebrated works, written by the giants of musical theater: Rodgers and Hammerstein, Leonard Bernstein, Stephen Sondheim, Lerner and Loewe, and Irving Berlin, among others. During this period, musicals such as *Carousel, South Pacific, The King and I, My Fair Lady*, and *West Side Story* dominated the stage, not only showcasing brilliant compositions but also tackling complex social issues. *South Pacific*, for example, explored themes of racial prejudice, while *West Side Story*, with music by Bernstein and lyrics by a young Sondheim, reimagined *Romeo and Juliet* in the context of urban gang violence and ethnic tensions.

Another key feature of the Golden Age was the rise of the director-choreographer, a single creative force guiding both the staging and the dance elements of a show. This new approach helped create a more cohesive vision for musicals, as seen in the works of Jerome Robbins, who revolutionized Broadway with his work on *West Side Story* and *Fiddler on the Roof*. Robbins was a master at using dance not just as a form of entertainment but as a means of driving the narrative forward and giving the audience deeper insights into the characters.

The Golden Age wasn't just about individual shows; it was about the entire Broadway ecosystem flourishing in a way that hasn't been replicated since. Audiences were flocking to theaters, eager to experience the magic of live musical performances. Broadway was at the heart of American culture, influencing not only theater but film, television, and popular music. Many Broadway hits were adapted into successful Hollywood films, extending their reach far beyond the confines of the Great White Way.

But as with all golden ages, this period eventually came to an end. By the late 1960s, the cultural and political landscape of America had shifted dramatically. The optimism and idealism of the post-World War II era gave way to the turmoil of the Vietnam War, the civil rights movement, and the counterculture revolution. Musicals like *Hair* and

Jesus Christ Superstar reflected these changes, pushing Broadway in new directions with rock music, edgier content, and more experimental storytelling techniques. The once-reliable formula of the traditional Broadway musical began to evolve, as audiences' tastes grew more diverse and fragmented.

Despite the end of the Golden Age, its influence continues to be felt. The musicals from this era remain a cornerstone of the Broadway repertoire, constantly revived and reinterpreted for new generations of theatergoers. *Oklahoma!* has been restaged with a stripped-down, darker aesthetic, while *West Side Story* has been given new life through both stage revivals and Steven Spielberg's 2021 film adaptation. The songs from these shows have become part of the American songbook, with numbers like "Some Enchanted Evening," "I Could Have Danced All Night," and "Tonight" remaining beloved classics.

The Golden Age of Broadway was a period of incredible creativity, collaboration, and artistic achievement. It not only gave birth to some of the greatest musicals ever written but also set the template for what a Broadway musical could be—a rich blend of music, storytelling, and spectacle that could entertain, inspire, and challenge its audiences. Today's musicals continue to build on the foundation laid during this time, pushing the boundaries of the form while paying homage to the great works that came before.

As we look to the future of Broadway, the lessons of the Golden Age remain relevant. The key to creating the next hit Broadway musical lies in understanding how the great masters of the past crafted their works, how they used music and storytelling to speak to their audiences, and how they dared to innovate while remaining true to the traditions that made Broadway the cultural powerhouse it still is today.

Legendary Shows: The Great Musicals That Shaped Broadway

Broadway's legendary shows are the cornerstones upon which modern musical theater has been built. These productions not only set new standards of excellence but also created the framework that contemporary musicals still follow. The great musicals that shaped Broadway each brought something fresh and innovative to the stage, whether through groundbreaking music, unforgettable characters, or daring storytelling techniques. By examining these iconic productions, we can better understand the evolution of Broadway and the elements that make a musical truly legendary.

One of the earliest and most important shows to shape Broadway was *Show Boat* (1927), with music by Jerome Kern and lyrics by Oscar Hammerstein II. *Show Boat* was revolutionary for its time because it dealt with serious social issues like racism and miscegenation, subjects rarely addressed in musical theater. The show broke away from the traditional, light-hearted operettas and vaudeville-style performances that were popular during the early 20th century. Instead, *Show Boat* wove a compelling narrative into its music, demonstrating that musicals could be vehicles for significant storytelling. The song "Ol' Man River" became an anthem for the struggles of the working class and minorities, and the show set the stage for future productions that would tackle complex themes.

Fast forward to 1943, and another game-changing show premiered: *Oklahoma!*. Created by the legendary duo of Richard Rodgers and Oscar Hammerstein II, *Oklahoma!* was the first fully integrated musical, where the songs, dances, and plot all worked together to tell a cohesive story. Before *Oklahoma!*, musical numbers were often added as mere entertainment, interrupting the flow of the narrative. But in *Oklahoma!*, the music was inseparable from the story, helping to define characters and move the plot forward. The dream ballet choreographed by Agnes de Mille was another innovation, using dance to explore the characters' inner emotions. *Oklahoma!* was a massive success and solidified the Rodgers and Hammerstein partnership as one of the most influential in Broadway history.

Rodgers and Hammerstein continued to dominate Broadway throughout the 1940s and 1950s with hit after hit, including *Carousel* (1945), *South Pacific* (1949), *The King and I* (1951), and *The Sound of Music* (1959). Each of these musicals introduced fresh ideas, from the deeply emotional storytelling in *Carousel* to the exploration of racial prejudice in *South Pacific*. *The King and I* broke new ground with its East-meets-West narrative and the creation of complex, multi-dimensional characters, while *The Sound of Music* showcased how personal family stories could become epic tales of resilience against tyranny.

During the 1950s, another landmark show emerged that would push the boundaries of what musical theater could achieve. *West Side Story* (1957), with music by Leonard Bernstein, lyrics by Stephen Sondheim, and choreography by Jerome Robbins, was a radical reinterpretation of Shakespeare's *Romeo and Juliet*. Set in the gritty streets of New York City, the show tackled themes of gang violence, immigration, and the American Dream. Robbins' electrifying choreography brought a new level of intensity to the dance sequences, particularly in iconic numbers like "America" and "The Dance at the Gym." Sondheim's lyrics were sharp, insightful, and emotionally charged, while Bernstein's score blended jazz, classical music, and Latin rhythms in a way that had never been heard on Broadway before. *West Side Story* was not just a musical; it was a social commentary, a work of art that reflected the turbulence and divisions of mid-century America.

Another great musical that left an indelible mark on Broadway is *My Fair Lady* (1956), written by Alan Jay Lerner and Frederick Loewe. Based on George Bernard Shaw's *Pygmalion*, the story follows the transformation of Eliza

Doolittle from a poor flower girl into a refined lady, underscoring themes of class, identity, and power. Rex Harrison's portrayal of the imperious Henry Higgins became iconic, and Lerner and Loewe's score, with songs like "I Could Have Danced All Night" and "Wouldn't It Be Loverly?", remains beloved by theatergoers to this day. *My Fair Lady* was celebrated not only for its witty dialogue and memorable music but also for its stunning costumes and set design, demonstrating how visual spectacle could enhance a show's appeal.

The 1960s ushered in a wave of change on Broadway, with musicals like *Fiddler on the Roof* (1964) taking center stage. With music by Jerry Bock, lyrics by Sheldon Harnick, and a book by Joseph Stein, *Fiddler on the Roof* tells the story of Tevye, a Jewish milkman in Tsarist Russia, struggling to maintain tradition in the face of changing times. *Fiddler on the Roof* was the first musical to focus on Jewish life and culture, and its themes of faith, family, and survival resonated deeply with audiences across the world. The score, featuring songs like "Tradition" and "If I Were a Rich Man," became instantly recognizable, while the show's emotional depth and universal themes of cultural identity made it a timeless classic.

As Broadway evolved, so too did the concept of what a musical could be. *Cabaret* (1966), with music by John Kander and lyrics by Fred Ebb, was a stark departure from the light-hearted fare of earlier decades. Set in 1930s Berlin, *Cabaret* uses the backdrop of the rise of Nazism to explore themes of decadence, political corruption, and societal collapse. The show's innovative use of a nightclub as both a setting and a metaphor for the larger political events taking place added layers of meaning to the story, while the Kit Kat Club's songs like "Willkommen" and "Maybe This Time" served as chilling reflections on the characters' struggles.

Perhaps no musical has had as lasting an impact on Broadway as *Hamilton* (2015), created by Lin-Manuel Miranda. *Hamilton* broke new ground by blending hip-hop, R&B, and traditional musical theater to tell the story of Alexander Hamilton and the founding of the United States. The show's diverse casting and innovative use of music brought Broadway to a new generation of theatergoers, while its exploration of themes like immigration, ambition, and legacy made it a defining cultural moment. *Hamilton* became a worldwide sensation, earning both critical acclaim and commercial success, and it demonstrated that musicals could still be at the forefront of both artistic and social change.

From *Show Boat* to *Hamilton*, these legendary shows have shaped Broadway and left an indelible mark on the world of theater. Each one pushed the boundaries of what a musical could achieve, whether through music, storytelling, choreography, or visual design. They stand as enduring examples of how the art form continues to evolve, inspiring future generations of creators to take bold risks and create the next great Broadway hit.

The Evolution of Broadway: Tradition Meets Innovation

Broadway is a living, breathing entity that has evolved dramatically over the decades. At its core, Broadway has always been about entertaining audiences, but what makes it truly remarkable is its ability to reflect the changing times while holding onto the traditions that made it great. The evolution of Broadway is a fascinating journey that demonstrates the balance between tradition and innovation—how the old guard and new ideas collide to create something fresh, relevant, and exciting.

The origins of Broadway lie in European theatrical traditions, including operettas, vaudeville, and melodramas that dominated the stage in the late 19th and early 20th centuries. Shows of that era, like *The Black Crook* (1866), are often credited with laying the foundation for the modern musical, blending dramatic storytelling with song and dance. These early productions were grand spectacles, full of elaborate costumes, sets, and choruses, designed to dazzle audiences. The focus was primarily on entertainment—light-hearted romance, comedy, and spectacle—with little emphasis on deep character development or thematic complexity.

As the 20th century progressed, a shift began to occur. Audiences were growing more sophisticated, and producers and writers sought to create works that were not just entertaining but also meaningful. This period brought the first waves of innovation in Broadway's evolution, particularly with shows like *Show Boat* (1927), which introduced the idea that musicals could tackle serious subjects. This was a groundbreaking moment in Broadway history, as the production delved into issues of race, class, and relationships. Jerome Kern and Oscar Hammerstein II's work signaled the beginning of Broadway's evolution from mere spectacle to a medium capable of telling deeper, more complex stories.

However, it was the arrival of Richard Rodgers and Oscar Hammerstein II's *Oklahoma!* in 1943 that marked a significant turning point in Broadway's tradition-meets-innovation narrative. *Oklahoma!* was revolutionary because it fully integrated music, dance, and story into a cohesive whole. For the first time, every element of the production served to advance the plot and develop the characters. This approach became the hallmark of the Golden Age of Broadway, which saw the emergence of legendary musicals like *South Pacific* (1949), *The King and I* (1951), and *West Side Story* (1957). The shows of this era adhered to traditional storytelling structures—typically the three-act format with a clear beginning, middle, and end—while pushing boundaries in terms of content, choreography, and emotional depth.

What's notable about this period is how innovation didn't come at the expense of tradition. Instead, it built on the foundational elements that had always defined Broadway—big numbers, catchy songs, memorable characters—while elevating the art form. Rodgers and Hammerstein in particular were masters at weaving serious themes into the fabric of their shows, without sacrificing the entertainment value that audiences craved. *South Pacific* dealt with racial prejudice, while *The Sound of Music* (1959) explored themes of family, love, and political resistance. These shows demonstrated that Broadway could maintain its appeal while offering thought-provoking content.

As the 1960s dawned, Broadway began to undergo yet another shift, as societal changes filtered into the theater world. The rise of the counterculture movement, along with political upheavals such as the civil rights movement and the Vietnam War, created an atmosphere ripe for experimentation. Musicals like *Hair* (1967) reflected the rebellious spirit of the times, breaking with traditional Broadway conventions in favor of a more raw, avant-garde style. The score of *Hair* was heavily influenced by rock and roll, marking a significant departure from the classical, jazz, and pop styles that had dominated the Broadway stage. It was also one of the first musicals to explicitly address social issues such as war, race, and sexuality. *Hair* was a sign that Broadway was not just evolving; it was adapting to the cultural pulse of the nation.

This period also saw the emergence of Stephen Sondheim, whose work would revolutionize the Broadway musical form. Sondheim's musicals, including *Company* (1970), *Follies* (1971), and *Sweeney Todd* (1979), were notable for their complex characters, intricate lyrics, and unconventional structures. Sondheim broke away from the linear, plot-driven format of traditional musicals, often focusing on themes of existentialism, alienation, and psychological complexity. In doing so, he pushed Broadway into new, more cerebral territory, showing that the musical theater format could be a vehicle for introspective, intellectual storytelling. His work continues to influence modern Broadway, and his approach to lyrics and narrative complexity is now considered a standard to aspire to.

The evolution of Broadway didn't stop there. The 1980s and 1990s brought another wave of innovation, this time in the form of large-scale, blockbuster productions that defined the era of the "megamusical." Shows like *Cats* (1981), *Les Misérables* (1987), *The Phantom of the Opera* (1988), and *Miss Saigon* (1989) were characterized by lavish sets, grandiose musical scores, and spectacle-driven storytelling. These productions were often driven by international collaboration, particularly from the British theater scene, and were geared toward global audiences. While they maintained many of the traditional elements of Broadway musicals, such as memorable songs and emotional narratives, they were also influenced by the demands of an increasingly globalized entertainment market. The rise of the megamusical exemplified Broadway's ability to adapt and innovate within the framework of tradition, appealing to modern audiences while staying true to its roots.

The new millennium brought yet more changes to Broadway, particularly in the ways musicals were produced and the types of stories that were being told. Productions like *Rent* (1996), *Wicked* (2003), and *The Book of Mormon* (2011) showed that Broadway was willing to embrace edgier, more contemporary subject matter. *Rent*, in particular, was a watershed moment for Broadway. Drawing inspiration from Puccini's *La Bohème*, the musical explored themes of poverty, AIDS, and artistic struggle in 1990s New York City. Its rock-infused score, diverse cast, and raw emotional content marked a significant departure from the glossy, polished productions that had dominated the 1980s.

Innovation reached a new peak with Lin-Manuel Miranda's *Hamilton* (2015). *Hamilton* was revolutionary not only because of its subject matter—telling the story of Alexander Hamilton through rap and hip-hop—but also because of its casting, which featured actors of color portraying the Founding Fathers of the United States. *Hamilton* fused modern music with historical storytelling in a way that captured the imagination of audiences around the world, reinvigorating Broadway and drawing in a younger, more diverse audience. The success of *Hamilton* is a testament to how innovation, when built on a foundation of tradition, can lead to cultural phenomena that redefine Broadway.

Today, Broadway continues to evolve, embracing technology, new storytelling methods, and diverse voices. Shows like *Dear Evan Hansen* (2016), *Hadestown* (2019), and *Six* (2021) exemplify the contemporary Broadway landscape, blending traditional musical elements with modern sensibilities, while experimenting with form, style, and content. These productions demonstrate that Broadway is far from static; it remains a dynamic and innovative force in the world of theater, continually finding new ways to balance tradition with modernity.

The future of Broadway will no doubt continue this tradition of innovation, as new generations of creators push the boundaries of what a musical can be. Yet, at the heart of it all will always be the elements that have made Broadway endure: compelling stories, unforgettable characters, and music that moves audiences. Tradition meets innovation on Broadway, and the result is an art form that remains as vital and exciting as ever.

The Architects of Success: Great Musical Writers and Producers

The story of Broadway's success is not just one of captivating performances and breathtaking productions; it is also the tale of the creative minds behind the scenes—the architects of success—who wrote, composed, and produced some of the most iconic musicals ever staged. These individuals transformed Broadway from a local entertainment hub into a global cultural phenomenon, shaping the very fabric of musical theater as we know it today. The great musical writers and producers are the backbone of Broadway's golden age, but their influence extends far beyond any one era. In this chapter, we will explore the work of a few of these monumental figures who contributed to making Broadway a world-renowned institution.

One of the most significant duos in the history of Broadway is Richard Rodgers and Oscar Hammerstein II. Together, they revolutionized the musical theater landscape with their series of groundbreaking productions in the mid-20th century. Rodgers, the composer, and Hammerstein, the lyricist and book writer, were responsible for some of Broadway's greatest hits, including *Oklahoma!*, *Carousel*, *South Pacific*, *The King and I*, and *The Sound of Music*. Their work defined what we now consider the classic Broadway musical: a show in which music, lyrics, and plot were tightly interwoven, with every song serving to advance the narrative. Rodgers and Hammerstein's musicals were not just entertaining; they tackled complex social issues like racism, class inequality, and war, all while maintaining a sense of optimism and hope. Their influence on musical theater is immeasurable, setting a standard of excellence that continues to inspire writers and composers today.

Stephen Sondheim, a protégé of Hammerstein, also redefined the Broadway musical in his own right. Sondheim's works are renowned for their lyrical complexity, emotional depth, and willingness to explore darker, more cerebral themes. His musicals, such as *Sweeney Todd*, *Into the Woods*, *Company*, and *Follies*, are often characterized by their intricate narratives and sophisticated music. Unlike the traditional Broadway musical, where songs often provide lighthearted entertainment, Sondheim's music is inextricably linked to character development and psychological nuance. His ability to blend wit, melancholy, and insight into the human condition has earned him a reputation as one of the greatest composers and lyricists in Broadway history. Sondheim's work is particularly noted for pushing the boundaries of what musical theater can be, challenging audiences to think deeply while being entertained.

Another towering figure in the world of Broadway is Andrew Lloyd Webber. While Rodgers and Hammerstein established the Broadway musical as we know it, Lloyd Webber helped to bring it into the modern era. His works, such as *Jesus Christ Superstar*, *Evita*, *Cats*, and *The Phantom of the Opera*, are synonymous with the rise of the "megamusical" in the 1980s and 1990s. Lloyd Webber's musicals are characterized by their grandiose scale, memorable melodies, and visual spectacle. He introduced rock and pop music to the Broadway stage in a way that had never been done before, opening the door for a new generation of musicals that appealed to younger, more diverse audiences. *The Phantom of the Opera*, which debuted in 1986, is still running today, making it the longest-running show in Broadway history—a testament to Lloyd Webber's enduring impact on the theater.

The late 20th century also saw the rise of another dynamic duo, composer John Kander and lyricist Fred Ebb, who made their mark with shows like *Cabaret* and *Chicago*. Kander and Ebb's musicals often had a distinct edge to them, using entertainment as a means to explore serious themes such as corruption, fame, and societal decay. *Cabaret*, set in pre-Nazi Germany, used the Kit Kat Club as a metaphor for the political instability and moral decline of the time. *Chicago*, a satire on the American obsession with celebrity, is one of the most revived and beloved musicals on Broadway. The biting wit and dark humor of Kander and Ebb's shows were a refreshing contrast to the more sentimental tone of other Broadway productions, offering audiences a new perspective on the genre.

Producers have also played a crucial role in shaping Broadway's success, often acting as the visionary leaders who bring creative teams together and oversee the financial and logistical aspects of a production. One of the most influential producers in Broadway history is Harold Prince. Prince's career spanned over five decades, and he was instrumental in producing and directing some of the most iconic shows of all time, including *West Side Story*, *Fiddler on the Roof*, *Cabaret*, and *The Phantom of the Opera*. Prince had a unique ability to identify groundbreaking material and bring it to life on stage, often taking risks on unconventional shows that others might have deemed too avant-garde or challenging for mainstream audiences. His collaborations with Stephen Sondheim, in particular, were legendary, resulting in critically acclaimed productions like *Sweeney Todd* and *Follies*. Prince's influence on Broadway can still be felt today, as he helped to elevate the role of the director-producer as a central figure in the creative process.

Cameron Mackintosh, another influential producer, is often credited with bringing the "megamusical" phenomenon to Broadway. Mackintosh produced global hits like *Les Misérables*, *The Phantom of the Opera*, *Miss Saigon*, and *Cats*, turning them into international sensations. His knack for marketing and branding these shows—transforming them into cultural phenomena with logos, merchandise, and touring productions—was revolutionary for the theater industry. Mackintosh's vision for Broadway went beyond the stage, recognizing the potential for musicals to become global brands that could attract audiences from all corners of the world. His approach to producing changed the way Broadway shows were marketed and financed, making it possible for large-scale productions to thrive in an increasingly competitive entertainment landscape.

Lin-Manuel Miranda represents the next generation of musical creators, combining the traditions of Broadway with modern influences like hip-hop, R&B, and Latin music. His work, particularly *Hamilton*, has reinvigorated Broadway and brought it to a new, younger audience. *Hamilton* not only tells the story of America's founding through a contemporary musical lens but also features a diverse cast, challenging the traditional perceptions of who gets to tell America's story on stage. Miranda's ability to blend modern music with historical narrative has redefined what a Broadway musical can be, making him one of the most important voices in contemporary theater. His earlier work, *In the Heights*, also demonstrated his knack for weaving cultural identity into his storytelling, a theme that continues to resonate with modern audiences.

In exploring the great musical writers and producers, it becomes clear that Broadway's success has been shaped by individuals who dared to innovate while respecting the traditions of the genre. From the groundbreaking work of Rodgers and Hammerstein to the boundary-pushing productions of Stephen Sondheim, Andrew Lloyd Webber, and Lin-Manuel Miranda, these architects of success have continually redefined what Broadway can be. Their influence goes beyond the stage, shaping popular culture and inspiring future generations of creators to dream big, take risks, and create the next hit musical that will captivate audiences worldwide.

The Spark of Genius: Discovering Your Next Hit Idea

The spark of genius that ignites the creation of a hit Broadway musical often seems elusive. How does one discover that perfect idea that will resonate with audiences, stand the test of time, and leave an indelible mark on the world of musical theater? This question has been asked by countless writers, composers, and producers over the years, and while there is no single formula for success, there are certain commonalities and methods that can help guide the creative process.

The journey to finding the next hit Broadway idea often begins with a deep understanding of human nature. At the core of every great musical is a compelling story that speaks to universal emotions and experiences. Whether it's love, loss, ambition, or redemption, the best musicals connect with audiences on a personal level, making them feel seen, understood, and inspired. The first step in discovering your hit idea is to tap into these universal themes and consider how your story can evoke powerful emotions. Ask yourself: What do I want my audience to feel? What kind of journey do I want to take them on? By starting with the emotional core of your idea, you can ensure that your musical will have a resonance that transcends time and place.

One way to spark a great idea is to look to the past for inspiration. Many successful Broadway musicals are based on pre-existing stories, whether they are novels, plays, films, or historical events. *Les Misérables* was adapted from Victor Hugo's epic novel, *The Phantom of the Opera* was inspired by Gaston Leroux's mystery novel, and *Hamilton* took its cue from American history. The key to adapting a pre-existing work is to find a fresh angle or perspective that will breathe new life into the story. Consider how your adaptation can offer something unique—whether it's through an innovative musical style, a reimagined setting, or a focus on previously unexplored characters. For example, Lin-Manuel Miranda's *Hamilton* took the historical narrative of the American Revolution and infused it with hip-hop, R&B, and a diverse cast, making the story feel contemporary and relevant to a modern audience.

Another powerful source of inspiration is personal experience. Some of the most compelling musicals are born from deeply personal stories or observations about the world. Jonathan Larson's *Rent*, for instance, was inspired by his own experiences living in New York City during the AIDS crisis. The musical's exploration of love, loss, and the fragility of life resonated with audiences because it was rooted in real human struggles. Similarly, *In the Heights*, written by Lin-Manuel Miranda, drew upon his experiences growing up in Washington Heights, a predominantly Latinx neighborhood in Manhattan. By telling a story that was intimately connected to his own background and community, Miranda created a musical that felt authentic and groundbreaking.

When searching for your next hit idea, it's also important to think about the larger cultural and social context. Broadway musicals have often reflected the times in which they were created, whether intentionally or not. *West Side Story*, for example, explored issues of gang violence and racial tension in 1950s New York, while *Hair* was a direct response to the counterculture movement of the 1960s. Today's audiences are drawn to stories that feel timely and relevant, addressing the pressing issues of our time. This doesn't mean that your musical needs to be explicitly political, but it's worth considering how your idea can engage with contemporary conversations. Whether it's through themes of identity, social justice, climate change, or technology, tapping into the cultural zeitgeist can help ensure that your musical resonates with today's audiences.

Another important consideration when discovering your hit idea is genre. Broadway musicals come in many forms, from romantic comedies to tragedies, from historical dramas to fantastical adventures. Each genre offers its own set of challenges and opportunities, and the key is to find the one that best serves your story. Comedy musicals like *The Producers* and *Avenue Q* succeed because they provide a welcome escape for audiences, offering laughter and levity in a world that often feels heavy. On the other hand, dramas like *Dear Evan Hansen* and *Next to Normal* thrive by offering deep emotional experiences that challenge audiences to think and feel in new ways. When conceptualizing your musical, consider what genre will best suit the story you want to tell, and don't be afraid to play with genre conventions or combine elements from different genres to create something new and exciting.

Once you've identified a compelling story and genre, it's time to think about the music. The music of your Broadway musical should not only complement the story but also elevate it. Great musicals use music to enhance the emotional stakes, to reveal character, and to drive the plot forward. Whether your score is rooted in classical Broadway traditions, like *Rodgers and Hammerstein*, or infused with contemporary sounds, like *Hamilton*, it should feel integral to the storytelling. Consider how different musical styles can help convey the themes and emotions of your show. For instance, jazz might evoke a certain time period or atmosphere, while rock can bring a sense of rebellion or intensity. The right musical style can make all the difference in setting your musical apart and creating a distinctive identity.

Another factor to consider in discovering your next hit idea is innovation. Broadway is a tradition-rich environment, but it is also a place where groundbreaking ideas can thrive. Many of the most successful musicals have pushed the boundaries of what was expected on stage, whether through their subject matter, musical style, or staging techniques. *Hamilton* revolutionized the Broadway musical not only through its use of hip-hop but also through its casting of actors of color in roles traditionally associated with white historical figures. This bold choice redefined how audiences saw American history and who had the right to tell that story. Similarly, *The Lion King* transformed Broadway with its use of puppetry and immersive visual design, creating a theatrical experience unlike anything audiences had seen before. Don't be afraid to take risks and explore unconventional ideas—innovation can be the key to creating a truly memorable musical. Finally, collaboration is an essential part of the creative process. While the initial spark of genius might come from a single individual, creating a hit Broadway musical is almost always a collaborative effort. Writers, composers, directors, choreographers, and producers all play a role in shaping the final product. Surround yourself with a team of talented and creative people who can help you refine your idea, push it in new directions, and bring it to life on stage. Collaboration can often spark new ideas and insights that you might not have considered on your own. In the end, discovering your next hit idea for Broadway is about tapping into the universal human experience, finding a story that resonates with your audience, and infusing it with creativity, innovation, and passion. Whether you draw inspiration from history, personal experience, or the world around you, the key is to stay true to your vision while remaining open to new possibilities. With the right idea, you could be on your way to creating the next Broadway sensation.

Elements of Success: What Makes a Hit Broadway Show?

The elements that make a Broadway show successful are a unique blend of artistry, timing, and execution. While the path to creating a hit musical is often unpredictable, there are certain key ingredients that have consistently contributed to the success of Broadway shows over the decades. Understanding these elements can help writers, composers, and producers craft a show that not only resonates with audiences but also stands the test of time.

At the heart of every successful Broadway musical is a compelling story. This might seem obvious, but the importance of storytelling cannot be overstated. Audiences are drawn to narratives that evoke emotion, feature complex characters, and explore universal themes. Whether it's the love and tragedy in *Les Misérables*, the coming-of-age journey in *Dear Evan Hansen*, or the political ambition in *Hamilton*, a strong, well-constructed story is the foundation upon which the entire musical is built. The best musicals are able to take these emotional journeys and make them accessible to a wide audience while maintaining depth and meaning. They create characters that audiences can root for, cry with, and ultimately remember long after the curtain falls.

But storytelling alone isn't enough. A hit musical must have unforgettable music, and this is where many Broadway shows distinguish themselves. The music in a Broadway show serves multiple purposes: it enhances the emotional experience, advances the plot, and gives the audience insight into the characters. In a successful musical, the score is more than just a collection of catchy tunes—it's an integral part of the storytelling. Think of how *West Side Story* uses music to express the tension between the Jets and the Sharks, or how *The Phantom of the Opera* creates an atmosphere of mystery and romance through its sweeping orchestral score. A hit Broadway show often has at least one or two iconic songs that capture the essence of the story and stick in the audience's minds. These songs become cultural touchstones, like "Defying Gravity" from *Wicked*, "Let It Go" from *Frozen*, or "You'll Be Back" from *Hamilton*.

Equally important is the seamless integration of music, lyrics, and dialogue. A successful Broadway musical achieves harmony between these elements, allowing the story to flow naturally from spoken word to song. This is one of the hallmarks of the "integrated musical," a form perfected by Rodgers and Hammerstein with *Oklahoma!* and continued by composers and lyricists like Stephen Sondheim and Lin-Manuel Miranda. In an integrated musical, every song has a purpose—whether it's to reveal a character's inner thoughts, to heighten dramatic tension, or to move the story forward. When music and lyrics are woven into the fabric of the show, the audience remains fully immersed in the world of the characters, and the emotional stakes are raised.

Another critical element of success is originality. While Broadway has seen its share of adaptations—from books, films, and even real-life events—the most successful shows bring something new to the table. Whether it's a fresh perspective, a bold artistic choice, or a new way of storytelling, originality helps a show stand out in a crowded market. Take *Hamilton*, for example. Lin-Manuel Miranda's decision to tell the story of America's founding fathers through hip-hop and R&B was unprecedented and immediately captured the attention of both Broadway insiders and the general public. Similarly, *The Lion King* was a familiar story to audiences, but the innovative use of puppetry, mask work, and immersive stage design transformed it into a Broadway spectacle like no other.

Speaking of spectacle, production values can often make or break a Broadway show. While a high-budget production isn't a guaranteed recipe for success, creative staging, set design, costumes, and lighting all contribute to the overall impact of a musical. Shows like *The Phantom of the Opera* and *Wicked* are known for their grandiose sets and stunning visual effects, which heighten the drama and transport the audience into the world of the story. However, it's not just about scale—sometimes simplicity can be equally powerful. *Dear Evan Hansen*, for instance, relies heavily on projections and minimalist staging to reflect the inner world of its teenage protagonist. The key is to ensure that the production elements serve the story and create an immersive experience for the audience.

Timing is another often-overlooked element of success. Sometimes, a show resonates because it taps into the cultural zeitgeist. *Rent* spoke to a generation dealing with issues like AIDS, poverty, and artistic struggle in 1990s New York. *Hair* captured the rebellious spirit of the 1960s counterculture, and *Hamilton* arrived at a moment when conversations about race, immigration, and the American Dream were dominating the national dialogue. A show that reflects or challenges contemporary social issues can capture the public's attention in a way that more timeless or escapist fare might not. That said, timing is unpredictable. A great show can flop if it comes out when the market isn't ready for it, and a mediocre show might succeed if it happens to land at just the right moment.

Another crucial component of a hit Broadway musical is casting. A well-cast show can elevate even the most ordinary material, while a poor casting choice can derail an otherwise promising production. Successful musicals often rely on star power or the right combination of actors to draw audiences in. However, it's not just about finding talented performers—it's about finding the right fit for each role. The chemistry between cast members, the ability to inhabit a character, and the way an actor connects with the audience can all make a significant difference in the overall impact of the show. Some actors, like Patti LuPone in *Evita* or Lin-Manuel Miranda in *Hamilton*, become synonymous with the roles they originate, creating performances that are inseparable from the success of the show.

Choreography is another factor that can make or break a Broadway musical. Dance sequences often serve as showstoppers, providing moments of pure spectacle or emotional release. Iconic choreography, such as the dream ballet in *Oklahoma!* or the intricate footwork in *West Side Story*, becomes a defining feature of the production. Successful musicals use choreography not just as filler between scenes but as an essential part of the storytelling, revealing character relationships, advancing the plot, or heightening tension. The best choreography feels organic to the narrative and leaves a lasting visual impression on the audience.

Behind the scenes, a great producer plays a pivotal role in the success of a Broadway show. Producers are responsible for securing financing, hiring the creative team, overseeing the production, and managing the marketing and promotion of the show. A skilled producer knows how to balance artistic vision with commercial viability, ensuring that the show appeals to both critics and audiences. Producers like Harold Prince and Cameron Mackintosh have had a significant impact on the success of some of Broadway's most iconic musicals, using their expertise to bring creative teams together and guide productions to their fullest potential.

Finally, audience engagement is essential for a Broadway show's success. Hit musicals often create a sense of community among their fans, whether through social media, fan events, or simply word of mouth. A show that resonates with its audience can develop a loyal fanbase that keeps coming back, spreading the word, and turning the musical into a cultural phenomenon. When audiences feel personally connected to a show, whether through its characters, themes, or music, they are more likely to champion it and help it achieve long-term success.

In conclusion, a hit Broadway show is the result of many factors working in harmony. A compelling story, memorable music, originality, production values, timing, casting, choreography, and strong producing all play a role in creating a successful musical. While there is no guaranteed formula for success, understanding and mastering these elements can significantly increase the likelihood of creating a Broadway show that resonates with audiences and becomes a hit.

From Concept to Script: Writing the Stage Play

The journey from concept to script is a critical phase in the development of a Broadway musical. This is where the foundation of the entire production is laid—the narrative arc, the characters, the dialogue, and the structure that will carry the music and lyrics to the stage. Writing the stage play requires not only creativity but also a deep understanding of how stories function within the context of live theater. It's about transforming an idea into a living, breathing world that unfolds on stage, engaging the audience from the first line of dialogue to the final bow.

The process of writing the stage play often begins with an idea or a concept. This could be a theme you're passionate about, a character you're intrigued by, or even a visual image that sparks your imagination. It's important to take some time to flesh out this idea before jumping into the scriptwriting process. Think about the core of your story—what is it that you want to communicate? What themes are you exploring, and what do you want the audience to feel? Whether your concept is rooted in romance, social justice, fantasy, or personal growth, clarity of vision is essential. A great stage play needs a strong, clear focus from the outset.

Once the concept is solidified, the next step is developing the structure of the story. Like most forms of storytelling, musicals often follow a three-act structure, though this can vary depending on the narrative style. In this structure, Act 1 introduces the main characters, sets up the central conflict, and establishes the world of the story. Act 2 deepens the conflict and explores the relationships between the characters, while Act 3 brings the story to its climax and resolution. In musicals, Act 1 typically ends with a major turning point that leaves the audience eager for the next act, and Act 2 usually contains the emotional core of the show, often ending with a cliffhanger or dramatic revelation. The final act resolves the central conflict, tying up loose ends and providing a satisfying conclusion. This structure, when done well, provides a strong narrative backbone that can guide your scriptwriting process.

After you've sketched out the basic structure of the story, it's time to focus on character development. In a Broadway musical, characters are everything. They drive the plot, engage the audience, and give life to the themes of the story. Great musicals often center on compelling protagonists who undergo significant transformations over the course of the show. Think of Elphaba in *Wicked*, who begins as an outcast and eventually becomes the feared Wicked Witch of the West, or Alexander Hamilton in *Hamilton*, whose rise and fall mirror the birth and growth of a nation. Your protagonist should have clear goals, internal conflicts, and a strong arc that reflects their personal journey.

In addition to the protagonist, it's important to create well-rounded supporting characters. These characters should have their own desires and conflicts, and they should serve to challenge or support the protagonist in meaningful ways. Whether they provide comic relief, emotional depth, or antagonistic tension, supporting characters enrich the world of the musical and add layers to the narrative. Take *The Lion King* as an example—Timon and Pumbaa are not just comedic sidekicks; they serve as a counterbalance to Simba's internal struggle, offering him a different perspective on life and helping him grow.

Dialogue is the next major component in writing the stage play. In a musical, dialogue serves as a bridge between the musical numbers, but it should never feel like filler. Every line of dialogue should have a purpose, whether it's revealing character, advancing the plot, or setting the tone for an upcoming song. One of the challenges of writing dialogue for musicals is ensuring that it transitions smoothly into the songs without feeling forced. This requires careful attention to the rhythm and pacing of the script. The best musicals weave dialogue and music together seamlessly, creating a natural flow that keeps the audience engaged. For instance, in *Les Misérables*, the shift from spoken dialogue to sung lyrics feels organic because the dialogue is often written with a musical cadence in mind.

While writing dialogue, it's also important to consider the limitations and opportunities of the stage. Unlike film, where close-ups and editing can convey subtle emotions, stage actors must rely on their voices, bodies, and facial expressions to communicate with the audience. This means that the dialogue needs to be clear and impactful. Every word should serve a purpose, whether it's to build tension, reveal character, or provide humor. Additionally, keep in mind that audiences in a theater may not have the same visual intimacy as a film audience, so moments of physical action and visual cues need to be clearly staged and integrated into the dialogue.

Once the dialogue is in place, it's time to think about the musical numbers. In a Broadway musical, the songs are as much a part of the script as the dialogue and should be treated as such. Each song must have a clear purpose within the story, whether it's to reveal a character's innermost thoughts, express a turning point in the plot, or heighten an emotional moment. As you write the stage play, think about where the songs will naturally fit into the narrative. Songs in musicals often occur at moments of heightened emotion—when characters can no longer express themselves through dialogue alone, they turn to song. This is why songs are often placed at key moments of transformation, conflict, or revelation.

It's also important to think about the pacing of the musical numbers. Too many songs back-to-back can overwhelm the audience, while too few can leave the show feeling sparse. Striking a balance between dialogue and music ensures that the show maintains a rhythm that feels natural and engaging. Additionally, the variety of musical styles can help shape the tone and atmosphere of the show. Some songs may be light-hearted and playful, while others might be intense and dramatic. This contrast helps keep the audience emotionally invested and prevents the show from feeling monotonous.

As the script takes shape, collaboration becomes key. Theater is inherently collaborative, and as the writer, you'll need to work closely with the composer, lyricist, director, and other creative team members to ensure that the dialogue, music, and staging all work together. This collaborative process often leads to revisions and refinements that strengthen the overall script. For example, the director may suggest changes to the staging that impact the flow of dialogue, or the composer may tweak a song's melody to better align with the emotional tone of a scene. Being open to feedback and willing to make adjustments is an essential part of writing a stage play.

In addition to collaboration, it's important to keep in mind the practicalities of staging. As you write the script, think about how the scenes will be physically realized on stage. Consider the limitations of space, set design, and costume changes. Can the scenes flow smoothly from one to the next? Are there opportunities for creative stagecraft or special effects that enhance the storytelling? Understanding the logistics of production will help you write a script that is not only artistically compelling but also feasible for the stage.

Finally, remember that writing a stage play for a musical is a process of continual refinement. Once the script is complete, it will likely go through workshops, readings, and rehearsals, where actors, directors, and producers will provide valuable feedback. Be prepared to make changes and embrace the idea that your script will evolve as it moves closer to production.

In conclusion, writing the stage play for a Broadway musical is a multifaceted process that requires careful planning, creativity, and collaboration. From developing a strong concept to crafting compelling characters, dialogue, and musical numbers, each element must come together seamlessly to create a cohesive and engaging theatrical experience. With persistence, flexibility, and a clear vision, you can take your idea from concept to script, bringing it one step closer to the Broadway stage.

Lyricism in Motion: Writing Compelling Lyrics

Writing compelling lyrics for a Broadway musical is an art form unto itself. While the music and melody often take center stage in the minds of audiences, the lyrics are what give voice to the characters, tell their stories, and connect the songs to the narrative. In many ways, the lyrics serve as the emotional heartbeat of the musical, offering insight into the characters' innermost thoughts, feelings, and desires. Crafting powerful, memorable lyrics is one of the most challenging and rewarding aspects of writing a musical, as it requires a unique blend of poetry, rhythm, storytelling, and musicality.

The first key to writing compelling lyrics is understanding the role that they play in the broader context of the musical. Unlike a stand-alone song, musical theater lyrics must serve a specific purpose within the story. Each song in a musical is an extension of the narrative, advancing the plot, revealing character, or heightening emotion at critical moments. The lyrics need to reflect the internal journey of the character singing them, as well as the larger themes and messages of the show. This requires a deep understanding of both the story and the characters. As a lyricist, your job is to make sure that each song feels integral to the overall narrative, not just a beautiful piece of music inserted for entertainment.

A great example of this can be found in Stephen Sondheim's *Into the Woods*. In the song "No One Is Alone," Sondheim uses lyrics to express themes of loss, fear, and hope, while offering characters a moment of introspection during a critical point in the story. The lyrics are simple yet profound: "You move just a finger / Say the slightest word / Something's bound to linger / Be heard." These lines reveal the emotional vulnerability of the characters while also reminding the audience that every action has consequences. The song reflects not only the internal emotional states of the characters but also the larger theme of the musical—navigating life's challenges and uncertainties. This is what makes compelling lyrics—they serve the character, the moment, and the larger story all at once.

Another important aspect of lyric writing is understanding the balance between simplicity and complexity. Some of the most memorable lyrics in Broadway history are deceptively simple, yet they convey profound emotions. A song like "Somewhere" from *West Side Story* relies on straightforward language to express a deep yearning for a better future: "There's a place for us, / Somewhere a place for us. / Peace and quiet and open air, / Wait for us, somewhere." The simplicity of the language allows the emotional intensity of the song to shine through. Similarly, in *Les Misérables*, the song "I Dreamed a Dream" uses direct, accessible lyrics to capture Fantine's tragic despair: "I had a dream my life would be / So different from this hell I'm living." The words are plain, but the emotions they evoke are powerful.

On the other hand, there are moments when lyrical complexity is needed to reflect the intricacies of a character's mind or the nuances of a situation. Sondheim is often praised for his ability to write intricate, multi-layered lyrics that challenge both the performers and the audience. In *Sweeney Todd*, the song "A Little Priest" uses dark humor and wordplay to express the characters' grim plans in a playful, clever way: "The history of the world, my love / Is those below serving those up above!" Sondheim's lyrics in this song are filled with double meanings and wit, reflecting the deviousness of the characters while keeping the audience engaged through sharp, humorous wordplay.

No matter the complexity, successful lyrics must always have a clear rhythm and flow. Musical theater lyrics need to fit within the structure of the music and work seamlessly with the melody. This means that, as a lyricist, you need to have a strong sense of musicality—even if you're not composing the music yourself. Understanding the rhythm of the music is crucial because the lyrics must feel natural as they are sung. Awkward phrasing or forced rhymes can take the audience out of the moment and disrupt the flow of the show. In contrast, when the lyrics and music are perfectly aligned, the song feels effortless and carries the audience along with it.

Consider "Defying Gravity" from *Wicked*. The song's lyrics are intricately woven into the rise and fall of the music, with phrases like "I'm through with playing by the rules of someone else's game" aligning perfectly with the shifting dynamics of the melody. The lyrics build in intensity, just as the music does, creating a sense of empowerment and liberation that matches the character's emotional journey in that moment. The seamless integration of words and music is what makes "Defying Gravity" such a powerful anthem and a defining moment in the show.

When writing lyrics, it's also important to consider the perspective of the character. Each song in a musical is sung by a character who has a specific point of view, emotional state, and motivation. The lyrics should reflect these elements and feel authentic to the character's voice. This requires a deep understanding of the character's psychology and backstory. For instance, in *Hamilton*, Lin-Manuel Miranda writes the song "My Shot" in a way that captures Alexander Hamilton's ambitious, restless energy. The rapid-fire delivery and clever wordplay mirror Hamilton's quick mind and relentless drive: "I'm past patiently waitin' / I'm passionately smashin' every expectation / Every action's an act of creation!" The lyrics reflect Hamilton's hunger for success, his determination to rise above his circumstances, and his belief in his own destiny. This character-driven approach to lyric writing helps the audience connect with the character on a deeper level and makes the songs feel more personal and impactful.

Another important aspect of lyric writing is the use of rhyme and wordplay. While not all lyrics need to rhyme, rhyming can add a musicality and cohesiveness to a song. Well-crafted rhymes can make the lyrics more memorable and pleasing to the ear. However, it's important to avoid "lazy rhymes" or rhymes that feel too predictable or forced. Instead, aim for rhymes that are inventive and feel natural within the context of the song. Sondheim, in particular, is known for his masterful use of rhyme, often employing internal rhymes and multi-syllabic rhymes to create a sense of complexity and sophistication. In *Company*, the song "The Ladies Who Lunch" features sharp, biting rhymes that enhance the character's acerbic wit: "Another long exhausting day, / Another thousand dollars, / A matinee, a Pinter play, / Perhaps a piece of Mahler's."

Finally, lyric writing for a Broadway musical requires an awareness of the audience. The lyrics need to be clear and accessible enough that the audience can follow the story, even if they're hearing the song for the first time. While it's tempting to be overly poetic or abstract, clarity is key in musical theater. Audiences need to understand the lyrics in real time, as they are being sung, so that they can stay engaged with the narrative. This doesn't mean the lyrics need to be overly simplistic, but they should be written with the audience's perspective in mind.

In conclusion, writing compelling lyrics for a Broadway musical is a delicate balance of storytelling, poetry, and musicality. The lyrics must serve the narrative, reveal character, and engage the audience, all while fitting seamlessly within the structure of the music. Whether they are simple or complex, humorous or heart-wrenching, the best lyrics evoke emotion, advance the plot, and leave a lasting impact. With careful attention to rhythm, rhyme, and character, lyricists can create songs that not only resonate with the audience but also become an integral part of the musical's legacy.

Crafting Melodies: Writing the Perfect Musical Score

Writing the perfect musical score is one of the most essential and creative aspects of crafting a Broadway musical. The score not only sets the emotional tone of the production but also elevates the story, making the characters' journeys more vivid and compelling. A well-composed score brings the lyrics to life, enhances the narrative, and creates unforgettable moments that resonate long after the curtain falls. From the opening overture to the final chord, the score is the heartbeat of the show, and crafting the melodies that make up that score is an art that requires both musical expertise and a deep connection to the story being told.

The first step in writing the perfect musical score is understanding the story and the characters inside and out. A score isn't just about creating beautiful music—it's about telling a story through sound. The music should reflect the characters' emotional states, desires, and conflicts. Before a single note is written, it's important to fully immerse yourself in the world of the musical. Who are the characters? What are they feeling at each moment? How do their emotions evolve over the course of the show? The answers to these questions will guide your musical choices and help you craft melodies that are authentic to the characters and the narrative.

One of the keys to creating a compelling score is developing a strong musical theme or motif that can be woven throughout the show. Many successful musicals use recurring musical themes to represent characters, ideas, or emotions. These motifs become musical signatures that help the audience connect with the story on a deeper level. For example, in *Les Misérables*, the melody of "Do You Hear the People Sing?" recurs throughout the show, representing the revolutionary spirit of the characters. In *The Phantom of the Opera*, Andrew Lloyd Webber uses the haunting "Phantom" motif to underscore the eerie presence of the title character, heightening the tension and drama. These musical themes help create continuity and cohesion within the score, giving the audience something familiar to latch onto as the story unfolds.

Another important element in writing a memorable score is ensuring that each song serves a distinct purpose within the narrative. In musical theater, songs occur at key moments when characters are experiencing heightened emotions, moments of transformation, or revelations. The melody of each song should reflect the emotional arc of the character in that moment. For example, a love ballad might have a sweeping, lyrical melody to capture the intensity of romantic feelings, while an upbeat, rhythmic tune might be used to express joy or excitement. The melody must align with the emotional content of the lyrics and dialogue, creating a seamless connection between what the characters are feeling and how the audience experiences those emotions through the music.

One challenge in crafting melodies for a Broadway musical is balancing complexity with accessibility. On one hand, you want to create intricate, interesting music that pushes the boundaries of musical theater and keeps the audience engaged. On the other hand, the melodies must be accessible enough for the audience to understand and remember after hearing them only once. Successful scores strike a balance between these two elements, offering moments of musical complexity while still delivering tunes that audiences can hum on their way out of the theater. A song like "The Room Where It Happens" from *Hamilton* is musically complex, with shifting rhythms and dynamic changes, but it also has a catchy, infectious melody that sticks with audiences. This balance helps to ensure that the music is both artistically rewarding and enjoyable for listeners.

When writing a musical score, it's also important to think about variety. A Broadway musical typically features a range of songs, from big, show-stopping numbers to quiet, introspective solos. Variety keeps the audience engaged and prevents the show from feeling monotonous. Consider the different musical forms you can incorporate into the score—ballads, duets, ensemble pieces, dance numbers—and how each type of song can serve the story. A show like *Wicked* is a masterclass in variety, featuring powerful ballads like "Defying Gravity," playful duets like "What Is This Feeling?," and emotionally driven solos like "I'm Not That Girl." Each song has a distinct mood and style, but they all contribute to the overall narrative and character development.

Melodic contrast is also a valuable tool in building a dynamic score. Contrasting different melodies within a song or across the show can help highlight emotional shifts and character development. For example, in *West Side Story*, the stark contrast between the romantic melody of "Tonight" and the energetic, syncopated rhythms of "America" reflects the tension between love and conflict in the story. This type of musical contrast adds depth to the score, keeping the audience emotionally engaged and enhancing the storytelling.

Harmonization is another critical aspect of crafting melodies in musical theater. The harmonies you choose can drastically affect the mood of a song. Rich, complex harmonies might be used to convey deep emotional turmoil, while simple, open harmonies can create a sense of purity or innocence. For example, in *Les Misérables*, the soaring harmonies in "One Day More" bring together multiple characters and their conflicting motivations, creating a sense of unity and anticipation. Harmonization also plays a role in ensemble pieces, where multiple characters may be singing different lines or melodies simultaneously. Skillful harmonization allows these voices to blend together in a way that enhances the complexity of the scene while still maintaining clarity.

Another crucial consideration when crafting melodies is the integration of the score with the lyrics. In musical theater, the lyrics and music must work hand-in-hand to tell the story. As you compose the score, think about how the rhythm and pacing of the melody will align with the natural flow of the lyrics. The melody should support the emotional content of the lyrics, heightening key moments and allowing the words to shine. For instance, in *Sweeney Todd*, the dark, lilting melody of "Johanna" underscores the character's longing and obsession, with the music and lyrics working in tandem to create a hauntingly beautiful expression of love and madness. The same can be seen in *Dear Evan Hansen*, where the melodies of songs like "Waving Through a Window" reflect the isolation and yearning expressed in the lyrics, creating an emotional resonance that is central to the character's journey.

Collaboration between the composer and lyricist is essential to achieving this balance. The composer must be attuned to the needs of the lyrics, while the lyricist must be flexible enough to adjust the words to fit the melody. This collaborative process often leads to the refinement of both the music and the lyrics, ensuring that they work together to create a unified, impactful song.

In addition to the melodies themselves, the orchestration plays a significant role in shaping the overall sound of the score. The choice of instruments can enhance the emotional impact of a song, create atmosphere, and help define the style of the musical. For example, the use of electric guitars and synthesizers in *Rent* gives the score a rock edge that reflects the bohemian, rebellious spirit of the characters, while the lush orchestration in *The Phantom of the Opera* contributes to the show's grand, gothic atmosphere. When writing the melodies, it's important to consider how they will be orchestrated and what instruments will best bring out the emotional qualities of the music.

Finally, flexibility is key when crafting a musical score. The melodies you write will likely go through several revisions as the show develops. During workshops, rehearsals, and previews, you'll have the opportunity to see how the music functions in the context of the full production. Be prepared to make changes based on feedback from directors, actors, and audiences. Sometimes a melody that sounds perfect on paper doesn't translate as well to the stage, and adjustments may be needed to improve the pacing, emotional clarity, or integration with the choreography.

In conclusion, writing the perfect musical score is a complex, multifaceted process that requires a deep connection to the story, characters, and themes of the show. The melodies must be crafted with care, balancing complexity with accessibility, and variety with cohesion. Recurring musical themes, melodic contrast, harmonization, and the integration of lyrics and music all contribute to the creation of a compelling, emotionally resonant score. With thoughtful composition, collaboration, and attention to detail, a well-crafted musical score has the power to elevate a Broadway show from good to unforgettable, creating moments that will stay with the audience long after they leave the theater.

The Music Comes to Life: Creating the Musical Arrangement

Creating the musical arrangement is where the music of a Broadway show truly comes to life. It's the stage in the creative process where the composer's melodies and the lyricist's words are transformed into fully realized pieces of theater. While composing the score lays the foundation, arranging is about adding depth, texture, and complexity, ensuring that each song has the right instrumentation, dynamics, and structure to support the emotional arc of the story. A well-crafted arrangement not only enhances the power of the music but also helps bring the narrative to the forefront, making the music feel as though it belongs in the world of the show.

The first step in arranging music for a Broadway musical is understanding the overall tone and style of the show. The arrangement must match the atmosphere, setting, and themes of the story. For example, a show like *Hamilton*, with its blend of hip-hop, R&B, and traditional musical theater, requires a very different arrangement than a classic Rodgers and Hammerstein show like *The Sound of Music*. The music in *Hamilton* is characterized by tight, rhythmic arrangements with a focus on percussion and modern instrumentation, while *The Sound of Music* relies on more traditional orchestration with strings and woodwinds to evoke the pastoral beauty of its setting. Before beginning the arrangement, it's essential to know how the music will interact with the show's visual and narrative elements.

One of the key elements of arranging is orchestration—choosing the instruments that will bring the score to life. Each instrument has its own tonal quality and emotional impact, so selecting the right combination is crucial. In a big Broadway production, the orchestra may include a wide range of instruments, from strings and woodwinds to brass, percussion, and keyboards. For a smaller, more intimate show, the arrangement might rely on a minimal ensemble, such as a piano, guitar, and drums. The choice of instruments helps define the mood and atmosphere of each song. For instance, the use of brass instruments in *Chicago* gives the score a jazzy, brassy energy that fits the show's 1920s setting, while the lush strings in *The Phantom of the Opera* create a sense of gothic romance.

In addition to choosing the instruments, the arranger must decide how those instruments will be used to support the melody. One of the arranger's main tasks is to take the composer's original melody and harmonies and expand them for a full orchestra or ensemble. This involves creating parts for each instrument, ensuring that they complement one another and contribute to the overall sound of the piece. In many ways, the arrangement is like a puzzle, with each instrument playing its role to build a cohesive and dynamic whole. A great arrangement allows the melody to shine while enhancing the emotional impact of the song.

An important aspect of arranging is balancing dynamics and texture. In a Broadway musical, the arrangement must reflect the emotional ebb and flow of the story. There will be moments of high intensity, where the music swells to match the drama unfolding on stage, and quieter moments, where a more restrained arrangement allows for introspection or intimacy. The arranger must carefully consider when to build the music and when to pull back, creating peaks and valleys that match the emotional arc of the song and the scene. For example, in *Les Misérables*, the song "One Day More" features a grand, full-orchestra arrangement that builds to a climactic moment as multiple characters sing together, reflecting their various hopes and fears. In contrast, a song like "On My Own" relies on a simpler, more intimate arrangement to reflect the character's loneliness and longing.

Another key element of arranging is rhythm. The rhythmic structure of a song plays a significant role in how it feels to the audience. In musical theater, rhythm can help drive the action forward or slow it down to create tension. Arranging the rhythm involves deciding how each instrument will contribute to the overall groove or pulse of the song. For an upbeat, energetic number, the arrangement might feature syncopated rhythms or driving percussion, while a ballad might have a more fluid, relaxed rhythm. Rhythm is especially important in dance numbers, where the arrangement must align with the choreography. In shows like *West Side Story*, the rhythms of the music are tightly linked to the movement of the dancers, creating a sense of unity between the music and the action on stage.

Harmony also plays a vital role in the arrangement. While the composer often outlines the basic harmonic structure of a song, the arranger has the opportunity to expand on these harmonies, adding richness and complexity. Harmonies can create tension, resolve emotional moments, or add depth to a vocal line. In ensemble numbers, harmony is often used to showcase multiple characters singing together, with each voice contributing to the overall texture of the piece. For example, in *Rent*, the song "Seasons of Love" features tight harmonies that bring the ensemble together, creating a powerful sense of unity and shared experience. The arrangement's harmonies elevate the song, making it one of the most memorable moments in the show.

In addition to harmony, the arranger must consider counterpoint—when different musical lines are played or sung simultaneously. Counterpoint can add layers of complexity to the arrangement, allowing different characters or instruments to express themselves independently while still contributing to the overall sound. This technique is often used in ensemble pieces where multiple characters are singing different lines at the same time. For example, in *Sweeney Todd*, the song "A Little Priest" features counterpoint between Sweeney and Mrs. Lovett, as they each sing their own twisted thoughts about their plan to bake people into pies. The counterpoint adds humor and depth to the song, as the audience can hear both characters' perspectives simultaneously.

Another aspect of arranging for musical theater is the use of musical motifs. A motif is a recurring musical phrase or theme that represents a particular character, idea, or emotion. These motifs can be woven throughout the score, creating continuity and helping the audience connect with the story. In *The Phantom of the Opera*, Andrew Lloyd Webber uses the "Phantom" motif throughout the show, reintroducing it at key moments to remind the audience of the Phantom's presence. The use of motifs in the arrangement helps to reinforce the narrative and give the score a sense of unity.

When arranging for a musical, the arranger must also consider the technical aspects of the production, such as scene changes, choreography, and dialogue. The music must align with the pacing of the show, providing the right energy for transitions, dance breaks, or moments of spoken dialogue. In some cases, the arrangement may need to include underscoring—music that plays softly in the background during dialogue or scene changes. Underscoring can help maintain the mood of the scene or subtly underscore the emotional subtext of the dialogue. For instance, in *Hamilton*, the underscoring during key moments of political debate heightens the tension and adds to the drama of the scene without overwhelming the dialogue.

Choreography is another element that must be considered when creating the musical arrangement. Dance numbers often require specific musical arrangements that complement the choreography, with rhythms and dynamics that match the movements on stage. In shows like *Chicago* or *Fiddler on the Roof*, the music is tightly integrated with the choreography, creating a seamless connection between the music and the dancers. The arranger must work closely with the choreographer to ensure that the music supports and enhances the movement, while still serving the overall narrative of the show.

Collaboration is key to creating the perfect musical arrangement. The arranger works closely with the composer, lyricist, director, and choreographer to ensure that the music aligns with the overall vision of the show. This collaboration often involves multiple revisions, as the arrangement is refined to match the needs of the production. The arranger must be flexible and open to feedback, adjusting the music as the show evolves during rehearsals and previews.

Finally, creating the musical arrangement is about bringing the music to life in a way that enhances the audience's experience. The arrangement should elevate the emotional impact of the songs, create atmosphere, and help the audience connect with the story and characters. A well-crafted arrangement can transform a simple melody into a powerful, memorable piece of theater, leaving a lasting impression on everyone who hears it.

In conclusion, arranging the music for a Broadway musical is a complex, collaborative process that requires a deep understanding of the story, characters, and emotional journey of the show. From orchestration and harmony to rhythm and dynamics, each element of the arrangement plays a crucial role in bringing the score to life. By carefully considering the needs of the production and working closely with the creative team, the arranger can create music that not only supports the narrative but also enhances the entire theatrical experience, turning a collection of melodies into a cohesive, compelling work of art.

The Art of Producing a Broadway Show

Producing a Broadway show is both an art and a business. It requires creativity, vision, leadership, and an acute understanding of the practicalities involved in bringing a theatrical production to life. The producer is the driving force behind a Broadway show, responsible for everything from securing financing and assembling a creative team to overseeing marketing and ensuring the show runs smoothly from development through closing night. While the creative team—writers, composers, directors, and actors—crafts the artistic elements of the show, it's the producer who ensures that the entire enterprise comes together and is financially viable.

The first step in producing a Broadway show is identifying the right project. Producers often receive pitches from writers, composers, and directors, but they also actively seek out new material by attending readings, workshops, and performances of off-Broadway or regional theater productions. A great producer has a strong sense of what stories will resonate with audiences and what ideas have the potential to become commercially successful Broadway shows. Finding the right material is crucial—whether it's an original story, an adaptation of a book or film, or a revival of a classic, the project must have both artistic merit and market appeal.

Once a producer has identified a project, the next step is acquiring the rights. If the show is an adaptation of a pre-existing work, the producer must negotiate with the original creators or rights holders (such as the author, screenwriter, or publishing house) to secure the rights to adapt the material for the stage. This process can be complex, as it involves not only financial terms but also creative control over the adaptation. Producers must ensure that the original creator's vision is respected while also having the freedom to develop the show for Broadway.

With the rights secured, the producer must begin assembling a creative team. This is one of the most important tasks for a producer, as the team will determine the artistic success of the show. The creative team typically includes the director, choreographer, set and costume designers, and the composer and lyricist (if they're not already attached to the project). A producer must have a keen eye for talent and a deep understanding of how to match the right people to the material. For instance, a show with elaborate dance numbers will require a choreographer with a strong vision, while a period drama may call for a set designer with expertise in historical accuracy. The director, in particular, is a crucial hire, as they will be responsible for guiding the entire production, shaping the performances, and ensuring that the creative elements come together cohesively.

One of the most challenging aspects of producing a Broadway show is securing financing. Broadway shows are expensive to produce, often costing millions of dollars to bring to the stage. The producer is responsible for raising the capital needed to cover all expenses, including paying the creative team, building sets, costumes, marketing, and securing a theater. To raise funds, producers typically turn to investors, known as "backers," who contribute money in exchange for a share of the profits if the show is successful. These investors are often individuals or organizations with a passion for theater and a willingness to take financial risks. Broadway is a high-stakes industry, and many shows never recoup their initial investments, so producers must be persuasive and strategic when pitching their projects to potential investors.

Budgeting is another critical aspect of producing. Once the financing is secured, the producer must create a detailed budget that accounts for all production costs. This includes everything from salaries for the cast and crew to the cost of renting a theater, building sets, and marketing the show. A good producer will work closely with the general manager to ensure that the budget is realistic and that expenses are carefully monitored throughout the production process. If costs begin to spiral out of control, it's the producer's responsibility to make tough decisions, whether that means cutting elements of the show, finding additional investors, or reallocating resources.

Another major responsibility of the producer is securing a theater. Broadway theaters are limited in number, and competition for available venues can be fierce. Securing the right theater is a crucial decision, as the venue must not only accommodate the technical requirements of the show (in terms of stage size, backstage facilities, etc.) but also fit the show's intended audience. For example, a large-scale musical with broad appeal may require a large-capacity theater, while an intimate, character-driven drama might work better in a smaller venue. Producers often need to negotiate with theater owners, and securing a theater can involve waiting for another show to close before a new one can move in.

Once the financing, theater, and creative team are in place, the production process begins in earnest. The producer oversees the entire production, making sure that everything stays on schedule and within budget. This includes monitoring rehearsals, coordinating with designers, and ensuring that all technical elements—sets, lighting, costumes, and sound—are being developed as planned. Producers must be able to solve problems quickly, whether it's dealing with creative disagreements, technical challenges, or budgetary issues. They are often the ones who mediate between the artistic and financial sides of the production, ensuring that creative vision is not compromised while keeping costs under control.

Marketing and promotion are another key responsibility of the producer. Even the best show won't succeed if no one knows about it, so producers work with marketing and PR teams to generate buzz for the production. This includes creating advertising campaigns, securing media coverage, and organizing events like press previews or special performances for industry insiders. Producers also play a role in determining ticket prices, creating discount strategies to attract different demographics, and managing the timing of the show's opening. Marketing a Broadway show requires creativity and strategy, as producers must find ways to stand out in a competitive market where multiple shows are vying for attention.

One of the most critical moments in the life of a Broadway show is the preview period, where the production is performed in front of live audiences before officially opening. Previews allow the creative team to test the show with audiences and make adjustments based on their reactions. Producers closely monitor audience feedback during previews and often work with the director and creative team to implement changes. This might involve cutting or reworking scenes, adjusting the pacing, or even making significant changes to the script or score. The producer's ability to balance the creative vision with audience expectations is crucial during this phase, as decisions made in previews can determine the ultimate success or failure of the show.

The official opening night is the culmination of months, or even years, of hard work. The producer's job is not done once the curtain rises, however. After the show opens, the producer continues to oversee the business side of the production, ensuring that ticket sales remain strong, managing day-to-day operations, and dealing with any unforeseen challenges. Producers also work with the PR team to manage reviews, awards campaigns, and other promotional efforts. If the show is successful, the producer may explore opportunities to expand the production through touring, licensing for regional theaters, or even adaptations for film or television.

The art of producing a Broadway show requires a unique combination of creativity, business acumen, and leadership. A great producer is both a visionary and a pragmatist, able to navigate the artistic and financial complexities of theater production while inspiring a team to bring a show to life. The producer's role is often behind the scenes, but their influence is felt in every aspect of the production, from the first idea to the final bow. Without the producer, the magic of Broadway simply wouldn't happen.

In conclusion, producing a Broadway show is a multifaceted, high-stakes endeavor that demands a balance of artistic vision and financial management. From acquiring the rights to assembling the creative team, securing financing, and promoting the show, the producer is responsible for every aspect of bringing the production to life.

Success requires not only a deep understanding of the theater industry but also the ability to solve problems, make tough decisions, and guide a creative project to its full potential. It is this combination of creativity and business savvy that makes producing one of the most challenging—and rewarding—roles in Broadway theater.

Making It Happen: Financing a Broadway Musical

Financing a Broadway musical is one of the most crucial and challenging aspects of bringing a show to the stage. While the creative vision is the heart of the project, the financial backing is what makes that vision a reality. Broadway shows are notoriously expensive to produce, with costs that can range from a few million dollars for a small-scale production to upwards of $20 million or more for a large musical with elaborate sets, costumes, and special effects. The producer's role in securing the necessary funds to cover these expenses is essential to getting the show off the ground.

The first step in financing a Broadway musical is creating a detailed budget. This budget will account for all production costs, including paying the creative team, cast, and crew; renting a theater; building sets and costumes; marketing and promotion; and various other operational expenses. A good producer must work closely with a general manager or financial expert to ensure that the budget is realistic and comprehensive. The budget will often include a contingency fund to cover unforeseen expenses that may arise during production or in the early weeks of the show's run. Once the budget is in place, the producer knows exactly how much money needs to be raised and can begin looking for investors.

Most Broadway musicals are financed through a combination of individual and institutional investors. These investors are often referred to as "backers" or "angels" and are typically wealthy individuals, theater enthusiasts, or companies willing to take the financial risk of investing in a Broadway production. In exchange for their financial contributions, investors receive a percentage of the profits if the show is successful. However, Broadway is a high-risk industry, and many shows fail to recoup their initial investment, meaning that investors could lose all or part of their money. Despite this risk, there are always investors willing to take a chance on Broadway, drawn by the possibility of being involved in a hit show or by their passion for the theater.

To attract investors, the producer must create a compelling pitch. This pitch typically includes an overview of the show, the creative team's credentials, and the producer's vision for the production. It also includes a breakdown of the budget and an explanation of how the money will be spent. The pitch must convince potential investors that the show has both artistic and commercial potential. In some cases, the producer may organize readings or workshops to give investors a preview of the material, allowing them to see the creative potential of the show before committing money. Producers may also show investors financial projections based on the show's potential to sell tickets, merchandise, or secure licensing rights for future productions.

For example, a successful producer may use the financial success of previous Broadway hits like *Hamilton* or *The Lion King* as a model to show investors what's possible. Broadway musicals that become hits can make enormous profits, with some shows running for decades and generating revenue not only from ticket sales but also from national tours, international productions, and film adaptations. However, producers must be careful not to over-promise, as the majority of shows do not achieve this level of success. Transparency and clear communication are key to building trust with investors.

Another option for financing a Broadway musical is securing institutional or corporate sponsorships. Companies may invest in a Broadway show as part of their marketing strategy, using their association with the production to enhance their brand image or reach a particular demographic. For example, major brands have sponsored Broadway shows by providing in-kind services, such as costume design or advertising, in exchange for promotional opportunities. Corporate sponsorships can provide valuable resources and help lower production costs, but producers must balance these partnerships carefully to ensure that they align with the artistic vision of the show and don't compromise its integrity.

Crowdfunding has also become a more viable option for some productions, particularly those with a built-in fan base or strong social media presence. Platforms like Kickstarter or GoFundMe allow producers to raise smaller amounts of money from a larger number of individual contributors. While this approach is more common for smaller-scale productions or off-Broadway shows, it has been successfully used in some cases to fund elements of larger Broadway projects. Crowdfunding can also help generate early buzz and build an audience for the show before it officially opens.

Once the producer has secured the initial financing to cover pre-production costs, they must begin managing the show's cash flow carefully. Unlike other businesses, Broadway shows typically don't start generating revenue until after they've opened and begin selling tickets. Pre-production costs—such as paying the cast and crew, building sets, and rehearsing—must be covered before the show opens, and there is no guarantee of immediate profit. This makes it essential for producers to have a well-structured financial plan to ensure that the show can stay afloat until it begins bringing in revenue.

The producer's financial responsibilities don't end once the show opens. Throughout the show's run, the producer must continue to manage expenses, monitor ticket sales, and ensure that the production stays within its operating budget. If ticket sales are slow, the producer may need to adjust marketing strategies, offer discounts, or consider moving the show to a smaller venue. Conversely, if the show is a hit, the producer may need to navigate the complexities of managing a long-running production, such as negotiating contract renewals with the cast or deciding when to launch a national tour or international productions.

Profit-sharing agreements between producers and investors typically involve a "recoupment" phase, during which all profits generated by the show go toward paying back the investors' initial contributions. Once the production has recouped its investment, the profits are split between the producers and investors according to a pre-agreed percentage. In some cases, the creative team—such as the director, composer, or lyricist—may also receive a percentage of the profits as part of their contract. The producer must carefully manage this profit-sharing process to ensure that all parties are paid fairly and according to the agreed terms.

One of the potential challenges in financing a Broadway musical is the unpredictable nature of the industry. Even with strong financing and a talented creative team, a show can still fail if it doesn't connect with audiences or receive positive reviews. Broadway is a high-risk, high-reward industry, and producers must be prepared to navigate the financial ups and downs that come with it. However, when a show does succeed, the rewards can be significant—not only in terms of financial profit but also in the cultural impact and legacy of the production.

In addition to managing the initial financing and cash flow of the production, successful producers often look for additional revenue streams to maximize profits. This can include selling merchandise, securing licensing deals for regional or international productions, or even adapting the show for other formats, such as a film or TV series. For example, shows like *Rent*, *Chicago*, and *The Phantom of the Opera* have all been successfully adapted into films, which generated additional revenue and expanded the show's audience beyond the theater.

Finally, producers must be strategic about planning for the future. Even a successful Broadway show has a finite run, and producers must think about what comes next. If a show is a hit, they may consider launching a national tour, licensing the show to other theaters, or creating an international production. These opportunities can provide ongoing revenue long after the Broadway production has closed. Producers may also explore ways to extend the life of the show through revivals or special anniversary productions.

In conclusion, financing a Broadway musical is a complex and high-stakes process that requires both financial acumen and creative vision. From creating a budget to securing investors, managing expenses, and exploring additional revenue streams, the producer plays a crucial role in ensuring that the show has the resources it needs to succeed. While Broadway is a risky business, the potential rewards—both financial and artistic—make it an exciting and rewarding venture for those willing to take the leap. With careful planning, strong financial management, and a bit of luck, financing can turn a creative idea into the next big Broadway hit.

Leading with Vision: Directing the Show

Directing a Broadway show is a multifaceted and highly demanding role, one that requires equal parts creative vision, leadership, and collaboration. The director is responsible for shaping every aspect of the production, from the performances of the actors to the overall look and feel of the show. They act as the glue that holds together the script, score, choreography, set design, and technical elements, ensuring that all of these pieces work in harmony to tell a compelling story on stage. To lead a production with vision means not only understanding the heart of the material but also inspiring the entire creative team to realize that vision in the most impactful way possible.

The first step for any director is to develop a deep connection to the material. Whether the show is an original production or a revival, the director must fully immerse themselves in the script, score, and characters. What are the core themes of the show? What is the emotional journey of each character? What is the overall tone and mood that the production needs to convey? Answering these questions helps the director shape their vision for the production. It's not enough to simply stage the scenes and songs—the director must understand the essence of the story and how to communicate that essence in every element of the show, from the pacing of the scenes to the lighting choices. A director with a strong vision will find ways to bring fresh, innovative ideas to the material while staying true to its core.

One of the director's key responsibilities is working closely with the actors to shape their performances. In a Broadway musical, this involves not only guiding the actors through their spoken lines but also helping them understand the emotional depth behind the songs they sing. The director must work with the actors to ensure that each character feels fully realized and believable. This involves exploring the character's motivations, relationships, and internal conflicts, often through a process of deep collaboration and rehearsal. The goal is to help each actor deliver a performance that not only fits within the overall vision of the show but also resonates on a personal, emotional level with the audience.

Directors must also be skilled communicators and collaborators, as they lead a team of artists and designers in creating the physical world of the show. This includes working with the set designer, lighting designer, costume designer, choreographer, and music director to bring the visual and auditory aspects of the production to life. A director with vision knows how to inspire their team, offering guidance and feedback while allowing each collaborator the freedom to contribute their expertise to the process. For example, the director might work closely with the set designer to create a stage that can transform seamlessly between different locations, enhancing the storytelling without overwhelming the performances. Similarly, the director might collaborate with the lighting designer to create atmospheric lighting that underscores the emotional beats of key scenes.

In musical theater, the choreography is a crucial element, and the director must work hand-in-hand with the choreographer to ensure that the movement on stage serves the story. Dance numbers in musicals are not just about spectacle—they are opportunities for characters to express themselves through movement. Whether it's a large ensemble dance or a more intimate duet, the choreography must feel organic to the characters and the narrative. The director's job is to make sure that the choreography flows seamlessly within the production, integrating it with the music and dialogue to create a unified whole.

One of the most important aspects of directing a Broadway show is shaping the pacing and rhythm of the production. A director with a strong sense of pacing knows how to build tension, create emotional highs and lows, and guide the audience through the story without losing momentum. This requires careful attention to the transitions between scenes and songs, ensuring that the energy of the production doesn't dip at crucial moments. In a musical, this also involves coordinating the timing of the musical numbers with the dramatic action. For instance, a show-stopping number like "Defying Gravity" from *Wicked* needs to come at just the right point in the story to maximize its emotional impact and leave the audience on the edge of their seats. The director's role is to make sure that these moments land with precision.

Directing a Broadway show also involves a significant amount of problem-solving. Broadway productions are complex, with numerous moving parts, from technical challenges to costume changes to managing a large ensemble cast. A director must be adaptable and resourceful, able to make quick decisions when issues arise. Whether it's adjusting the blocking because a set piece isn't working as planned, or finding a way to rework a scene that's not resonating with the actors, the director must be a creative problem-solver who can think on their feet.

The director also plays a critical role during the rehearsal process. Rehearsals are where the director's vision truly starts to take shape, as the actors, musicians, and technical crew work together to bring the production to life. The director must create a productive, supportive environment during rehearsals, where the cast and crew feel comfortable experimenting and taking creative risks. At the same time, the director must keep everyone focused on the ultimate goal: bringing the vision of the show to its full realization. This often involves giving detailed notes, refining performances, and making adjustments to staging or timing as necessary.

In the weeks leading up to the show's opening, the director also works closely with the producer and creative team to prepare for previews. Previews are a critical phase in the production process, where the show is performed in front of live audiences before officially opening. During previews, the director must be open to feedback from both the audience and the creative team, making necessary changes to improve the show. This might involve trimming scenes, tightening transitions, or even reworking entire sequences if they aren't landing with the audience. The ability to remain flexible and open to change is essential during this period, as the show evolves based on real-time feedback.

Leading with vision also means understanding the broader cultural and social context in which the show is being produced. Broadway musicals do not exist in a vacuum—they are part of a larger cultural conversation, and great directors know how to make their productions feel relevant and timely. Whether addressing contemporary social issues, reinterpreting a classic work for a modern audience, or finding new ways to engage with timeless themes, a director with vision understands the power of theater to reflect and influence the world around us. For example, *Hamilton* revolutionized Broadway by reimagining the story of America's founding fathers through a modern lens, using hip-hop music and a diverse cast to tell a familiar story in a fresh, exciting way.

Finally, a director's vision must extend beyond opening night. Once the show is up and running, the director may need to continue working with the cast to maintain the quality of the performances and ensure that the production remains consistent over time. Directors may also be involved in decisions about touring productions, revivals, or adaptations of the show for other formats, such as film or television. Leading a show to success on Broadway is just the beginning—the director's role can continue long after the final curtain falls.

In conclusion, directing a Broadway show is an intricate balance of artistry, leadership, and collaboration. A great director leads with vision, shaping every aspect of the production to create a cohesive, emotionally resonant experience for the audience. From guiding the actors to collaborating with the creative team, the director is the driving force behind the production, ensuring that the story, music, and design come together seamlessly. With the ability to solve problems, inspire creativity, and shape the pacing and rhythm of the show, a director can turn a collection of songs and scenes into a powerful, unforgettable theatrical experience.

Movement and Magic: The Importance of Dance and Choreography

In a Broadway musical, dance and choreography are much more than mere spectacle; they are integral components of the storytelling. The movement on stage serves as a powerful tool to convey emotion, character development, and even plot progression. When done effectively, dance creates a visceral connection between the performers and the audience, elevating the music and narrative to new heights. Choreography allows the audience to experience the story not just through words and music, but through movement, providing a dynamic and often magical layer to the production.

The importance of choreography in a Broadway show cannot be overstated. Dance has the power to express what words and music alone cannot. While a character may sing about their feelings, movement can give those emotions a physical form. For instance, in *West Side Story*, the iconic dance sequences choreographed by Jerome Robbins do more than entertain; they express the tension, rivalry, and passion between the Jets and the Sharks. The aggressive movements, precise footwork, and athletic jumps reflect the volatile emotions of the characters, turning the dance into a form of dialogue. Robbins' choreography tells the story as much as the music and lyrics, and without it, the show would lose much of its emotional impact.

One of the primary functions of choreography in musical theater is to heighten emotional moments. A well-placed dance sequence can make a joyful celebration feel more exuberant, a romantic duet more intimate, or a climactic showdown more intense. Dance can amplify the emotional stakes of a scene, allowing the audience to experience the character's joy, pain, or inner turmoil in a more immersive way. For example, in *The Lion King*, Garth Fagan's choreography uses animalistic movements to bring the savannah to life, but it also amplifies the emotional resonance of scenes like "Circle of Life," where the choreography's grand, sweeping motions capture the majesty and spiritual depth of the moment.

Another crucial role of choreography is to develop character. In musical theater, how a character moves on stage is as important as what they say or sing. A skilled choreographer will work closely with the director and actors to ensure that the character's personality, background, and emotional arc are reflected in their movements. For instance, the character of Eliza Doolittle in *My Fair Lady* transforms from a scrappy, unpolished flower girl into a poised lady. Her movements, which start out rough and unrefined, become more graceful and controlled as the story progresses, mirroring her internal transformation. In this way, choreography is not just about creating beautiful or entertaining dance numbers—it's about using movement as a storytelling tool to show character growth and change.

Choreography also plays a vital role in setting the tone and atmosphere of a musical. The style of dance used in a production can establish the time period, location, and overall mood of the show. For instance, Bob Fosse's distinctive jazz-influenced choreography in *Chicago* immediately sets the tone for the show's gritty, cynical portrayal of fame, crime, and corruption in 1920s Chicago. His sharp, angular movements, sultry poses, and rhythmic isolation of body parts create a stylized world that feels both seductive and dangerous. The choreography not only reflects the themes of the show but also helps create the dark, satirical tone that *Chicago* is known for.

In addition to enhancing the narrative and character development, dance in musical theater is often used to convey subtext or themes. Choreography can add layers of meaning to a scene, providing the audience with visual cues about relationships, power dynamics, or internal conflicts. In *Fiddler on the Roof*, Jerome Robbins' choreography for "Tradition" visually demonstrates the tension between old customs and modern challenges. The dancers' movements are rooted in traditional folk dance styles, but the increasingly complex choreography mirrors the growing conflict between maintaining tradition and adapting to change. Through the choreography, the audience can see the struggle that Tevye and his community face, even without a single word being spoken.

The collaborative nature of dance in a musical production is another key aspect of its importance. The choreographer works closely with the director, music director, and set designer to ensure that the dance numbers are integrated seamlessly into the show. The choreography must align with the music's rhythms, the emotional beats of the story, and the technical aspects of the set. This requires careful planning and collaboration, as the choreographer must create movement that not only looks beautiful but also fits within the constraints of the stage design, lighting, and costumes. For example, in *Hamilton*, Andy Blankenbuehler's choreography is intricately tied to the musical's rhythm, with the movement often reflecting the rapid-fire nature of the dialogue and music. The choreography is also designed to fit within the minimalist set, using the performers' bodies to create dynamic visuals that fill the stage and enhance the storytelling.

Dance numbers in a musical also serve as pivotal moments of spectacle. Broadway audiences expect to be dazzled, and a show-stopping dance sequence can leave a lasting impression. Think of the electrifying choreography in *42nd Street*, where the ensemble's synchronized tap dancing creates a thrilling, high-energy performance that exemplifies the glitz and glamour of Broadway itself. Or consider the Act 1 finale of *Wicked*, where Elphaba's ascent into the air during "Defying Gravity" is made even more dramatic by the choreography that builds up to that moment. The visual and kinetic energy of these dance sequences captures the audience's attention and often becomes one of the most memorable aspects of the show.

Another significant element of choreography in musical theater is the way it can enhance ensemble numbers. Large dance ensembles provide an opportunity to create intricate, visually stunning performances that fill the stage with movement. These ensemble numbers can represent larger groups within the story, such as communities or opposing factions, and can add depth to the narrative. In *Les Misérables*, the ensemble's choreography in "Do You Hear the People Sing?" turns the stage into a rallying cry for revolution, using coordinated movement to express unity and collective action. The choreography reinforces the song's message and helps create a powerful sense of momentum, drawing the audience into the revolutionary spirit of the moment.

In musical theater, the choreography must also be adaptable to the skills and abilities of the cast. While many Broadway performers are trained dancers, not all leading actors are professional dancers. A good choreographer will design movement that highlights the strengths of the cast, creating choreography that feels natural for the performers while still maintaining the artistic integrity of the show. For instance, in *The King and I*, the choreography for "Shall We Dance?" is designed to be graceful and elegant, allowing the performers to communicate the growing connection between Anna and the King without requiring overly complex dance steps. The choreography enhances the emotional tension of the scene while allowing the actors to focus on the chemistry between their characters.

Choreographers must also consider the demands of the entire production when creating dance sequences. A Broadway musical typically runs eight performances a week, so the choreography must be designed with stamina and repetition in mind. While the choreography needs to be visually impressive, it also has to be sustainable for the performers, who must repeat the movements night after night without risking injury or fatigue. A skilled choreographer finds the balance between creating challenging, dynamic movement and ensuring that the dancers can maintain the energy and precision needed for each performance.

Finally, choreography in a Broadway musical can be a transformative experience for the audience. Dance has a universal, wordless power to evoke emotions, transcending language barriers and cultural differences. A beautifully choreographed dance sequence can transport the audience into the emotional world of the characters in a way that spoken dialogue or even song cannot. It can make the audience feel the character's joy, sorrow, love, or fear on a more visceral level. Dance can make the world of the musical feel more alive, more vibrant, and more immediate, leaving a lasting emotional impact.

In conclusion, dance and choreography are essential elements of a Broadway musical that go far beyond spectacle. Choreography serves as a powerful tool for storytelling, helping to express emotion, develop characters, and reinforce themes. It plays a crucial role in shaping the tone, atmosphere, and visual identity of the show, while also providing moments of magic and excitement that captivate audiences. Whether through intimate character duets, large ensemble numbers, or iconic showstoppers, the movement on stage is an integral part of the musical's success, transforming music and lyrics into a living, breathing experience. When dance and choreography are used to their full potential, they elevate the entire production, turning a great show into an unforgettable theatrical event.

Injecting Humor: How Comedy Enhances the Musical

Humor is one of the most powerful tools in a Broadway musical, bringing levity, charm, and relatability to the stage. While musicals often explore deep emotions, dramatic conflicts, or complex themes, comedy plays a crucial role in making these stories accessible and enjoyable for audiences. Injecting humor into a musical can create moments of relief, enhance character development, and even deepen the audience's connection to the story. In many ways, comedy serves as the glue that holds the emotional and narrative elements of a musical together, providing contrast, balance, and moments of pure entertainment.

The first and most obvious benefit of humor in a musical is its ability to entertain and engage the audience. A well-timed joke, a clever bit of physical comedy, or a funny song can capture the audience's attention and keep them invested in the story. Musicals like *The Producers*, *Avenue Q*, and *Something Rotten!* are built around humor, using wit, satire, and absurdity to entertain the audience from start to finish. In these shows, comedy is the driving force behind the narrative, but even in more serious or dramatic musicals, humor can be a vital tool for maintaining the audience's interest and making the story more enjoyable.

One of the key ways that comedy enhances a musical is by providing moments of relief from emotional or dramatic tension. Musicals often deal with intense themes, from love and heartbreak to loss and societal conflict, and the audience can become emotionally overwhelmed if there is no balance. Injecting humor at strategic points in the narrative can lighten the mood and give the audience a chance to breathe before diving back into the heavier elements of the story. This technique is often referred to as "comic relief," and it can be found in many musicals. For example, in *Les Misérables*, the song "Master of the House" provides a humorous break from the show's darker, more dramatic moments. The antics of the innkeeper, Thénardier, and his wife inject a burst of comedy into an otherwise somber narrative, giving the audience a moment to relax and enjoy the characters' absurd behavior before returning to the tragic arc of the story.

Humor also enhances character development, making characters more relatable and human. When characters make jokes, engage in playful banter, or find themselves in funny situations, the audience gets to see a more lighthearted side of them, which can make them more endearing. In *Wicked*, the song "Popular" is a humorous, upbeat number that reveals Glinda's bubbly personality and her somewhat shallow desire to be liked. While the song is comedic, it also serves to deepen Glinda's character, showing her insecurities and her genuine, if misguided, attempts to help Elphaba fit in. The humor in this song makes Glinda more relatable and lovable, helping the audience connect with her on a deeper level.

In many musicals, comedy arises naturally from character interactions and relationships. The dynamic between characters often provides fertile ground for humor, particularly when their personalities clash or when they find themselves in absurd or awkward situations. For example, in *The Book of Mormon*, the mismatched pairing of the overly optimistic Elder Price and the socially awkward Elder Cunningham creates comedic tension throughout the show. Their contrasting personalities lead to misunderstandings, awkward moments, and hilarious situations, which not only entertain the audience but also drive the character arcs forward. By using humor to explore character relationships, musicals can create richer, more dynamic interactions that deepen the audience's understanding of the characters.

Physical comedy is another way that musicals inject humor into their narratives. Broadway is a visual medium, and physical comedy—whether it's slapstick, exaggerated movements, or choreographed pratfalls—can create laugh-out-loud moments that transcend dialogue and lyrics. Shows like *The Producers* and *Spamalot* use physical comedy extensively, with actors engaging in elaborate physical gags, over-the-top dance numbers, and exaggerated facial expressions. This type of humor adds a layer of fun to the performance, showcasing the actors' physicality and timing while providing a burst of energy that keeps the audience engaged.

Musical numbers themselves can be a source of comedy, using lyrics, melody, and performance to create humor. A song can be funny because of its lyrics, its context within the story, or the way it's performed. Take "A Little Priest" from *Sweeney Todd*, for example. The song is darkly comedic, with Sweeney and Mrs. Lovett discussing how they will bake people into pies while making pun-filled jokes about the different "flavors" of meat. The humor here arises from the contrast between the grisly subject matter and the playful tone of the song, making it both unsettling and hilarious. Similarly, *Avenue Q* is filled with humorous songs like "Everyone's a Little Bit Racist" and "The Internet is for Porn," where the comedy comes from the irreverent and unexpected subject matter being delivered in a catchy, upbeat musical style.

Another way that comedy enhances a musical is by allowing the show to address serious or controversial topics in a more palatable way. Satire is a powerful tool in musical theater, using humor to critique societal norms, politics, or cultural issues. Shows like *Urinetown*, *The Book of Mormon*, and *Hairspray* use comedy to tackle issues like corporate greed, religion, racism, and body image. By wrapping these serious topics in humor, the musicals make their critiques more accessible and entertaining, encouraging the audience to think critically while still enjoying the show. Satire can be both biting and entertaining, and when done well, it adds depth to the musical by offering a commentary on real-world issues.

In some cases, humor in musicals is used to break the fourth wall and engage directly with the audience. Shows like *Something Rotten!* and *The Drowsy Chaperone* often poke fun at the conventions of musical theater itself, using meta-humor to create a playful relationship with the audience. This type of comedy not only generates laughs but also invites the audience to be in on the joke, creating a more interactive and self-aware experience. For example, in *Something Rotten!*, the song "A Musical" humorously explains the absurdity of musical theater to a character who has never heard of such a thing, while simultaneously poking fun at the tropes and clichés of the genre. The audience gets to laugh at the conventions of musicals while still appreciating the craft behind them.

Comedy can also be used to create contrast and make emotional moments more impactful. By juxtaposing humor with more serious or dramatic scenes, musicals can heighten the emotional impact of key moments. For example, in *The Lion King*, the characters Timon and Pumbaa provide comic relief with their carefree attitude and humorous interactions. However, their lightheartedness also serves to underscore the gravity of Simba's journey. When the show shifts from Timon and Pumbaa's antics to Simba's moment of self-realization and confrontation with his past, the contrast makes Simba's emotional transformation feel even more powerful. Comedy, in this case, helps to highlight the depth of the dramatic moments, making them stand out more vividly.

Lastly, humor can be an essential tool in making musicals more relatable to contemporary audiences. Modern musicals often reflect current cultural sensibilities, and humor is a way to connect with the audience in a way that feels fresh and relevant. Shows like *Mean Girls* and *The Prom* use humor to comment on the social dynamics of high school, identity politics, and the pressures of fitting in, while still delivering heartfelt messages about friendship and acceptance. The humor in these shows resonates with younger audiences, who see their own experiences reflected on stage in a way that is both entertaining and meaningful.

In conclusion, injecting humor into a musical enhances the production by making it more entertaining, accessible, and emotionally engaging. Comedy provides relief from dramatic tension, deepens character development, and creates dynamic interactions between characters. Whether through witty dialogue, clever lyrics, physical gags, or satirical commentary, humor plays a vital role in shaping the tone and pacing of a musical. It can also be a powerful tool for addressing serious topics and making them more approachable for the audience. When used effectively, comedy enhances the overall experience of the musical, turning it into a multi-dimensional production that can make audiences laugh, think, and feel all at once.

The Emotional Core: Drama in the Broadway Musical

Drama is the emotional heart of the Broadway musical, providing the depth and intensity that makes a story resonate with audiences. While musicals are often celebrated for their vibrant songs, dazzling choreography, and moments of humor, it is the drama—the conflict, the relationships, the struggles—that gives the story weight and meaning. The emotional stakes of a musical are what draw audiences in, making them care about the characters and their journeys. Drama is the thread that ties together the music, lyrics, and performance, creating a rich, immersive experience that stays with the audience long after the final curtain falls.

At its core, drama in a Broadway musical is about conflict. Conflict drives the story forward, pushing characters to confront their fears, desires, and the obstacles in their way. Whether it's internal conflict, like a character's struggle with self-doubt or guilt, or external conflict, like a battle against societal expectations or an antagonist, the tension created by these challenges fuels the dramatic arc of the musical. In *Les Misérables*, for instance, the conflict between Jean Valjean and Javert represents a moral and philosophical battle that drives the entire narrative. Valjean's quest for redemption and Javert's unyielding belief in the law create a dramatic tension that keeps the audience engaged throughout the show.

One of the key ways that drama enhances a Broadway musical is by creating an emotional connection between the audience and the characters. When characters face adversity or grapple with difficult choices, the audience becomes invested in their journey. This emotional investment is what makes the stakes of the story feel real and significant. In *Dear Evan Hansen*, Evan's internal struggles with loneliness, anxiety, and guilt create a deeply personal drama that resonates with many audience members. The raw emotion of songs like "Waving Through a Window" and "You Will Be Found" draws the audience into Evan's world, making them feel his pain and isolation. The emotional core of the drama allows the musical to explore themes of identity, belonging, and mental health in a way that feels both authentic and impactful.

Drama in a musical is often expressed through the relationships between characters. Romantic relationships, family dynamics, and friendships are all fertile ground for dramatic tension. The highs and lows of these relationships provide the emotional fuel for many of the most powerful moments in musical theater. In *West Side Story*, the forbidden love between Tony and Maria is at the center of the drama. Their relationship is filled with passion, hope, and despair, as they try to navigate their love in a world filled with violence and hatred. The dramatic tension between the lovers and the rival gangs is what drives the tragic narrative, and the audience becomes emotionally invested in the outcome of their story.

Another vital aspect of drama in musical theater is the exploration of personal growth and transformation. Characters in musicals often undergo significant changes over the course of the show, and this evolution is typically marked by moments of intense drama. These moments of crisis and resolution are what make the characters' journeys so compelling. In *Wicked*, for example, the character of Elphaba undergoes a dramatic transformation from an idealistic young woman to the feared Wicked Witch of the West. Her journey is filled with moments of internal conflict, as she struggles with her desire to do good and her realization that the world may never accept her. The song "Defying Gravity" is a pivotal dramatic moment in the show, marking Elphaba's decision to embrace her own power and destiny, regardless of the consequences.

Drama also allows musicals to explore complex themes and social issues. Broadway musicals have long been a platform for addressing topics like injustice, inequality, and the human condition. The drama in these musicals helps bring these issues to life in a way that is emotionally resonant and thought-provoking. In *Rent*, for instance, the characters face the challenges of poverty, illness, and the struggle for creative expression in the midst of the AIDS epidemic. The dramatic tension in the show comes from the characters' battles with these external forces, as well as their internal struggles with love, loss, and survival. The emotional weight of the drama helps convey the urgency of the show's themes, making the audience feel the impact of the characters' experiences.

In many musicals, drama is heightened by the use of music. Music has the unique ability to amplify emotions, and in a musical, songs often serve as the emotional high points of the drama. When characters sing, they are often expressing feelings that are too intense to be conveyed through dialogue alone. A song can capture a character's deepest fears, hopes, and desires, allowing the audience to experience their emotions in a more direct and powerful way. For example, in *Les Misérables*, the song "I Dreamed a Dream" is a heartbreaking expression of Fantine's despair and disillusionment. The combination of the raw emotion in the lyrics and the sweeping melody creates a moment of intense drama that leaves a lasting impact on the audience.

Dramatic tension in a musical can also be created through pacing and structure. The way a story unfolds—when revelations are made, when conflicts come to a head, and when resolutions are reached—can create a sense of suspense and anticipation that heightens the drama. In *Hamilton*, the pacing of the show mirrors the rise and fall of Alexander Hamilton's life. The first act builds momentum as Hamilton rises to power, culminating in the explosive drama of the Revolutionary War and his role in shaping the new nation. The second act, in contrast, slows down to focus on Hamilton's personal and political struggles, leading to the climactic duel with Aaron Burr. The structure of the musical creates a sense of inevitability, with each dramatic event building on the one before, making the audience feel the weight of Hamilton's choices and their consequences.

Conflict resolution is another key element of drama in musicals. The resolution of dramatic tension—whether through reconciliation, triumph, or tragedy—often provides the emotional climax of the show. In *The Phantom of the Opera*, the final confrontation between the Phantom, Christine, and Raoul brings all the dramatic tension of the story to a head. The Phantom's unrequited love and inner torment, Christine's fear and compassion, and Raoul's determination to save her all collide in this intense moment. The resolution of this drama, with Christine's act of kindness and the Phantom's ultimate decision to let her go, provides a cathartic release for the audience, leaving them emotionally spent but deeply moved.

Another important aspect of drama in musical theater is the way it can reflect real-life struggles. Audiences often connect most deeply with stories that reflect their own experiences, whether it's the pain of loss, the joy of love, or the challenge of overcoming adversity. Musicals like *Next to Normal* tackle issues like mental illness and family dynamics with unflinching honesty, creating a drama that feels both raw and real. The emotional intensity of the show's drama is what makes it so powerful, as it forces the audience to confront difficult emotions and situations. The honesty and vulnerability of the drama allow audiences to see themselves in the characters, making the story resonate on a personal level.

Finally, drama in a Broadway musical creates opportunities for performers to showcase their emotional range and depth. Musicals are a uniquely demanding art form because they require actors to combine singing, acting, and often dancing, all while maintaining the emotional truth of their character. Dramatic moments in a musical allow performers to delve into the most intense emotions of their characters, whether it's heartbreak, rage, or joy. These moments often become the defining performances of a show, with actors pouring their hearts into the roles and leaving everything on the stage. Performers like Patti LuPone in *Evita* or Ben Platt in *Dear Evan Hansen* became iconic not only because of their vocal talents but because of their ability to convey deep emotional truths through their performances, bringing the drama of their characters to life in a way that deeply moved audiences.

In conclusion, drama is the emotional core of a Broadway musical. It provides the conflict, tension, and emotional stakes that make a story compelling, allowing the audience to connect deeply with the characters and their journeys. Through conflict, relationships, personal growth, and thematic exploration, drama gives a musical its weight and resonance. When combined with music, structure, and performance, drama elevates a musical from entertainment to an emotionally immersive experience that can leave a lasting impact on the audience. Whether through moments of triumph, tragedy, or transformation, the drama of a Broadway musical is what makes it unforgettable.

Finding the Stars: The Art of Casting

Casting is one of the most critical and delicate tasks in producing a Broadway musical. Finding the right performers to bring characters to life on stage is an art form that requires a deep understanding of both the material and the talent pool. The casting process involves not only finding actors with the right vocal, acting, and sometimes dancing abilities but also discovering performers who embody the essence of their characters and have the ability to connect with the audience emotionally. Casting decisions can make or break a production, and when done well, they elevate a show from good to unforgettable.

The first step in casting a Broadway musical is understanding the characters. Each role in the production has specific traits, motivations, and an emotional journey that must be portrayed with authenticity. Before auditions even begin, the director, producer, and casting director must have a clear idea of what they're looking for in each character. What are the character's strengths and weaknesses? What are their primary emotional beats? What is their arc throughout the show? This understanding helps shape the casting process, guiding the team to look for performers who can not only sing and act but also capture the character's depth.

For a leading role, casting requires finding a performer with both star quality and the ability to carry the emotional weight of the show. Lead performers often have to navigate intense emotional moments while delivering complex songs and, in some cases, intricate choreography. It's essential that they have the stamina to perform multiple shows per week while maintaining the integrity of their performance. This is why casting a lead role is often a lengthy and meticulous process. Take *Wicked*, for example: the role of Elphaba is vocally and emotionally demanding, requiring a performer who can belt out showstopping numbers like "Defying Gravity" while also conveying the character's inner turmoil and transformation. Casting directors must find a performer who can excel in all areas, blending technical skill with emotional depth.

While vocal ability is often the first quality that comes to mind in casting a musical, acting skills are just as important. The best musical performers are not only great singers but also great actors. They must be able to convey the nuances of their characters through their facial expressions, body language, and line delivery, even when they are singing. A powerful voice is meaningless if the audience can't feel the character's emotions. For example, in *Hamilton*, the role of Alexander Hamilton requires an actor who can handle the rapid-fire rap lyrics while delivering a performance that makes the audience feel Hamilton's ambition, vulnerability, and eventual downfall. Lin-Manuel Miranda, who originated the role, brought a raw emotional energy to the character that resonated deeply with audiences. His casting not only helped define the show but also showcased the importance of finding actors who can bring layered, authentic performances to the stage.

For supporting roles, casting is equally important. These characters often provide comedic relief, emotional grounding, or additional layers to the narrative. They may not have as much stage time as the leads, but their presence is crucial to the overall dynamic of the show. In *Les Misérables*, characters like Éponine and Javert are not the primary protagonists, but their performances are pivotal to the emotional impact of the story. Finding the right actors for these roles requires a focus on chemistry—how they interact with the lead actors and how they fit into the overall ensemble.

Ensemble casting is another vital element of the process. The ensemble provides the musical's backbone, filling out the world of the production with supporting characters, dancers, and chorus members. Ensemble performers must be versatile, as they often play multiple roles throughout the show, and they must be strong dancers and singers, capable of blending harmoniously with the rest of the cast. In shows like *West Side Story* or *The Lion King*, the ensemble carries much of the visual and choreographic storytelling. The energy and cohesiveness of the ensemble can significantly affect the show's overall impact, and casting directors must find performers who not only fit into the production's aesthetic but also have the ability to adapt to different roles and moments on stage.

Chemistry between actors is another key factor in casting. Even the most talented performers may not succeed in a role if they lack chemistry with their co-stars. Whether it's the romantic tension between a leading couple or the camaraderie between a group of friends, the dynamic between performers must feel authentic and compelling. This is why many casting processes include callback auditions where actors are paired with one another to test their chemistry. Directors and producers often spend hours watching different combinations of actors read or sing together to see if the emotional connection is there. In *Dear Evan Hansen*, for example, the relationship between Evan and his mother is central to the show's emotional arc. Casting actors who can convincingly portray the vulnerability and tension in that relationship is crucial to making the audience feel the weight of the story.

Physical appearance can also play a role in casting, though it is often a secondary consideration to talent and chemistry. Directors may have a specific vision for how they want certain characters to look, based on the source material or the overall design of the show. However, modern casting practices have become increasingly flexible, with more emphasis on diversity and inclusion. Productions like *Hamilton* have broken the mold by casting actors of color in roles traditionally associated with white historical figures, proving that talent and storytelling transcend race. The goal of casting should always be to find the performers who can best embody the spirit of the characters, regardless of physical appearance.

Casting decisions are also influenced by the overall tone and style of the production. A traditional musical like *The Sound of Music* requires a different casting approach than a contemporary, edgy show like *Spring Awakening*. Directors and producers must ensure that the performers they choose fit the stylistic demands of the show. For example, in *Chicago*, the sharp, sultry jazz choreography and vaudeville-inspired performances require actors who can embody the show's bold, cynical tone. Meanwhile, in *Next to Normal*, the emotional realism and rawness of the family drama require actors who can deliver subtle, nuanced performances that feel deeply personal and authentic.

The audition process itself is an essential part of casting. It's where the director, producer, and casting director have the opportunity to see how actors perform under pressure and how they interpret the material. Auditions typically include singing, acting, and sometimes dancing, depending on the role. A great audition is not just about hitting the right notes or delivering lines perfectly—it's about capturing the essence of the character and showing potential. Many legendary Broadway performers, like Audra McDonald and Idina Menzel, have wowed casting directors not just with their talent but with their ability to bring something unique and personal to their auditions.

In some cases, producers may seek out established stars to cast in key roles, particularly for high-profile productions or revivals. While star casting can help sell tickets and generate buzz, it also presents challenges. The performer must not only have name recognition but also the talent and work ethic to handle the demands of a Broadway production. For example, when Hugh Jackman was cast in the revival of *The Music Man*, his star power drew significant attention to the production, but it was his proven musical theater skills that made him a perfect fit for the role. Producers must weigh the benefits of casting a celebrity against the risk of overshadowing the show itself or compromising the integrity of the performance.

Once the cast is assembled, the director's work is far from over. Throughout rehearsals, the director continues to shape and refine the performances, helping the actors develop their characters and build chemistry with one another. Casting is just the first step in a collaborative process that brings the story to life. A well-cast production becomes a cohesive ensemble where every performer contributes to the overall impact of the show.

In conclusion, the art of casting a Broadway musical requires a combination of intuition, collaboration, and careful judgment. Finding the right actors is about more than just talent—it's about finding performers who can embody the characters, connect with the material, and create chemistry with their co-stars. From lead roles to the ensemble, every casting decision plays a crucial role in shaping the success of the production. When done well, casting elevates a show, bringing its characters to life in ways that are emotionally compelling and unforgettable for the audience.

Dressing the Part: Costuming for Broadway

Costuming is a critical element in any Broadway musical, playing a pivotal role in helping to define characters, set the tone, and enhance the storytelling. Costumes do more than simply clothe the actors; they become part of the world being created on stage, adding visual depth, authenticity, and emotional resonance to the production. The art of costume design for Broadway requires an understanding of the narrative, character arcs, historical accuracy (when relevant), and the physical demands of live theater. The right costume can transform a performer into their character, making them look and feel the part while also contributing to the overall aesthetic and atmosphere of the show.

One of the most important aspects of costume design is how it helps define character. Costumes reflect a character's personality, status, occupation, and emotional state. They can be bold and flamboyant or understated and simple, depending on the needs of the role. For example, in *The Phantom of the Opera*, the costumes are opulent and grand, mirroring the Gothic romance and mystery that permeates the show. Christine's elegant gowns reflect her transformation from innocent chorus girl to the Phantom's muse, while the Phantom's dark, dramatic cape and mask symbolize his isolation and power. Each costume tells the audience something about the character before they even speak or sing, helping to set the stage for their story.

Costumes are also instrumental in showing the evolution of a character throughout a musical. As characters go through personal growth, challenges, or transformations, their costumes often reflect these changes. In *Wicked*, Elphaba's costumes evolve from a simple, schoolgirl outfit in muted tones to her iconic black dress and hat as she fully embraces her identity as the "Wicked Witch of the West." This change in her wardrobe symbolizes her journey from idealism and naivety to power and defiance. Similarly, Glinda's sparkling, glamorous gowns highlight her ascent into popularity and superficiality, reinforcing the contrast between the two characters. Costuming in this case not only adds to the visual appeal of the production but also serves as a subtle narrative tool that enhances character development.

Historical accuracy is often a key factor in costume design, particularly for period musicals. Shows like *Les Misérables* or *Hamilton* require costumes that reflect the time periods in which they are set, adding authenticity to the production and helping to immerse the audience in the story's world. In *Hamilton*, the costumes are inspired by 18th-century American revolutionary fashion, with the soldiers wearing waistcoats, breeches, and boots. However, the design choices are also modernized with sleek silhouettes and a more stylized approach to fabric and tailoring, creating a visual blend of historical reference and contemporary flair. This approach reflects the musical's innovative fusion of historical narrative with modern musical styles like hip-hop and R&B.

In period pieces, costume designers must conduct extensive research to ensure that the details of the clothing—fabrics, accessories, cuts, and colors—are accurate to the era. These details help transport the audience to a different time, grounding the story in its historical context. For example, in *The King and I*, the elaborate costumes worn by the King of Siam and his court reflect traditional Thai royal attire, adding authenticity to the production while also showcasing the cultural differences between the King and Anna, the British governess. The contrast in their costumes visually underscores the cultural and personal conflicts at the heart of the story.

However, costume design isn't limited to historical or realistic accuracy. In many musicals, particularly fantasy or abstract productions, costumes can be more stylized or symbolic. Designers have the freedom to use bold colors, exaggerated shapes, and fantastical elements to create a visual language that enhances the themes and emotions of the show. In *The Lion King*, for instance, Julie Taymor's innovative costume designs blend elements of traditional African dress with avant-garde puppetry, creating stunning visual representations of the animal kingdom. The actors wear elaborate headdresses and masks that evoke the spirit of lions, zebras, and other animals, while their costumes incorporate natural textures and patterns to reflect the savannah. These designs transport the audience into a world that is both familiar and otherworldly, heightening the theatrical experience.

Another essential aspect of costume design is color. Color is a powerful tool that can evoke emotions, highlight themes, and help distinguish characters from one another. Costume designers often use specific color palettes to convey mood, contrast characters, or symbolize different aspects of the story. For example, in *West Side Story*, the rival gangs—the Jets and the Sharks—are distinguished not only by their body language and attitudes but also by their contrasting costumes. The Jets, representing white working-class youth, wear cooler tones like blues and grays, while the Sharks, representing Puerto Rican immigrants, are dressed in warmer colors like reds and purples. This visual distinction enhances the tension between the two groups and reinforces their cultural differences.

In addition to supporting the narrative, costume design on Broadway must also address the practical demands of live performance. Actors need to be able to move freely and perform complex choreography while wearing their costumes, so designers must find ways to balance style with functionality. Costumes must be durable enough to withstand multiple performances each week, quick changes, and the physicality of live theater. For example, in *Chicago*, the dancers' costumes are sleek, sexy, and designed to allow for the sharp, precise movements required by Bob Fosse's iconic choreography. The minimalistic costumes not only enhance the sensuality and energy of the show but also provide the flexibility needed for the demanding dance routines.

Costume changes are another logistical challenge for designers. In many musicals, actors must change costumes multiple times throughout the show, often within a matter of seconds. Quick-change costumes are designed with hidden zippers, snaps, or Velcro to allow the actors to change outfits quickly and efficiently without disrupting the flow of the performance. In *The Phantom of the Opera*, Christine's costume changes are frequent and elaborate, requiring backstage precision and the careful design of garments that can be slipped on and off in seconds while maintaining their luxurious appearance.

Costuming also plays a critical role in creating spectacle. Broadway musicals often rely on grand visual moments to captivate the audience, and costumes are a key part of that spectacle. Elaborate, detailed costumes can transform the stage into a world of fantasy, luxury, or historical grandeur. In *Aladdin*, the costume design is integral to the show's lavish, opulent atmosphere. The vibrant, jewel-toned costumes, adorned with intricate beading and embroidery, evoke the magical, exotic world of Agrabah. The Genie's sparkling blue ensemble, in particular, creates a sense of wonder and whimsy, aligning with the character's larger-than-life personality and the magical tone of the production.

Similarly, in *Frozen*, the costumes are not only beautiful but also technically complex. Elsa's iconic transformation during the song "Let It Go" is a standout moment in the show, and her costume plays a pivotal role in creating that magic. As she sings, Elsa's plain dress is seamlessly replaced with her shimmering ice-queen gown, an effect that relies on both costume design and precise stagecraft. These kinds of moments demonstrate how costumes can enhance the drama and magic of a musical, leaving a lasting impression on the audience.

Another essential aspect of Broadway costuming is how it reflects the cultural or thematic layers of a production. In *In the Heights*, the costumes help ground the characters in the vibrant, multicultural world of Washington Heights, New York. The characters' clothing reflects their identities, occupations, and personal styles, from Usnavi's casual streetwear to Vanessa's fashionable, urban-chic outfits. The costumes reflect the neighborhood's diverse Latinx community, adding authenticity to the portrayal of the characters' lives and struggles.

Collaboration is key in costume design, as the designer must work closely with the director, set designer, lighting designer, and choreographer to ensure that the costumes complement the overall vision of the production. The costumes must fit within the world of the set, work with the lighting to enhance visibility and atmosphere, and accommodate the physical demands of the choreography. Costume designers often attend rehearsals to see how the performers move in their costumes and make adjustments to ensure that everything works seamlessly in performance.

In conclusion, costuming for a Broadway musical is a blend of artistry, practicality, and storytelling. It helps define characters, establish time and place, and enhance the emotional and visual impact of the production. Whether through historically accurate designs, stylized fantasy creations, or simple, modern clothing, costumes play a crucial role in creating the world of the musical and bringing the characters to life. The right costume not only supports the actor's performance but also becomes an integral part of the narrative, making it an essential element of any successful Broadway show. When executed with creativity and precision, costume design elevates a musical, turning it into an immersive, unforgettable theatrical experience.

Staging the Magic: Finding the Right Venue for Your Show

Finding the right venue is a crucial step in bringing a Broadway musical to life. The theater where the show will be staged serves as more than just a physical location—it becomes an integral part of the overall production, influencing everything from the visual presentation to the audience experience. The venue must align with the scale, style, and technical requirements of the show while also providing a comfortable and engaging environment for the audience. Choosing the right venue is a strategic decision that involves careful consideration of the theater's size, technical capabilities, location, and the specific needs of the production.

The first factor in selecting a venue is the size of the theater. Broadway theaters vary widely in capacity, with some seating fewer than 500 people and others accommodating over 1,500. The size of the theater has a direct impact on the audience's experience and the overall atmosphere of the show. A large, grandiose musical like *The Lion King* or *Wicked* benefits from a larger venue, where the scale of the production can be fully appreciated, and the elaborate sets and special effects can be maximized. The expansive seating allows for bigger musical numbers, more elaborate staging, and greater spectacle, which are essential to the success of these shows.

On the other hand, a more intimate musical, such as *Dear Evan Hansen* or *Next to Normal*, might be better suited to a smaller venue where the emotional nuances of the performances can resonate more deeply with the audience. In a smaller theater, every gesture, expression, and lyric can be felt more personally, creating a closer connection between the performers and the audience. The intimacy of the space enhances the emotional impact of the show, allowing for a more focused and introspective experience.

Technical capabilities are another critical consideration when choosing a venue for a Broadway musical. The technical demands of modern Broadway productions can be immense, with complex lighting designs, automated set pieces, elaborate sound systems, and, in some cases, special effects like pyrotechnics or flying rigs. The venue must be able to accommodate all of these technical requirements to ensure that the show runs smoothly and achieves its full visual and auditory potential. For example, a show like *Aladdin* requires a theater with advanced rigging systems for the magic carpet sequence, as well as the space and infrastructure to support large, ornate set pieces that transport the audience to the fictional world of Agrabah.

Theater facilities such as backstage space, dressing rooms, and rehearsal areas also play a role in the decision-making process. Productions with large casts, intricate costumes, and frequent quick changes need ample backstage space to manage the flow of actors, props, and costumes during the performance. In *Les Misérables*, for instance, the rapid costume changes and the large ensemble cast require a well-organized and spacious backstage area to ensure smooth transitions between scenes. Without adequate backstage space, the cast and crew may struggle to maintain the pace of the show, leading to delays and logistical issues.

The venue's acoustics are another important factor, particularly in musicals where live music plays a central role. The theater's design and acoustics can significantly affect how the music and dialogue are heard by the audience. A theater with poor acoustics might distort the sound, making it difficult for the audience to understand the lyrics or dialogue, which can detract from the overall experience. In contrast, a venue with excellent acoustics can enhance the clarity and emotional power of the music, allowing the audience to fully appreciate the score. Shows like *Hamilton*, with its intricate wordplay and fast-paced lyrics, require a venue where the acoustics allow every word to be heard clearly, ensuring that the audience can follow the narrative.

Location is another key consideration when choosing a venue. Broadway theaters are all located in New York City's famed Theater District, but even within this concentrated area, location can impact a show's success. A theater that is closer to major landmarks, public transportation, or popular tourist destinations may attract more foot traffic and casual theatergoers, boosting ticket sales. Location can also affect the accessibility of the venue for audiences, especially for visitors who may not be familiar with navigating New York City. Producers often consider how easy it is for audiences to find and access the theater when making a decision.

The financial aspects of securing a venue are also significant. Renting a Broadway theater is a major expense, and the costs vary depending on the size, location, and prestige of the theater. Larger, more prominent theaters in high-traffic areas tend to come with higher rental fees, while smaller or less well-known theaters may offer more affordable options. Producers must carefully balance the desire for a prime location and ideal technical facilities with the financial realities of their budget. In some cases, a more affordable venue may allow the production to allocate more resources to other areas, such as marketing or set design, while a higher-cost theater may come with the added benefit of drawing larger audiences or enhancing the show's visibility.

For new or smaller-scale productions, off-Broadway theaters are often an attractive option. Off-Broadway venues, which typically seat between 100 and 499 people, offer a more intimate setting and lower costs, making them ideal for shows that may not yet have the budget or audience base for a full Broadway production. Many successful Broadway musicals, including *Rent, Hamilton*, and *Dear Evan Hansen*, started off-Broadway before transferring to a larger Broadway venue once they had built a strong following. Off-Broadway theaters provide an opportunity to refine the production, test audience reactions, and make adjustments before committing to the higher stakes of a Broadway run.

Once the show is ready for Broadway, the transfer to a larger venue can be a turning point in its success. A larger venue offers more visibility, higher ticket sales potential, and the chance to reach a wider audience. However, transferring a show from off-Broadway to Broadway comes with its own set of challenges, including scaling up the production to fit a larger space, reworking technical elements, and adjusting the pacing to account for the size and layout of the new venue. Producers and directors must carefully plan for these changes to ensure that the show retains its integrity and impact in a larger setting.

Another factor in selecting a venue is the theater's history and reputation. Some Broadway theaters are iconic, with a long history of hosting legendary shows, and securing one of these venues can add prestige to a production. A show staged at a theater with a rich history may benefit from the theater's association with past successes, drawing in theatergoers who are excited by the venue's legacy. For example, theaters like the Winter Garden Theatre, where *Cats* ran for years, or the Richard Rodgers Theatre, home to *Hamilton*, are known for hosting groundbreaking productions. Performing in such a venue can create an added sense of anticipation and excitement around the show.

In addition to the physical and technical considerations, the venue's ambiance and design play a role in shaping the audience's experience. Some theaters are ornate and grand, with classic architecture and luxurious interiors that evoke a sense of old-world Broadway glamour. Others are more modern and minimalist, creating a different atmosphere that may suit certain productions better. The theater's design can help set the tone before the show even begins, influencing how the audience perceives the production.

Staging a musical in the right venue can also create a sense of community and intimacy. Some theaters are known for fostering close relationships between the audience and the performers, particularly in smaller venues where the audience feels more connected to the action on stage. This sense of connection can be especially important for emotionally charged or character-driven musicals, where the audience's engagement with the story and characters is key to the show's success.

In conclusion, finding the right venue for a Broadway musical is a complex process that requires balancing artistic vision with practical considerations. From the size and technical capabilities of the theater to its location, acoustics, and financial implications, every aspect of the venue impacts the production's success. The theater becomes an extension of the musical itself, influencing how the story is told, how the performers interact with the audience, and how the audience experiences the magic of the show. Whether it's a grand, large-capacity theater or an intimate off-Broadway venue, the right stage can elevate a musical, turning it into an unforgettable experience for all who attend.

Building the World: Props and Stage Design

Props and stage design are fundamental to creating the immersive world of a Broadway musical. Together, they not only set the physical scene but also establish the tone, enhance the narrative, and support the emotional journey of the characters. While the actors, music, and choreography bring a story to life, it is the design of the stage and the use of props that ground the audience in the world of the production. Every piece of scenery, every set detail, and every carefully chosen prop contributes to the visual storytelling, working in harmony with the performances to create a seamless theatrical experience.

Stage design is where the overall visual concept of the musical comes to life. The set serves as the physical environment in which the story unfolds, and it must reflect the world of the characters while aligning with the director's vision for the show. Whether it's the grandeur of a king's palace, the gritty streets of New York, or a fantastical realm of magic, the stage design creates the first impression for the audience and sets the tone for the entire performance.

One of the most important functions of stage design is to establish a sense of place. For example, in *The Phantom of the Opera*, the elaborate, gothic set design immerses the audience in the dark, mysterious world of the Paris Opera House. The grand chandelier, winding staircases, and subterranean lair all serve to transport the audience into the Phantom's domain, where beauty and terror coexist. The set not only establishes the physical location but also mirrors the themes of the story, with its grandeur and decay reflecting the Phantom's tortured inner world. In this way, the set design becomes an extension of the characters and the narrative.

Stage design is often shaped by the style and genre of the musical. A realistic, historically grounded musical like *Les Misérables* requires a set that convincingly portrays 19th-century France, from the grimy streets of Paris to the barricades of the revolution. In contrast, a more fantastical or abstract production, like *Wicked* or *The Lion King*, allows for a more imaginative and symbolic approach to set design. In *Wicked*, the set evokes the whimsical and dangerous world of Oz, with its emerald cityscapes, twisted gears, and fantastical structures reflecting the magical and political tensions of the story. Meanwhile, *The Lion King* uses a minimalist set design paired with innovative puppetry and costumes to evoke the vast, open landscapes of the African savannah, allowing the audience to focus on the movement and symbolism of the animals rather than on intricate, literal scenery.

In some musicals, the set design is highly interactive and dynamic, with moving pieces, revolving stages, and elaborate mechanisms that create a sense of fluidity and transformation. In *Hamilton*, for instance, the rotating stage is used to create a sense of motion and passage of time, helping to enhance the choreography and storytelling. The simple but versatile set allows the focus to remain on the performers while still offering enough flexibility to shift between different locations and emotional moments. This dynamic set design becomes a vital part of the show's energy and pacing, keeping the action moving and drawing the audience deeper into the world of the musical.

Another critical aspect of stage design is how it enhances the thematic elements of the musical. The set should support the mood and atmosphere of the production, helping to convey the underlying messages or emotions of the story. In *Rent*, the industrial, minimalist set design reflects the grittiness and struggles of the characters living in New York's East Village. The exposed scaffolding, makeshift apartments, and neon signage all reinforce the themes of survival, creativity, and rebellion in the face of hardship. The set's raw, unfinished quality mirrors the characters' lives, which are also incomplete and uncertain. In this way, the set becomes a metaphor for the themes of the musical, subtly reinforcing the emotional core of the story.

In addition to the set design, props play a crucial role in bringing the world of the musical to life. Props are the objects that actors interact with on stage, and they often have significant symbolic or narrative importance. A well-chosen prop can add layers of meaning to a scene, help define a character, or advance the plot. For example, in *Les Misérables*, the small red flag carried by the revolutionaries becomes a powerful symbol of their rebellion and sacrifice. The simple act of raising the flag transforms it from a mere object into a visual representation of hope, defiance, and unity.

Props can also be used to define the time period or setting of the musical. In a historical musical like *Hamilton*, the use of quills, parchment, and old-fashioned pistols helps ground the story in the 18th century, while in a modern musical like *Dear Evan Hansen*, the presence of smartphones, laptops, and social media feeds makes the world of the musical feel current and relevant. These props are not just background details; they actively shape the way the audience engages with the story and the characters.

In many cases, props are used to reveal key aspects of a character's personality or motivations. In *Sweeney Todd*, for instance, the barber's razor is more than just a tool; it becomes an extension of Todd's anger, revenge, and madness. The razor's prominence in the story symbolizes Todd's descent into violence and obsession, and every time he picks it up, the tension in the scene increases. Props like this one are carefully chosen to enhance the emotional stakes of the narrative, becoming iconic elements of the production.

Similarly, in *The Phantom of the Opera*, the Phantom's mask is not just a prop but a vital part of his character. The mask represents both his physical deformity and the emotional scars that drive him into isolation and madness. When the mask is removed, it reveals his vulnerability and rage, creating a dramatic moment that is central to the character's identity. The use of props like the Phantom's mask shows how integral they can be to the storytelling process, adding layers of complexity to the characters and their relationships.

Stage design and props must also work in harmony with the technical elements of the production, such as lighting, sound, and special effects. The lighting design, for example, can transform the appearance of a set, casting shadows, highlighting key areas, or creating an atmosphere of warmth, danger, or mystery. In a show like *The Phantom of the Opera*, lighting plays a crucial role in enhancing the gothic mood of the story, with spotlights and shadowy effects creating an eerie, otherworldly atmosphere. Similarly, in *Hadestown*, the use of red and golden lighting gives the set a mythic, underworld quality, heightening the sense of foreboding as the characters descend deeper into Hades.

Sound design also works hand-in-hand with props and the set. For instance, in *The Lion King*, the sound of animals moving across the savannah is integrated with the visual elements of the puppets and costumes, creating a fully immersive environment for the audience. The rustling of grass, the roar of a lion, or the thundering hooves of a wildebeest stampede all help build the world of the play, making the stage feel alive and dynamic.

In some productions, special effects are integral to the stage design and the use of props. In *Wicked*, Elphaba's broomstick is a key prop in her transformation from a misunderstood young woman to the Wicked Witch of the West. The broomstick, combined with the rigging that allows her to fly, creates one of the most iconic moments in modern musical theater—the "Defying Gravity" sequence. The illusion of flight, supported by the physical prop, stage machinery, and lighting effects, turns the broomstick into a symbol of Elphaba's empowerment and rebellion, leaving a lasting impression on the audience.

Stage design also needs to account for the flow and pacing of the production. In many musicals, sets must transform quickly to move the story from one scene to the next without interrupting the momentum of the show. For example, in *Les Misérables*, the famous barricade set must be constructed and dismantled quickly during the revolution scenes, creating a sense of urgency and chaos. Set designers often use rotating platforms, modular pieces, or sliding walls to create these transitions smoothly, ensuring that the visual storytelling keeps pace with the music and action.

In conclusion, props and stage design are essential to the success of a Broadway musical, serving as the foundation of the world in which the story unfolds. Through careful design and thoughtful choices, the set and props help create an immersive experience that enhances the emotional impact of the narrative. Whether through grand, elaborate sets or simple, symbolic props, these elements work together to transport the audience into the world of the characters, making the story more vivid, engaging, and unforgettable. When executed with creativity and precision, stage design and props become more than just background details—they become integral parts of the storytelling, elevating the musical to new heights and leaving a lasting impression on all who witness the magic of the stage.

Technical Mastery: Sound Equipment and Design for the Stage

Sound equipment and design are integral to the success of a Broadway musical, playing a critical role in ensuring that every word, note, and sound effect reaches the audience with clarity, power, and emotional impact. Sound design on Broadway is more than just amplification; it is about creating an auditory experience that enhances the storytelling, supports the performances, and immerses the audience in the world of the musical. From microphones and speakers to sound effects and orchestration, the technical mastery required for sound design is essential to bringing the show to life.

One of the most fundamental aspects of sound design is ensuring that the actors' voices are heard clearly by every member of the audience, no matter where they are seated. In a Broadway musical, where songs often convey key emotional beats and narrative elements, every lyric and line of dialogue must be intelligible. To achieve this, sound designers use a combination of microphones, speakers, and audio mixing equipment to amplify the performers' voices in a way that feels natural and balanced.

Broadway productions typically use body microphones (commonly called lavalier or "lav" mics), which are small, discreet microphones worn by the actors. These microphones are often placed near the actor's hairline, on the forehead, or hidden in wigs or costumes to capture their voice without being visible to the audience. The placement of these mics is crucial to ensuring that the sound is consistent and clear, even during intense dance sequences or when actors turn away from the audience. The sound team must carefully balance the volume of each microphone to ensure that no performer is too loud or too soft, creating a smooth and cohesive auditory experience.

The quality of the sound equipment used in a Broadway musical is of paramount importance. High-quality microphones, speakers, and mixers ensure that the sound is not only loud enough to fill the theater but also free from distortion, feedback, or unwanted noise. The speakers must be strategically placed throughout the theater to create an even distribution of sound, so that every audience member, whether in the front row or the balcony, has the same immersive audio experience. Subwoofers are often used to enhance the lower frequencies of the sound, adding depth and resonance to the music and sound effects.

Sound engineers play a key role in mixing the audio during the performance, ensuring that the levels of the actors' voices, the orchestra, and any sound effects are perfectly balanced. This requires a high level of technical skill and precision, as the mix must constantly be adjusted in real-time to account for changes in dynamics, actor movement, and the acoustics of the theater. A sound engineer must have an intimate understanding of the show's score, dialogue, and overall pacing to ensure that the audio mix supports the emotional and narrative flow of the performance.

In addition to amplifying the actors' voices, sound design must also account for the music, which is a central element of any Broadway musical. The orchestra, whether it is located in the pit or offstage, must be amplified and balanced in a way that complements the actors' voices without overpowering them. Sound designers often use separate microphones for each instrument or section of the orchestra, allowing them to fine-tune the mix and ensure that the music sounds rich and full throughout the theater. The challenge is to create a balance where the music enhances the drama and energy of the performance while still allowing the lyrics to be clearly understood.

In musicals where the orchestra is a key part of the experience, such as *The Phantom of the Opera* or *Les Misérables*, the sound design must create a sense of grandeur and scale, allowing the audience to feel fully immersed in the music. This is achieved through careful orchestration of the sound, using a combination of speakers and microphones to create a surround-sound experience that envelops the audience. The use of digital sound processing allows sound designers to manipulate the audio in real-time, creating effects like reverb, echo, or delay that enhance the music and make it feel more immersive.

Another important aspect of sound design is the creation and integration of sound effects. Sound effects help build the world of the musical, adding depth and realism to the scenes and supporting the visual storytelling. In some musicals, sound effects are used to underscore key moments of action or emotion. For example, in *The Lion King*, the sound of rustling grass, animal calls, and thunder adds to the atmosphere of the African savannah, making the setting feel alive and dynamic. Similarly, in *Wicked*, the use of sound effects during Elphaba's flying scenes enhances the magical quality of the moment, making the audience feel as if they are soaring along with her.

In more technologically advanced productions, sound effects are often synchronized with visual elements, such as lighting or projections, to create a cohesive sensory experience. For example, in *Harry Potter and the Cursed Child*, the sound design is a key part of creating the magic on stage, with sound effects for spells, transformations, and time travel working in tandem with visual effects to make the magical world feel real. The timing and precision of these effects are crucial, as even a slight delay in the sound can break the illusion and take the audience out of the moment.

Sound design also plays a significant role in shaping the emotional arc of a musical. Subtle sound cues can heighten tension, build anticipation, or enhance moments of joy or sorrow. In *Les Misérables*, for instance, the sound of the barricade collapsing or the distant cannons during the battle scenes creates a visceral impact that reinforces the gravity of the characters' struggle. The sound of gunfire, explosions, and clashing swords, combined with the swelling orchestration, adds to the intensity of the revolution, immersing the audience in the chaos of the moment.

In more intimate musicals, sound design can be used to create a sense of closeness and vulnerability. In *Next to Normal*, the sound design helps create a heightened emotional atmosphere, where the inner struggles of the characters are amplified through the use of echo, reverb, and other subtle sound manipulations. The music and sound effects work together to reflect the mental and emotional states of the characters, drawing the audience deeper into their psychological world.

The acoustics of the theater itself also play a role in sound design. Each theater has its own unique acoustic properties, influenced by its architecture, size, and layout. Sound designers must account for these factors when planning the audio for a show. A theater with a more "live" acoustic (where sound reverberates more easily) may require different sound levels and speaker placements than a theater with more "dead" acoustics (where sound is absorbed by the walls and seating). The goal is to create a consistent and balanced sound across the entire theater, so that no part of the audience experiences an overly loud or muffled performance.

The use of modern sound technology has expanded the possibilities for sound design on Broadway. Digital soundboards, wireless microphones, and advanced speaker systems allow sound designers to achieve greater precision and control over the audio mix. In some productions, sound designers use digital audio processing to create immersive, three-dimensional soundscapes that move with the action on stage. For example, sound can be panned from one side of the theater to the other to create the illusion of movement, or layered effects can be used to create a sense of depth and complexity in the sound.

Collaboration is key in sound design. The sound designer must work closely with the director, music director, and other members of the creative team to ensure that the sound supports the overall vision of the production. This includes working with the lighting and set designers to coordinate sound cues with visual elements, as well as collaborating with the performers to ensure that their voices and performances are enhanced by the sound design, not hindered by it.

In conclusion, sound equipment and design are essential to the technical mastery of a Broadway musical. From amplifying the actors' voices and orchestra to creating immersive sound effects and shaping the emotional arc of the story, sound design plays a pivotal role in bringing a show to life. The goal of sound design is to enhance the audience's experience, ensuring that every note, lyric, and sound is heard clearly and with the emotional impact that the story demands. With the right equipment, expertise, and creative vision, sound design transforms the auditory landscape of a Broadway musical, turning it into an unforgettable sensory experience that fully immerses the audience in the magic of live theater.

Illuminating the Story: The Role of Lighting in Broadway Musicals

Lighting design is an essential element in any Broadway musical, transforming the stage into a dynamic canvas that enhances the storytelling, mood, and emotional impact of a production. While often working in the background, lighting plays a pivotal role in shaping how the audience experiences a musical, influencing everything from the intensity of key moments to the subtle nuances of a character's emotional arc. Through creative and strategic use of light, designers illuminate the story in ways that are both visual and symbolic, enhancing the actors' performances, drawing attention to specific elements, and heightening the theatrical experience.

At its core, lighting design serves to direct the audience's focus. In a Broadway musical, the stage is filled with multiple layers of action, set pieces, and performers, and lighting helps guide the audience's attention to the most important elements of the scene. A well-placed spotlight can single out a performer in a crowded scene, emphasizing a key moment of dialogue or a solo performance. In *Les Misérables*, for example, the iconic image of Jean Valjean standing center stage, illuminated by a single beam of light as he sings "Who Am I?," uses lighting to focus attention on his internal struggle. The stark contrast between light and darkness in this moment not only isolates Valjean physically but also symbolically represents his moral dilemma, making the scene resonate deeply with the audience.

Lighting also sets the tone and atmosphere of a musical, creating the visual mood that supports the story's emotional arc. Warm, soft lighting can evoke feelings of comfort and intimacy, while harsh, cool lighting can create tension or unease. In *The Phantom of the Opera*, lighting plays a crucial role in establishing the gothic, mysterious atmosphere that permeates the show. The use of shadows, dim lighting, and dramatic spotlights highlights the eerie, haunting world of the Phantom, adding to the sense of danger and romance that defines the production. The lighting design becomes an extension of the Phantom's psychological torment, creating a mood that mirrors the themes of love, obsession, and isolation.

Color is another powerful tool in lighting design, helping to evoke emotions, reinforce themes, and differentiate between scenes or characters. Lighting designers use color to visually communicate what the characters are feeling or what the audience should be sensing in a particular moment. For example, in *Wicked*, the predominant use of green lighting is a visual cue that aligns with the character of Elphaba, who is associated with the color green throughout the show. The green light not only defines her character but also symbolizes her connection to magic, nature, and the idea of "otherness." In contrast, the use of warm, golden light in scenes with Glinda reinforces her status as the popular, beloved figure, creating a visual contrast that enhances the dynamic between the two characters.

The lighting in a musical also plays a crucial role in transitions between scenes, often serving as a bridge that helps shift the audience's attention from one moment to the next. In shows with complex, multi-location settings or large ensemble numbers, lighting helps create smooth transitions that maintain the flow of the production. For instance, in *Hamilton*, lighting is used not only to highlight specific moments of action but also to move the story forward as scenes shift rapidly between the political, personal, and battlefield arenas. The use of a rotating stage in *Hamilton* is complemented by precise lighting changes that keep the audience engaged, signaling shifts in time, space, and perspective without the need for extensive set changes.

Lighting can also be symbolic, adding layers of meaning to a musical's narrative. By playing with light and shadow, designers can reflect the internal states of characters or underscore thematic elements. In *Hadestown*, the lighting design plays a pivotal role in distinguishing the worlds of the living and the dead. The warm, amber glow of the upper world contrasts sharply with the cold, industrial blues and grays of the underworld, visually representing the divide between hope and despair, life and death. As Orpheus descends into the underworld to retrieve Eurydice, the lighting shifts dramatically, pulling the audience into the dark, foreboding world of Hades. This use of lighting as a symbolic element enhances the storytelling, adding emotional depth and visual clarity to the production's mythic themes.

In musicals that involve fantasy or supernatural elements, lighting can create a sense of magic and wonder. In *The Lion King*, lighting design is used to evoke the grandeur and beauty of the African savannah. The use of naturalistic lighting techniques—such as creating the illusion of sunrise, sunset, or the vibrant colors of the sky—brings the stage to life, allowing the audience to feel as if they are immersed in the vast, open landscapes of the Serengeti. During musical numbers like "Circle of Life," the lighting becomes an integral part of the visual storytelling, with golden hues washing over the stage to evoke the warmth of the African sun and the cyclical nature of life.

Another important aspect of lighting design is how it interacts with the set and costumes. Lighting designers must work closely with set designers and costume designers to ensure that the lighting complements the visual aesthetic of the production. Certain materials and fabrics respond differently to light, and the colors chosen for costumes or sets can change dramatically under different lighting conditions. In *Aladdin*, for example, the glittering costumes and jewel-toned set pieces are enhanced by vibrant, saturated lighting that reflects the opulence and magic of Agrabah. The lighting design amplifies the visual spectacle of the show, making the colors pop and creating a dazzling atmosphere that feels larger than life.

Lighting can also help create a sense of movement and rhythm in a musical. In shows with extensive choreography, such as *Chicago* or *West Side Story*, lighting is often used to highlight key moments in the dance sequences, creating visual emphasis on certain moves or formations. In *Chicago*, the use of stark, angular lighting complements the sharp, stylized choreography of Bob Fosse, enhancing the sleek, jazzy feel of the show. The lighting design reinforces the rhythm of the dance, turning the stage into a dynamic, ever-changing visual landscape that mirrors the energy of the music and movement.

In more technologically advanced productions, lighting design often incorporates elements of projection mapping or special effects. In *Harry Potter and the Cursed Child*, for example, lighting is combined with projections to create stunning visual effects that bring the magical world of Harry Potter to life on stage. Spells, transformations, and time-travel sequences are all enhanced by the interplay of light and projection, creating an immersive experience that feels both magical and real. This fusion of lighting and technology demonstrates how innovative design can push the boundaries of what is possible on stage, creating moments of wonder that captivate the audience.

One of the key challenges for lighting designers is working within the physical and architectural constraints of the theater. Every Broadway theater has its own unique layout, size, and technical capabilities, and the lighting design must be tailored to the specific venue. For example, a theater with a deep stage might require different lighting angles and placements than a theater with a shallower stage. The goal is to create a consistent and balanced lighting design that works for every seat in the house, ensuring that the visual storytelling reaches the entire audience. This requires a deep understanding of both the technical aspects of lighting and the artistic vision of the production.

Collaboration is essential in lighting design. The lighting designer works closely with the director, set designer, costume designer, and sound designer to create a cohesive visual and auditory experience. Lighting must complement the other elements of the production without overpowering them. It is the lighting designer's job to ensure that the lighting enhances the performances, supports the mood and tone of the show, and aligns with the director's overall vision. This collaborative process often involves extensive rehearsals, where lighting cues are timed to the music, dialogue, and choreography, creating a seamless integration of light and performance.

In conclusion, lighting design is a vital component of Broadway musicals, shaping the way the audience experiences the story, characters, and emotions of the production. Through the strategic use of light, color, and shadow, lighting designers create the visual language that supports the narrative, heightens the emotional impact of key moments, and enhances the overall theatrical experience. Whether through subtle, atmospheric lighting or bold, dynamic effects, the role of lighting in a musical is to illuminate the story in ways that are both artistic and functional. When executed with creativity and technical precision, lighting design transforms the stage into a living, breathing world that captivates the audience and brings the magic of Broadway to life.

Beyond the Curtain: Promoting Your Broadway Musical

Promoting a Broadway musical is as vital to its success as the creative elements themselves. Even the most compelling, well-executed show can struggle if it fails to attract an audience. In a competitive environment like Broadway, where multiple productions are vying for attention at any given time, a strong promotional strategy is essential for generating interest, selling tickets, and sustaining a show's run. Promoting a Broadway musical involves a multi-layered approach, combining traditional marketing methods with digital media, public relations efforts, and audience engagement initiatives to build excitement and awareness.

One of the first and most important steps in promoting a Broadway musical is crafting a clear and compelling message about the show. This includes defining what makes the production unique, who the target audience is, and what the overall tone and experience of the musical will be. The promotional campaign needs to capture the essence of the show and convey why it stands out from other productions. For example, the marketing for *Hamilton* highlighted its groundbreaking blend of hip-hop and history, positioning it as a revolutionary theatrical experience. The campaign focused on how *Hamilton* was not just another historical musical but a cultural event that redefined the genre. By communicating a clear identity, the show became instantly recognizable and generated significant buzz before it even opened on Broadway.

The visual branding of a Broadway musical plays a key role in its promotion. The logo, posters, and other promotional imagery need to be eye-catching, memorable, and representative of the show's themes. These visuals are the first impression many potential audience members will have, so they must convey the energy and spirit of the production. For example, the iconic yellow logo of *The Lion King*—with its stylized depiction of a lion's face—immediately evokes the grandeur and majesty of the show, while also suggesting its African setting and themes of leadership and family. Similarly, the green-and-black color scheme of *Wicked*, featuring the silhouette of Elphaba in her witch's hat, visually communicates the show's magical, dark, and subversive tone.

Once the branding is established, the promotional campaign can roll out across multiple platforms. Traditional marketing methods, such as posters, billboards, and print advertisements, remain an important part of promoting a Broadway musical. In New York City's Theater District, large posters and digital displays dominate Times Square, offering prime real estate for shows to capture the attention of both locals and tourists. These physical advertisements often include quotes from early reviews, images of key cast members, and taglines that entice potential theatergoers. For example, *The Phantom of the Opera* has long used its iconic mask imagery on billboards and subway posters to create an air of mystery and intrigue, appealing to those unfamiliar with the story while drawing in long-time fans.

Public relations efforts also play a significant role in promoting a Broadway musical. Press releases, media interviews, and feature stories in major publications help build credibility and generate buzz around the show. Producers and publicists work to get early coverage of the musical in both theater-specific outlets, such as *Playbill* and *BroadwayWorld*, as well as mainstream media like *The New York Times*, *The Wall Street Journal*, and entertainment magazines. Having the cast and creative team featured in interviews or behind-the-scenes articles can provide audiences with a deeper connection to the production, increasing interest in seeing the show.

Previews and special events are another powerful promotional tool. Many Broadway shows hold preview performances before their official opening night, offering audiences a chance to see the production while it is still being fine-tuned. These previews allow for word-of-mouth promotion, as early audience reactions can spread quickly, especially through social media. Additionally, producers may organize special events, such as opening night galas, celebrity appearances, or charity performances, to generate buzz and media attention. For example, when *Rent* opened on Broadway, it held benefit performances to raise awareness about AIDS, which not only tied into the themes of the show but also attracted media coverage and heightened interest.

Digital marketing has become increasingly important in promoting Broadway musicals, especially in reaching younger and more tech-savvy audiences. Social media platforms like Instagram, Twitter, Facebook, and TikTok offer powerful tools for engaging with potential theatergoers in creative and interactive ways. Shows can use social media to share behind-the-scenes content, teaser trailers, cast announcements, and rehearsal footage, building anticipation leading up to the opening. For instance, *Dear Evan Hansen* used social media to great effect by posting videos of the cast recording songs in the studio, sharing clips from rehearsals, and engaging directly with fans who connected with the show's themes of loneliness and social media. By creating a strong online presence, the show fostered a dedicated fan base before it even opened.

Digital advertising, including Google Ads, YouTube promotions, and social media ads, also plays a crucial role in driving ticket sales. These ads can be highly targeted, reaching specific demographics based on age, location, and interests. For instance, a show that appeals to families, such as *Aladdin*, might use Facebook ads to target parents looking for kid-friendly entertainment in New York City. Similarly, a more edgy or avant-garde production could use Instagram and TikTok to reach younger, trend-conscious audiences by showcasing its bold design and high-energy performances.

In recent years, viral marketing has become a game-changer for Broadway musicals. When a show captures the public's imagination, whether through a viral video, meme, or social media challenge, it can generate massive attention and bring in new audiences. The *#Ham4Ham* performances—where *Hamilton* cast members would perform mini-shows outside the theater before a lottery drawing for discounted tickets—became a viral sensation, spreading the word about the show and creating a sense of community around it. Fans who couldn't afford to attend the show itself still felt connected to it through these videos, which helped build *Hamilton*'s massive cultural presence.

Collaborations and partnerships with brands or organizations can also help promote a Broadway musical. Some shows partner with popular brands to create co-branded content or promotions. For example, a musical with a strong fashion element might collaborate with a clothing brand to create themed merchandise, while a show aimed at families might partner with a toy company to create collectible items related to the characters. These partnerships not only help promote the show but also extend its reach into new markets.

Engaging with influencers and theater bloggers is another key promotional strategy. Influencers in the theater world, including social media personalities, critics, and YouTubers, often have dedicated followings that can amplify a show's message. By inviting these influencers to early performances or press events, producers can tap into their audience's enthusiasm for theater, generating word-of-mouth excitement. Additionally, theater bloggers often review shows early in their run, and positive reviews can quickly spread across social media, building momentum for ticket sales.

Discount ticket platforms, such as TodayTix, TKTS, and Goldstar, are also valuable tools for promoting Broadway shows. These platforms cater to budget-conscious theatergoers and can help fill seats during a show's initial run, generating buzz and encouraging positive word-of-mouth. Offering discounted tickets can attract tourists, students, and locals who might not otherwise attend a Broadway show, broadening the audience base and increasing visibility.

Merchandising is another effective promotional tactic. Branded merchandise, such as T-shirts, posters, mugs, and cast recordings, allows fans to take a piece of the show home with them, deepening their connection to the production. Merchandise can also serve as free advertising, as fans wear or use items featuring the show's logo, helping spread awareness to others. Shows like *Wicked*, *The Lion King*, and *Hamilton* have developed extensive merchandising lines that generate significant revenue while also reinforcing their brands in the broader culture.

One of the most effective promotional strategies is building a loyal fan base through interactive experiences. Shows can create immersive marketing campaigns that allow fans to engage directly with the content of the musical. For example, immersive pop-up experiences or behind-the-scenes tours of the theater can give fans a deeper connection to the show. For musicals with passionate fan followings, offering exclusive access, special meet-and-greets with the cast, or interactive events helps create a sense of community and excitement around the production.

In conclusion, promoting a Broadway musical requires a carefully coordinated strategy that combines traditional marketing, digital media, public relations, and audience engagement. By crafting a compelling message, building a strong visual brand, and using a mix of media to reach diverse audiences, producers can create buzz, generate ticket sales, and sustain a successful run. Whether through viral marketing, social media campaigns, or special events, the goal is to create excitement around the show and ensure that it reaches as many people as possible. In the fast-paced world of Broadway, a strong promotional strategy is essential for turning a musical into a hit and keeping it in the spotlight long after opening night.

Driving Sales: The Art of Selling Tickets

Selling tickets is the lifeblood of any Broadway musical. No matter how exceptional the performances, stage design, or story, the success of a show ultimately hinges on its ability to fill seats. The art of selling tickets requires a combination of pricing strategies, targeted marketing, partnerships with ticket platforms, and audience engagement. To drive sales effectively, producers and marketers must balance the need to attract theatergoers with varying budgets while ensuring that the show generates enough revenue to sustain its run. This process involves understanding audience behavior, leveraging technology, and creating incentives that make ticket purchases feel accessible and exciting.

The first step in selling tickets is developing a comprehensive pricing strategy. Ticket pricing on Broadway is often dynamic, meaning prices fluctuate based on factors like demand, seat location, and time of purchase. Theaters usually offer different pricing tiers, with premium seats commanding higher prices and seats farther from the stage available at lower rates. The goal is to create a range of price points that appeal to different segments of the audience—from tourists willing to splurge on premium seats for a once-in-a-lifetime experience to budget-conscious locals looking for affordable entertainment.

Premium pricing is a strategy commonly used to maximize revenue from high-demand shows. Producers set aside prime seating, such as front-row or center orchestra seats, at a higher price for patrons willing to pay for the best view in the house. For blockbuster shows like *Hamilton, Wicked,* or *The Lion King,* premium seats can sell for several hundred dollars or more. Offering premium tickets capitalizes on the demand for high-quality experiences, especially from audiences who are willing to pay a premium for exclusive or up-close seating. However, balancing these high-priced seats with affordable options is crucial to ensure that the show appeals to a broad audience.

To attract a wider audience, Broadway shows often offer discount tickets through various platforms and initiatives. Platforms like TodayTix, TKTS, and Goldstar provide discounted tickets, often at 30% to 50% off, for same-day or near-future performances. These platforms are especially valuable for budget-conscious theatergoers, such as students, tourists, and locals looking for last-minute deals. Discounted tickets help fill seats that might otherwise go unsold, which in turn can generate word-of-mouth buzz and build momentum for the show.

One of the most well-known discount strategies is the use of lottery or rush tickets. These deeply discounted tickets are offered through a daily lottery system or first-come, first-served rush at the theater. For example, *Hamilton's* daily lottery, known as *Ham4Ham,* became iconic for offering $10 tickets to lucky winners. Shows like *Dear Evan Hansen* and *The Book of Mormon* also use digital lotteries, making it easier for fans to participate without physically lining up outside the theater. Rush tickets, on the other hand, are typically sold at the box office on the day of the performance for a significantly reduced price. Both lottery and rush systems create a sense of excitement and accessibility, making the Broadway experience more affordable while fostering a sense of loyalty among fans who regularly try their luck for tickets.

Group sales are another important component of ticketing strategies. Broadway shows often offer discounted rates for groups of 10 or more, encouraging schools, corporate events, tourist groups, and organizations to purchase blocks of tickets. Group sales help fill seats, especially during matinees or weekdays when individual ticket demand may be lower. Producers work with group sales agents who specialize in marketing to schools, businesses, tour companies, and special interest groups. Group sales not only provide a steady source of revenue but also help build long-term audience relationships, as attendees who enjoy the show are likely to recommend it to others or return for another performance.

Seasonal promotions and special events are also effective tools for driving ticket sales. During holiday seasons, Broadway shows often see an increase in ticket demand, as tourists and locals look for festive entertainment. Producers may offer special holiday pricing, family packages, or themed performances to capitalize on the seasonal boost. Similarly, special events such as talkbacks with the cast, behind-the-scenes tours, or meet-and-greet opportunities can create additional incentives for ticket purchases. Limited-time offers, such as exclusive merchandise or VIP experiences, can also attract audiences looking for a more immersive or memorable theater experience.

Digital marketing plays an increasingly critical role in ticket sales, as more theatergoers turn to online platforms to research and purchase tickets. Many Broadway shows invest in digital advertising through Google Ads, social media platforms, and targeted email campaigns. Producers use these digital channels to reach potential ticket buyers based on demographic data, interests, and browsing behavior. For instance, a show like *Hadestown* might target ads to fans of folk music, mythology, or previous Broadway productions, while a family-friendly show like *Aladdin* might target parents and tourists planning a trip to New York. Personalized ads, combined with compelling visuals and special offers, can drive traffic to ticketing websites and convert interest into sales.

The growing use of mobile apps and ticketing websites has transformed how audiences purchase tickets. Platforms like TodayTix and Broadway.com make it easy for theatergoers to browse available shows, compare prices, and purchase tickets with just a few clicks. These apps often feature user-friendly interfaces, digital ticketing options, and real-time updates on availability. TodayTix, for example, offers flash sales and exclusive deals, allowing users to quickly snag discounted tickets. The convenience and accessibility of mobile ticketing have expanded the reach of Broadway shows, making it easier for people to buy tickets on the go or at the last minute.

Social media is another powerful tool for driving ticket sales, as it allows shows to engage directly with fans and build excitement around performances. Many shows use platforms like Instagram, Twitter, and TikTok to share promotional content, behind-the-scenes footage, and cast interactions, encouraging fans to buy tickets and share their experiences online. Viral campaigns, social media challenges, and influencer partnerships can generate significant buzz, especially among younger audiences. For example, *Be More Chill* gained a massive following on social media before transferring to Broadway, driven by fan-created content, memes, and a strong presence on platforms like Tumblr and TikTok.

Engaging with theatergoers post-performance is also essential for building long-term ticket sales. Encouraging audiences to share their experience on social media, leave reviews, or recommend the show to friends can create a ripple effect, spreading word-of-mouth excitement and drawing in new potential ticket buyers. Many Broadway shows use hashtags, photo booths in the theater lobby, or branded backdrops to encourage audience members to take photos and share them online. This user-generated content can act as free promotion, as theatergoers share their positive experiences with their social networks.

Email marketing remains a valuable tool for promoting ticket sales and engaging with a dedicated fan base. Broadway shows often build email lists by offering incentives, such as exclusive content, early access to tickets, or special discounts for subscribers. Regular newsletters keep audiences informed about upcoming performances, cast changes, or special events, while personalized offers based on previous ticket purchases can encourage repeat attendance. For instance, if a theatergoer has attended a family-friendly show, they may receive email promotions for similar productions or family package deals for future performances.

Collaborations with discount platforms like TKTS and TodayTix, combined with partnerships with travel agencies or tourism boards, help Broadway shows reach a wider audience, particularly tourists. Tourists often make up a significant portion of Broadway ticket buyers, and targeting this demographic through hotel partnerships, travel websites, or city guides can boost ticket sales, especially during peak tourist seasons. Offering packages that combine

Broadway tickets with dining experiences, hotel stays, or sightseeing tours can make the experience more attractive to visitors, providing a seamless way for them to enjoy multiple aspects of New York City.

Broadway shows also benefit from positive reviews and award recognition, which can drive ticket sales significantly. Shows that receive strong reviews from reputable critics in publications like *The New York Times*, *Variety*, or *The Wall Street Journal* often see an immediate boost in sales. Similarly, winning major theater awards, such as the Tony Awards, can elevate a show's profile and attract new audiences who want to see the "must-see" production. Shows like *Hamilton* and *Dear Evan Hansen* experienced huge surges in ticket demand after winning multiple Tony Awards, leading to sold-out performances for months, or even years, following their wins.

In conclusion, driving ticket sales for a Broadway musical involves a combination of strategic pricing, targeted marketing, digital engagement, and creative incentives that cater to diverse audience segments. By understanding the behaviors and preferences of theatergoers, producers can implement effective ticket-selling strategies that maximize revenue while making the show accessible to a broad range of people. Whether through premium pricing, discounted platforms, social media campaigns, or special events, the art of selling tickets is about building excitement, maintaining momentum, and ensuring that the theater is filled with enthusiastic audiences eager to experience the magic of live Broadway performances.

Critical Response: Navigating Reviews and Awards

Navigating reviews and awards is a crucial aspect of a Broadway musical's journey, as both critical response and recognition can significantly impact a show's success. Positive reviews and prestigious awards can drive ticket sales, build buzz, and establish a musical as a cultural phenomenon, while negative reviews or a lack of award nominations can pose challenges. How producers, creative teams, and performers manage this process, engage with critics, and respond to award recognition often determines the long-term viability of a show. Understanding how to leverage praise and handle criticism effectively is an art in itself, and doing so can make or break a production's legacy.

The critical response to a Broadway musical typically begins during its preview performances. Previews are essential not only for fine-tuning the production but also for gauging audience and critic reactions before the official opening. Producers and directors use previews to address any potential issues in pacing, performances, or technical elements, ensuring that the show is as polished as possible before critics file their reviews. It's during this period that adjustments might be made—whether cutting scenes, changing choreography, or tweaking dialogue—in response to early feedback from industry insiders and test audiences.

Once a musical officially opens, the reviews from major critics are often published within hours of the first performance. In New York City, publications like *The New York Times*, *Variety*, *The Wall Street Journal*, and *The New Yorker* have a significant influence on Broadway's critical landscape. A glowing review from a prominent critic can propel a show to immediate success, while a harsh critique can dampen ticket sales and the show's overall momentum. For instance, *The New York Times* critic Ben Brantley famously praised *Hamilton* and its revolutionary approach to musical theater, helping to solidify its status as a groundbreaking production. On the other hand, mixed or negative reviews from such influential critics can create challenges that producers must navigate with care.

When reviews are overwhelmingly positive, producers use them as powerful marketing tools. The best quotes from reviews are often highlighted in advertisements, posters, and social media campaigns, with phrases like "Critics are raving!" or "A must-see masterpiece!" Positive reviews can also create a sense of urgency for theatergoers, as they heighten demand for tickets, making people feel like they need to see the show before it potentially sells out. A strong critical response also opens doors for national tours, international productions, and film or television adaptations, all of which can further the show's legacy.

For instance, *Dear Evan Hansen* received universal acclaim from critics, with many praising its emotional depth, contemporary relevance, and the performance of Ben Platt. These reviews not only helped drive ticket sales but also positioned the show as a frontrunner during the awards season, eventually leading to its multiple Tony Award wins, which further elevated its cultural presence.

When reviews are mixed or negative, the challenge becomes managing public perception while addressing any potential flaws in the production. Negative reviews don't necessarily mean the end of a Broadway musical; many shows have found success despite critical pushback. However, producers need to be strategic in how they respond. Some shows embrace their niche appeal, understanding that they may resonate more with certain audiences than others. In cases where the reviews focus on specific issues, such as pacing, performances, or design elements, producers may opt to make adjustments and reframe the marketing to focus on the show's strengths.

In some instances, a show may lean into its divisiveness, turning a negative review into an opportunity for conversation. Shows like *Spider-Man: Turn Off the Dark* received widespread negative reviews, but the sheer spectacle of the production, combined with its media attention, continued to draw curious audiences. While *Spider-Man* ultimately closed, its response to negative reviews highlights how a show can still generate buzz, even when it isn't critically beloved.

Awards season plays a pivotal role in the long-term success of a Broadway musical. Winning major theater awards like the Tony Awards, Drama Desk Awards, or Outer Critics Circle Awards can give a production a significant boost, attracting new audiences, generating media attention, and solidifying the show's reputation. The Tony Awards, in particular, are considered the highest honor in American theater, and winning a Tony can elevate a show's status, often leading to extended runs, touring productions, and adaptations.

Tony Award nominations typically create a surge in ticket sales, as theatergoers flock to see the nominated productions before the awards ceremony. For shows like *Hamilton*, *The Book of Mormon*, and *Hadestown*, multiple Tony nominations and subsequent wins led to a spike in demand, with tickets becoming nearly impossible to obtain for months or even years after their wins. For a musical, winning the Tony Award for Best Musical is the ultimate accolade, often ensuring a place in Broadway history.

In addition to the prestige and publicity that come with winning awards, there are also financial benefits. Shows that win major awards tend to see an increase in both ticket sales and merchandise revenue. Additionally, producers can leverage these accolades in future marketing campaigns, using phrases like "Tony Award-Winning Musical" to draw in new audiences. A Tony win can also secure the future of a show's national tour or international productions, as theaters and audiences worldwide seek out award-winning productions.

However, not all shows win the awards they are expected to, and navigating award snubs or losses is another challenge. If a show is critically acclaimed but overlooked during awards season, producers must work to keep momentum going without the added boost of awards recognition. Some shows choose to refocus their marketing efforts on other strengths, such as strong box office performance or audience loyalty. For example, *Waitress* did not win any Tony Awards despite being a fan favorite, but it continued to perform well due to its strong fan base, beloved score, and relatable story.

Even for shows that don't receive critical acclaim or major awards, there are opportunities for niche appeal and cult status. Some productions, like *Rocky Horror Show*, initially received mixed reviews but went on to become cult classics with a devoted fan base. In these cases, word of mouth and audience engagement become more important than critical praise, as fan communities take ownership of the show's legacy.

Ultimately, the key to navigating reviews and awards is adaptability. Producers and creative teams must be prepared for both the highs and lows of critical response and find ways to keep their musical in the public consciousness. Whether through adjusting the production, focusing on audience engagement, or leveraging positive reviews and awards wins, navigating the critical landscape is about maintaining momentum and ensuring the longevity of the show.

In conclusion, reviews and awards play a central role in the success of a Broadway musical, influencing public perception, ticket sales, and the show's cultural impact. While positive reviews and major awards can elevate a production to new heights, negative critiques and award snubs present challenges that require thoughtful navigation. By understanding how to manage critical response and leverage awards recognition, producers can maximize a show's potential, ensuring that it finds its audience and thrives on Broadway and beyond.

Bringing It Together: Integrating the Script, Music, and Dance

Bringing together the script, music, and dance in a Broadway musical is a complex and dynamic process, but when done successfully, it creates a seamless, captivating experience that transcends the sum of its parts. Each of these elements plays a distinct role in telling the story, developing characters, and evoking emotion, but the magic happens when they all come together in harmony. Integrating the script, music, and dance requires close collaboration among the creative team—playwrights, composers, lyricists, choreographers, directors, and performers—all working to ensure that each element complements the others in service of the story.

At the heart of this process is the script, or the book of the musical. The script lays the foundation for the story, defining the characters, plot, and dialogue that anchor the production. It provides the structure within which the music and dance are built, and it is essential that the script creates a strong narrative arc that can support these other elements. In a well-integrated musical, the script flows naturally into the songs and dance numbers, with each transition feeling organic and motivated by the story.

In many cases, the script sets up key moments that will later be expanded upon or explored more deeply through music and dance. For instance, in *West Side Story*, the dialogue between Tony and Maria builds the romantic tension between them, but it is through the song "Tonight" and the accompanying dance sequences that their love truly blossoms. The music and choreography give emotional depth and express what cannot be fully conveyed through words alone. This ability to move fluidly between spoken dialogue, music, and movement is what distinguishes a musical from other forms of theater, allowing for a richer, more multi-layered form of storytelling.

Music is a vital tool for conveying emotion and advancing the plot in a musical. Songs often serve as emotional high points, where characters express their deepest fears, desires, or conflicts. The composer and lyricist work together to ensure that each song fits seamlessly within the story, capturing the tone of the scene and the character's state of mind. The integration of music with the script is crucial for maintaining the flow of the production, and the best musicals know how to use music to heighten the drama rather than interrupt it.

In *Les Misérables*, for example, the song "I Dreamed a Dream" allows Fantine to express her despair and hopelessness, emotions that are rooted in the story but brought to life through music. The haunting melody and raw lyrics reveal the depth of her suffering in a way that dialogue alone could not achieve. Here, the song becomes an extension of the character's arc, making the emotional impact of the scene even more powerful. The music not only supports the script but elevates it, turning a simple moment of despair into one of the most memorable and heartbreaking moments in musical theater.

Just as music enhances the emotional dimension of a musical, dance often brings the physicality and energy that words and music cannot fully capture. Choreography adds movement and visual dynamism to the story, expressing ideas and emotions through motion and rhythm. Dance sequences are typically used to heighten dramatic moments, convey group dynamics, or give the audience insight into a character's inner world.

In *Hamilton*, the choreography by Andy Blankenbuehler plays an integral role in advancing the story. The fast-paced, precise movements of the ensemble reflect the high-stakes political and personal struggles of the characters. The dancers' movements often mirror the rhythm of the music, creating a sense of urgency and momentum that propels the story forward. For example, the "Rewind" sequence during "Satisfied" uses both music and choreography to replay the events from Angelica's perspective, visually and sonically showing how she rethinks her choices. Here, dance is not just an added flourish but a critical storytelling device, deepening the audience's understanding of the characters and their relationships.

The integration of dance into a Broadway musical requires careful attention to timing, space, and energy. The choreography must feel like a natural extension of the characters and the world they inhabit. In *The Lion King*, for example, the dance and movement of the characters are designed to evoke the fluid, animalistic grace of the African savannah. The dancers embody the lions, zebras, and other animals through precise, stylized movements, making the world of the musical feel alive and immersive. The choreography is deeply connected to the music, with each movement reflecting the rhythm and pulse of the score.

To successfully integrate the script, music, and dance, the creative team must collaborate closely throughout the development and rehearsal process. The director plays a central role in guiding this integration, working with the writers, composers, choreographers, and designers to ensure that each element serves the overall vision of the production. It is the director's job to find the balance between these elements, making sure that one does not overpower the others but rather that they all work in concert to tell the story.

The rehearsal process is where much of this integration happens in real time. Actors, singers, and dancers must learn to move fluidly between dialogue, song, and movement, ensuring that each transition feels natural and seamless. Timing is critical in these moments, as even a slight misstep can break the flow of the production. For instance, in *Wicked*, the iconic song "Defying Gravity" is not just a vocal showpiece but a complex technical and emotional moment that requires precise coordination between the music, lights, flying rig, and performance. Elphaba's literal rise into the air must be perfectly timed with the music and her emotional crescendo, creating a powerful moment of transformation. This kind of integration requires extensive rehearsal and collaboration between the technical crew, performers, and creative team to ensure that everything comes together smoothly.

The integration of the script, music, and dance also extends to the design elements of the show. The set, lighting, and costumes must complement the choreography and musical numbers, creating a cohesive visual and auditory experience. For example, in *Chicago*, the minimalistic set and sharp lighting design mirror the sleek, stylized choreography of Bob Fosse. The costumes, with their bold, 1920s-inspired designs, further reinforce the show's themes of seduction, manipulation, and showbiz glitz. The visual and musical elements work together to create a world that feels both glamorous and gritty, enhancing the storytelling and immersing the audience in the world of vaudeville and jazz.

Ultimately, the goal of integrating the script, music, and dance is to create a unified experience for the audience. When all the elements come together seamlessly, the result is a production that feels cohesive, emotionally resonant, and deeply engaging. The audience becomes fully immersed in the world of the musical, experiencing the story not just through words, but through sound, movement, and visual spectacle. This integration is what makes Broadway musicals such a unique and powerful form of storytelling, allowing audiences to experience the full range of human emotion through a blend of narrative, song, and dance.

In conclusion, bringing together the script, music, and dance in a Broadway musical requires collaboration, creativity, and meticulous attention to detail. Each element plays a vital role in telling the story, but it is their integration that creates the magic of musical theater. When the script, music, and choreography are in harmony, they enhance one another, creating a richer, more immersive experience for the audience. It is through this delicate balance that musicals can transcend individual moments, offering a holistic emotional and sensory journey that leaves a lasting impact on everyone who experiences it.

The Art of Rehearsals: Polishing the Performance

Rehearsals are the heart and soul of preparing a Broadway musical, where the cast, creative team, and crew come together to shape and refine every element of the production. It is during rehearsals that the vision of the musical is brought to life, as the actors develop their characters, the choreography is polished, and the music is perfected. The rehearsal process is where the magic happens—it's a journey of discovery, problem-solving, and artistic growth that ensures every performance is polished, precise, and emotionally resonant.

The art of rehearsals begins with the table read. In this early stage, the cast gathers to read through the script together for the first time, accompanied by the director, music director, choreographer, and other key members of the creative team. This initial read-through allows the actors to familiarize themselves with the script and their characters, giving them a sense of the story's overall flow and emotional beats. It's also an opportunity for the creative team to hear how the dialogue sounds aloud, which may lead to adjustments or rewrites. During the table read, the director will often discuss the overarching themes of the show and the characters' journeys, setting the tone for how the performances will develop in rehearsals.

Once the script has been explored, the musical elements come into play. Rehearsing the songs is a critical aspect of the process, led by the music director and vocal coaches. The cast works through each number, learning harmonies, dynamics, and timing. It's important that every singer knows their part intimately and understands how their voice fits within the ensemble. For solo numbers, the music director collaborates closely with the actor to shape the performance—ensuring that the song conveys the appropriate emotions and supports the character's arc.

In *Les Misérables*, for instance, the music is deeply tied to the characters' emotional journeys. During rehearsals, actors must work to connect their vocal performance with the raw emotions their characters experience. For a song like "Bring Him Home," the actor playing Jean Valjean needs to evoke a sense of prayerful desperation while maintaining perfect control over his vocal delivery. Rehearsals give the actor time to explore the emotional layers of the song while fine-tuning the technical aspects of the performance.

Rehearsing the choreography is another vital component of the process, particularly in dance-heavy musicals like *West Side Story* or *Chicago*. The choreographer works with the dancers to perfect each movement, ensuring that the physicality aligns with the music and the story. Rehearsals are where dancers learn not only the steps but also how to convey emotion through movement. In *West Side Story*, for example, the aggressive, high-energy dance numbers reflect the tensions between rival gangs, while the more romantic, flowing movements of Tony and Maria express their love. The cast must not only master the choreography technically but also perform it in a way that serves the narrative.

REHEARSING DANCE NUMBERS involves repetition and refinement. Dancers practice the same sequences over and over to ensure precision and unity within the ensemble. This process can be physically demanding, as the cast must build stamina and muscle memory to perform these intricate routines eight times a week. In musicals with complex choreography, rehearsals also focus on spatial awareness, as the cast must navigate the stage, props, and each other in a way that looks effortless to the audience.

Blocking—the staging of the actors' movements—is a key aspect of rehearsals led by the director. In blocking rehearsals, the director works with the actors to determine where they should be on stage at any given moment, how they move between scenes, and how they interact with the set and props. Blocking is crucial for creating a sense of flow and rhythm in the production, ensuring that the actors' movements feel natural and purposeful while maintaining visual interest. During these rehearsals, actors begin to develop their physicality and learn how their characters occupy space. Whether it's a grand gesture or a subtle shift in posture, every movement must be intentional and in service of the story.

For example, in *Wicked*, the famous "Defying Gravity" scene is carefully blocked to build tension and emotional power. Elphaba's ascent into the air is timed with the climax of the music, and the actor's movements are choreographed to create a sense of rising power and defiance. Blocking rehearsals ensure that the technical aspects of the flying rig align perfectly with the actor's performance, lighting, and music to create a seamless and breathtaking moment.

Character development is another central focus of the rehearsal process. Under the director's guidance, actors delve into their characters' motivations, backstories, and emotional arcs. This is where the actors explore how their characters think, feel, and react, shaping performances that are nuanced and deeply felt. Rehearsals provide a safe space for experimentation—actors can try different approaches to a scene or a line until they find the version that feels most authentic.

For a musical like *Dear Evan Hansen*, character development is particularly important, as the story relies heavily on the emotional truth of its characters. During rehearsals, the actor playing Evan must navigate the character's anxiety, loneliness, and moral dilemmas, finding the balance between vulnerability and self-deception. These rehearsals often involve deep conversations between the actor and director, as they work to uncover the emotional beats of each scene and ensure that Evan's journey feels truthful and resonant.

Rehearsals also involve building chemistry between the cast members. In a musical, relationships between characters are often conveyed through song, dance, and dialogue, and it's essential that the actors develop a strong rapport with one another. Whether it's the romantic chemistry between two leads or the camaraderie of an ensemble, the rehearsal room is where these connections are nurtured. Directors may lead exercises or improvisations designed to help the cast build trust and find their rhythm together, making their interactions on stage feel more organic and authentic.

Technical rehearsals are a crucial stage of the process, where all the elements of the production—sets, lighting, sound, and costumes—are integrated with the performances. During tech rehearsals, the actors rehearse on the actual set with the full technical team, ensuring that everything runs smoothly and safely. These rehearsals focus on timing, scene transitions, and how the technical elements support the storytelling. It's in tech rehearsals that all the pieces of the production come together, and adjustments are often made to ensure that the lighting complements the choreography, the sound levels are balanced, and the set transitions are smooth.

Dress rehearsals are the final step before the show is ready for previews or its official opening. In dress rehearsals, the cast performs the show in full costume, with all technical elements in place, as if it were a live performance. This is where the production is polished to its final form, with the creative team fine-tuning any last-minute details. Dress rehearsals allow the actors to adjust to their costumes and make any necessary adjustments to their performances based on how the costumes impact movement or character portrayal. It's also a chance for the director and creative team to see how the show looks and feels as a complete experience, making final adjustments to pacing, timing, and transitions.

Throughout the rehearsal process, one of the most important aspects is collaboration. The director, choreographer, music director, and designers must work together to ensure that every element of the production supports the others. This requires open communication, flexibility, and a shared vision for the show. Rehearsals are a time for problem-solving, and adjustments are often made in real-time to ensure that the show runs smoothly and that all the creative elements align.

In conclusion, the art of rehearsals is where a Broadway musical takes shape. It is a time of discovery, collaboration, and refinement, where the cast and creative team work together to bring the script, music, and choreography to life. Through careful preparation and attention to detail, rehearsals ensure that every element of the performance is polished and ready for the stage. Whether it's building character, perfecting choreography, or integrating technical elements, rehearsals are essential to creating the magic that audiences experience in a live performance. They are the invisible work behind the seamless, breathtaking moments that make Broadway musicals so unforgettable.

A Singular Vision: Aligning Director, Writer, and Composer

Aligning the vision of the director, writer, and composer is critical to the success of a Broadway musical. These three roles form the creative backbone of the production, and when they work in harmony, the result is a cohesive and emotionally powerful experience. Each brings a unique perspective and set of skills to the table: the writer crafts the narrative and characters, the composer infuses the story with music, and the director shapes the overall vision, guiding the performances, design, and pacing of the show. Ensuring that these creative voices are aligned requires clear communication, collaboration, and mutual respect, as all three must share a common understanding of the story they are telling.

At the heart of this collaboration is the story. The writer's script serves as the foundation of the production, defining the plot, characters, themes, and dialogue. The writer's vision is the narrative thread that connects every element of the musical. However, the story's emotional depth and resonance are brought to life through music and performance, and this is where the composer and director come in. The composer must understand the emotional beats of the story, crafting music that complements and enhances the writer's vision, while the director must guide the actors in bringing both the script and the score to life in a way that feels cohesive and true to the intended experience.

One of the first steps in aligning the director, writer, and composer is defining the tone and style of the musical. This involves conversations about how the story should feel: Is it a sweeping romantic epic like *The Phantom of the Opera*, or is it a gritty, contemporary drama like *Rent*? Is the tone whimsical and fantastical, like *Wicked*, or is it satirical and cutting-edge, like *The Book of Mormon*? These decisions about tone and style are crucial because they influence every creative choice, from the structure of the score to the choreography and design.

For example, in *Hamilton*, the writer (Lin-Manuel Miranda) and director (Thomas Kail) worked closely to ensure that the show's unique blend of hip-hop, R&B, and traditional musical theater styles supported the historical narrative. Miranda's script and music were groundbreaking in their use of modern musical genres to tell the story of America's founding, and Kail's direction was instrumental in ensuring that the tone was both accessible and historically grounded. This alignment of vision allowed the show to transcend genre and create a new kind of theater experience that felt fresh, dynamic, and deeply emotional.

Once the tone and style are agreed upon, the next step is integrating the music into the script. The composer works with the writer to identify key moments where songs can elevate the emotional stakes or reveal deeper aspects of the characters. Songs in musicals often serve as turning points, allowing characters to express emotions that they might not be able to convey through dialogue alone. The writer and composer collaborate to ensure that the songs feel organic to the story and that the transitions between spoken dialogue and musical numbers are seamless.

In *Wicked*, for example, Stephen Schwartz (the composer) and Winnie Holzman (the writer) created moments where the music became an extension of the characters' emotional journeys. In the iconic number "Defying Gravity," the music swells as Elphaba reaches her breaking point, choosing to embrace her power and independence. The song reflects her transformation, and the powerful music mirrors the character's internal struggle. This integration of music and script only works when the composer and writer are in sync, understanding how to use music as a storytelling device, rather than a distraction from the narrative.

The director plays a pivotal role in maintaining the unity of the production, acting as the bridge between the writer and composer, and guiding how their work is realized on stage. Directors are responsible for interpreting the script and score, bringing their own vision to the table while respecting the intentions of the writer and composer. A strong director will ensure that the performances, choreography, set design, and lighting all align with the creative vision, making decisions about pacing, tone, and staging that keep the musical cohesive.

In *Les Misérables*, director Trevor Nunn's interpretation of Victor Hugo's epic novel, along with the score by Alain Boublil and Claude-Michel Schönberg, required careful coordination between all elements of the production. Nunn's staging choices—such as the use of the revolving stage and the decision to stage the climactic barricade scenes in a visually powerful, immersive way—complemented the sweeping, emotional score. The director's vision was not separate from the work of the writer and composer, but rather an extension of it, ensuring that all elements were working toward the same emotional and narrative goals.

Effective collaboration between the director, writer, and composer often starts early in the development process, long before rehearsals begin. Workshops and readings are key to shaping the musical, allowing the creative team to test ideas, make adjustments, and see how the different elements fit together. In these settings, the writer, composer, and director can experiment with how songs interact with dialogue, how characters' emotional journeys evolve, and how the pacing of the show feels when it's performed. Feedback from these early workshops is crucial, as it often leads to rewrites, new musical arrangements, or changes in staging.

For example, *Dear Evan Hansen* underwent multiple workshops and revisions before arriving on Broadway. Writer Steven Levenson, composers Benj Pasek and Justin Paul, and director Michael Greif worked together to fine-tune the balance between the script and the score, ensuring that the emotional weight of the story—particularly Evan's struggle with anxiety and social isolation—was supported by both the music and the performances. This collaborative process allowed the team to create a musical that felt deeply personal and authentic, resonating with audiences on a profound emotional level.

Communication is key to aligning the creative vision. The writer, director, and composer must remain open to each other's ideas, working through challenges and making compromises where necessary. Disagreements are inevitable in any creative process, but the most successful collaborations are those where the creative team is united in their goal of serving the story. Trust and respect between the collaborators are essential, as they ensure that each person's voice is heard and valued, while also maintaining a shared commitment to the larger vision.

In some cases, a musical's success is built on long-term partnerships between directors, writers, and composers who have a deep understanding of one another's strengths. These partnerships allow for an intuitive understanding of how the different elements of the musical should come together. For example, the partnership between Stephen Sondheim (composer/lyricist) and James Lapine (director/writer) has produced some of Broadway's most innovative and beloved musicals, including *Into the Woods* and *Sunday in the Park with George*. Their collaborations are marked by a shared artistic vision and a deep trust in each other's ability to push the boundaries of musical theater while staying true to the story.

When all three creative roles are aligned, the result is a musical that feels cohesive, emotionally resonant, and artistically unified. The audience experiences a seamless integration of dialogue, music, and performance, where every element feels like it belongs and serves the larger narrative. In shows like *Wicked, Hamilton, Les Misérables,* and *Dear Evan Hansen*, this alignment has led to critically acclaimed productions that continue to captivate audiences year after year.

In conclusion, aligning the director, writer, and composer in a Broadway musical is a delicate yet essential process. It requires a shared vision, open communication, and a deep respect for each other's contributions. When these elements come together, the result is a musical that resonates on every level—emotionally, visually, and musically. The process of integrating these creative voices ensures that the final production is more than the sum of its parts, creating a powerful, unified theatrical experience that can move audiences and stand the test of time.

Storytelling through Song: The Role of Music in the Narrative

Music in a Broadway musical plays a unique and powerful role in storytelling, shaping the narrative in ways that dialogue alone cannot. While the script provides the framework for the plot and character development, music brings emotional depth, heightens dramatic tension, and conveys ideas and emotions that transcend words. Storytelling through song allows audiences to connect with characters on a visceral level, immersing them in the emotional stakes of the narrative while advancing the plot in dynamic and memorable ways. In this chapter, we explore how music becomes an essential narrative tool, from shaping character arcs to reinforcing themes and creating unforgettable moments in a Broadway musical.

At the heart of musical storytelling is the idea that songs express emotions, desires, and conflicts that dialogue alone cannot fully capture. When a character begins to sing, it signals a shift in the emotional landscape—something significant is happening that requires a heightened form of expression. In musicals, songs often serve as turning points, where characters reveal their innermost thoughts, make important decisions, or confront key challenges. These musical moments are not interruptions of the story but rather essential components of the narrative, providing insight into the characters' inner worlds.

For instance, in *Les Misérables*, the character of Jean Valjean sings "Who Am I?" as he wrestles with his conscience and moral identity. In this song, Valjean confronts the dilemma of whether to reveal his true identity and risk imprisonment or continue living under a false name. The song is not just a reflection of his internal struggle but also a critical moment of character development that propels the plot forward. Through the music, the audience experiences Valjean's anguish and the weight of his decision, making the song an essential part of the narrative.

Music in a Broadway musical also plays a vital role in shaping character arcs. Through songs, characters can express their growth, transformation, and emotional journey over the course of the story. In many musicals, the character's "I Want" song serves as a defining moment early in the show, where the protagonist reveals their deepest desires and sets the stage for their journey. These songs often establish the central conflict of the story and give the audience a clear sense of what the character is striving for.

For example, in *The Little Mermaid*, Ariel's song "Part of Your World" expresses her longing to live on land and experience a world beyond the ocean. This song not only introduces the audience to Ariel's dream but also sets the stakes for the rest of the musical, as her desire to be "part of that world" drives the plot forward. Similarly, in *Wicked*, Elphaba's "The Wizard and I" reveals her ambition to meet the Wizard of Oz and achieve greatness. This song establishes her goals and foreshadows the personal and political conflicts that will shape her journey throughout the musical.

As characters evolve, their songs often reflect their changing perspectives, emotions, and circumstances. In *Hamilton*, Alexander Hamilton's character arc is closely tied to his musical numbers. Early in the show, his songs like "My Shot" are fast-paced, filled with ambition and urgency, reflecting his relentless drive to make a name for himself. As the story progresses, the tone of his songs shifts, particularly in numbers like "It's Quiet Uptown," where Hamilton grapples with personal loss and regret. The slower tempo and more introspective lyrics reflect his emotional maturity and the consequences of his earlier actions. In this way, the music helps to chart Hamilton's growth, providing the audience with a deeper understanding of his internal struggles.

Music also serves as a narrative tool by reinforcing themes and motifs throughout the musical. Composers often use recurring musical phrases or motifs to tie together different parts of the story, creating a sense of continuity and thematic unity. These motifs can signal key emotional moments, connect characters, or symbolize broader themes within the narrative. By repeating certain musical themes in different contexts, the composer can subtly remind the audience of earlier events or foreshadow future developments.

In *The Phantom of the Opera*, for example, Andrew Lloyd Webber uses the haunting "Phantom's Theme" as a recurring motif to represent the Phantom's presence and influence over Christine. This motif recurs throughout the musical, often during moments of tension or mystery, reinforcing the idea that the Phantom is always lurking in the background, shaping the events of the story. Similarly, in *Les Misérables*, the melody of "Do You Hear the People Sing?" becomes a rallying cry for revolution, with its stirring tune reappearing in different contexts to symbolize hope, unity, and resistance.

Musical numbers can also function as dramatic punctuation, emphasizing key moments of conflict or resolution. In many cases, the climax of a musical is marked by a powerful song that encapsulates the emotional stakes of the story and brings the narrative to a head. These songs often serve as emotional releases for both the characters and the audience, allowing the characters to confront their deepest fears or desires in a highly charged moment of song.

For example, in *Wicked*, the climactic number "Defying Gravity" is not only a vocal showstopper but also a turning point in Elphaba's journey. As she embraces her power and defies those who seek to control her, the soaring music and bold lyrics capture the magnitude of her decision. This song crystallizes the themes of independence, rebellion, and empowerment that have been building throughout the show, making it a defining moment in the narrative.

In addition to advancing the plot and developing characters, music in a Broadway musical often serves to create atmosphere and enhance the emotional tone of a scene. Composers use different musical styles, rhythms, and instrumentation to evoke specific emotions, settings, or cultural influences. For instance, the use of hip-hop and rap in *Hamilton* not only reflects the modern, revolutionary spirit of the characters but also brings a fresh, energetic sound to the historical narrative. The fast-paced, rhythmic nature of the music mirrors Hamilton's relentless ambition and the urgency of the political environment, immersing the audience in the high-stakes world of the American Revolution.

In contrast, the lush, sweeping melodies of *The Phantom of the Opera* create a sense of romance and grandeur, reflecting the opulent setting of the Paris Opera House and the intense emotions of the characters. The music helps to transport the audience into the world of the story, making the opera house feel both enchanting and foreboding.

Furthermore, music often helps to define relationships between characters in a musical. Duets and ensemble numbers provide opportunities for characters to interact musically, revealing their dynamics and emotional connections. In *West Side Story*, the love between Tony and Maria is expressed through the song "Tonight," where their harmonies blend beautifully, symbolizing their unity in the face of external conflict. In contrast, songs like "A Boy Like That" reveal the tension between Maria and her friend Anita, with their clashing melodies and rhythms reflecting their differing views on love and loyalty.

Ensemble numbers, in particular, can be used to showcase the collective emotions or actions of a group, offering insight into the larger world of the story. In *Rent*, the song "La Vie Bohème" brings the entire cast together in a celebration of bohemian life and artistic freedom. The ensemble nature of the song emphasizes the sense of community among the characters, while the music's upbeat, rebellious tone reinforces the show's themes of defiance and self-expression.

In conclusion, the role of music in a Broadway musical is far more than a series of pleasant tunes—it is an essential narrative tool that drives the story forward, shapes character development, and deepens emotional engagement. Through song, characters reveal their inner thoughts and motivations, face their challenges, and share their desires with the audience in ways that dialogue alone cannot. Music creates a heightened emotional experience, weaving together motifs, themes, and melodies to create a cohesive and compelling narrative. When storytelling through song is done effectively, it transforms a musical into a rich, immersive journey that resonates with audiences long after the final note fades.

Finding the Emotional Heart: Character Arcs in Musicals

In a Broadway musical, character arcs are the emotional backbone of the story, driving the narrative forward and creating a journey that audiences can connect with on a deeply personal level. Unlike in straight plays or films, where character development is primarily conveyed through dialogue and action, musicals have the added dimension of music and song to explore a character's inner world. This combination of script, music, and performance allows for richer, more dynamic character arcs, where emotional growth and transformation are expressed through moments of song, dance, and heightened performance.

A character arc refers to the personal journey a character undergoes from the beginning to the end of the story. In musicals, character arcs often revolve around themes of self-discovery, love, loss, redemption, or ambition. As the character faces challenges, makes decisions, and evolves, their songs become a powerful means of conveying these changes, offering insight into their thoughts, emotions, and motivations. Finding the emotional heart of a musical involves identifying and developing these character arcs so that the audience can fully invest in the characters' growth and transformation.

One of the most common types of character arcs in musicals is the "hero's journey" or transformation arc, where the protagonist begins the story in one state—often inexperienced, conflicted, or unsure of their identity—and ends in a place of clarity, empowerment, or fulfillment. This type of arc can be seen in many of the most successful Broadway musicals, where the protagonist's emotional journey is central to the story's themes and resolution.

For example, in *The Lion King*, Simba's arc follows a classic hero's journey. At the beginning of the story, Simba is a young, carefree cub, unaware of the responsibilities that await him as the future king. His arc takes him through loss, guilt, and self-doubt, until he finally reclaims his identity and embraces his role as king. The emotional heart of *The Lion King* lies in Simba's internal struggle to reconcile his past with his future, and this is powerfully expressed through key musical moments like "Hakuna Matata" (his attempt to avoid responsibility) and "He Lives in You" (his ultimate acceptance of his destiny). The music underscores his emotional growth, guiding the audience through his transformation.

Similarly, Elphaba in *Wicked* undergoes a major transformation arc. At the start of the musical, she is an idealistic, misunderstood young woman, hoping to use her magical abilities to make the world a better place. However, as the story progresses, she is forced to confront the corrupt realities of the world around her and ultimately embraces her role as the "Wicked Witch of the West." Elphaba's arc is one of empowerment and defiance, and it reaches its emotional climax in the song "Defying Gravity," where she fully accepts her identity and takes control of her own destiny. This turning point in the character's arc is not just a powerful vocal moment but also a crucial step in her emotional evolution, as she transforms from a hopeful outsider to a self-determined figure of rebellion.

In contrast to the transformation arc, some musicals focus on tragic or downward character arcs, where the protagonist faces insurmountable obstacles or makes choices that lead to their downfall. These arcs can be just as compelling and emotionally resonant, as they explore themes of fate, loss, and the consequences of one's actions. In *Les Misérables*, for instance, Jean Valjean's arc is one of redemption, but the arcs of characters like Javert and Fantine are much more tragic. Javert's rigid adherence to the law ultimately leads to his suicide, and Fantine's descent into poverty and despair culminates in her untimely death. Both characters' tragic arcs are powerfully conveyed through music—Javert's final song, "Javert's Suicide," is a chilling reflection of his internal conflict, while Fantine's "I Dreamed a Dream" captures the devastating loss of hope that defines her journey.

In *West Side Story*, the love story between Tony and Maria follows a similarly tragic arc. Their relationship, built on love and hope in the midst of violence and hatred, ultimately ends in tragedy. Songs like "Somewhere" and "Tonight" express the optimism and passion of their love, while the darker realities of their world close in on them. By the end of the musical, Maria's grief and loss are palpable, and her character arc underscores the devastating consequences of intolerance and violence.

Musicals also often explore character arcs through relationships—romantic, familial, or friendships. In these stories, the emotional heart of the musical lies in how these relationships evolve and change the characters. For instance, in *Dear Evan Hansen*, Evan's arc is closely tied to his relationship with the Murphy family and his own mother. His emotional growth is reflected in his struggle to belong and be seen, and much of the musical's emotional weight comes from the shifting dynamics between Evan and those around him. Songs like "Waving Through a Window" and "You Will Be Found" reveal Evan's deep loneliness and desire for connection, while "Words Fail" exposes the pain of his dishonesty and his ultimate realization of the harm he has caused. Evan's arc is a deeply emotional one, centered on themes of truth, identity, and redemption.

In some musicals, character arcs focus on the tension between individual desires and societal expectations. In *Fiddler on the Roof*, Tevye's arc is about navigating tradition and change. As a father and a devout Jewish man, Tevye struggles with the changing world around him, especially as his daughters make choices that challenge his deeply held beliefs. His arc is about learning to balance his love for his family with his commitment to tradition, and this tension is expressed through songs like "If I Were a Rich Man," where Tevye dreams of a life of comfort, and "Tradition," where he asserts the importance of cultural continuity. Throughout the musical, Tevye's character is tested, and his eventual acceptance of his daughters' choices represents his emotional growth and adaptability in the face of change.

In *Hamilton*, many characters have distinct and compelling arcs that interweave with the broader narrative of revolution and legacy. Alexander Hamilton's arc is one of ambition and drive, as he rises from an impoverished immigrant to one of the most influential figures in American history. His arc, however, also includes hubris and downfall, particularly in his personal life, as his relentless ambition leads to personal betrayals and, ultimately, his death. On the other hand, Aaron Burr's arc is one of caution and restraint, constantly contrasting Hamilton's boldness. Burr's internal conflict and envy of Hamilton's daring decisions come to a head in "The World Was Wide Enough," when Burr tragically becomes the instrument of Hamilton's demise. Both characters' arcs are defined by their contrasting approaches to life, with the musical exploring the consequences of their choices.

Music serves as the key medium through which these character arcs are expressed, with each song representing a step along the journey. In *Wicked*, for instance, Glinda's arc is reflected in her songs as much as Elphaba's. Glinda begins the musical as a shallow, self-centered young woman, but her arc sees her grow into a more thoughtful and self-aware character. Songs like "Popular" show her initial vanity and superficiality, while later numbers, like "For Good," reveal the depth of her relationship with Elphaba and her recognition of the importance of their friendship. By the end of the musical, Glinda has matured, and her emotional growth is as central to the story as Elphaba's.

Even supporting characters in musicals often have well-defined arcs that contribute to the emotional complexity of the story. In *Rent*, the character of Angel undergoes a transformative arc despite being a supporting figure. Angel's generosity, love, and eventual death have a profound impact on the other characters, particularly Collins and Mark, shaping their emotional journeys. The song "I'll Cover You (Reprise)" is one of the most emotionally charged moments in the musical, capturing the depth of Angel's impact and the pain of loss, even as the characters continue to celebrate love and community.

In conclusion, character arcs are the emotional heart of a Broadway musical, providing the framework for personal growth, transformation, and the exploration of themes like love, identity, ambition, and loss. Music plays a crucial role in shaping these arcs, allowing characters to express emotions that go beyond dialogue and bringing their internal journeys to life. Whether the arc is one of empowerment, tragedy, or redemption, a well-developed character arc engages the audience on an emotional level, making the musical experience not only entertaining but deeply moving. Through their songs, decisions, and relationships, characters in musicals undergo journeys that resonate long after the curtain falls.

Building Tension: Conflict and Resolution on Stage

Conflict and resolution are at the core of any compelling Broadway musical, driving the plot forward and keeping the audience emotionally invested in the characters' journeys. In musicals, conflict is often heightened by the combination of dialogue, music, and choreography, making it more immediate, visceral, and impactful. The way a musical builds tension through these elements and ultimately resolves its conflicts is crucial to its emotional and narrative success. Whether the story is one of triumph, tragedy, or bittersweet compromise, the balance between conflict and resolution is what gives the musical its dramatic arc, creating moments of suspense, intensity, and catharsis.

At its most basic level, conflict in a musical arises from opposing desires, goals, or values between characters, or between a character and their external circumstances. This conflict can take many forms: internal struggles within a character, interpersonal conflicts between characters, or broader societal or environmental challenges. The way a musical builds and escalates this conflict often determines the emotional stakes of the story, as the audience becomes invested in seeing how the characters navigate their challenges.

In *West Side Story*, the central conflict revolves around the rivalry between two street gangs, the Jets and the Sharks, and the forbidden love between Tony and Maria, who belong to opposing sides. The tension builds as the characters are caught between their love for each other and their loyalty to their respective communities. The music and choreography in *West Side Story* play a pivotal role in heightening this tension. The iconic "Dance at the Gym" scene, for instance, starts as a vibrant, energetic number but quickly becomes a battleground where the rivalry between the gangs is palpable. The escalating tension in the music and dance mirrors the growing hostility between the groups, setting the stage for the tragic conflicts to come.

Musicals often use songs to externalize internal conflicts, giving the audience direct access to a character's emotional turmoil. In *Wicked*, Elphaba's internal conflict is between her desire to do good and the way the world perceives her as "wicked." This struggle reaches its peak in the song "Defying Gravity," where Elphaba embraces her power and rejects the labels others have placed on her. The soaring music and powerful lyrics build to a dramatic crescendo, reflecting the internal and external conflicts she faces. By the end of the song, the tension has reached its highest point, with Elphaba making a defiant decision that sets her on a new path and further intensifies the story's conflict.

Interpersonal conflict, often between a protagonist and an antagonist, is another key source of tension in musicals. In *Les Misérables*, the conflict between Jean Valjean and Javert serves as one of the central driving forces of the narrative. Javert's rigid belief in law and order is in direct opposition to Valjean's quest for redemption and mercy. Their conflict plays out in a series of confrontations throughout the musical, each one escalating in intensity. Songs like "Confrontation" bring their opposing values to the forefront, with the music underscoring the tension between the characters. The resolution of this conflict, with Javert's eventual suicide, is a powerful moment of release, but it also leaves the audience grappling with the complexities of justice, mercy, and morality.

Conflict in musicals is often heightened by external factors, such as societal pressures, war, or systemic injustice. In *Hamilton*, the central conflicts revolve around Alexander Hamilton's ambition, the political battles of the American Revolution, and the personal rivalries that define his life. The tension between Hamilton's desire to rise to greatness and the opposition he faces from figures like Aaron Burr builds throughout the show. Songs like "The Room Where

It Happens" and "Your Obedient Servant" reflect the growing tension between Hamilton and Burr, with the music creating an almost frenetic energy that mirrors the characters' mounting frustrations. The ultimate resolution of their conflict, in the form of the infamous duel, is both inevitable and tragic, providing a dramatic conclusion to the personal and political tensions that have been simmering throughout the musical.

Music and choreography in a musical are essential tools for building tension, often amplifying the emotional stakes and providing cues to the audience about the escalating conflict. Fast-paced, driving rhythms can create a sense of urgency, while dissonant harmonies or sudden shifts in dynamics can convey tension or unease. In *Sweeney Todd: The Demon Barber of Fleet Street*, for example, the music plays a crucial role in creating an atmosphere of suspense and dread. The recurring musical motif in "The Ballad of Sweeney Todd" builds tension by reminding the audience of the looming violence and moral ambiguity of Sweeney's quest for revenge. The music mirrors Sweeney's growing obsession, building tension that culminates in the show's bloody resolution.

Choreography also contributes to the development of conflict in musicals, especially in productions where dance is a central element. In *West Side Story*, the physicality of the dance numbers reflects the aggression and competition between the Jets and the Sharks. The iconic "Rumble" scene is a masterclass in using choreography to build tension—each movement is charged with emotion and violence, creating a palpable sense of danger that leads to the fatal confrontation between the two gangs. The combination of movement, music, and character dynamics heightens the tension, making the eventual resolution all the more devastating.

The pacing of a musical is another critical factor in building and releasing tension. A well-structured musical knows how to escalate conflict over time, allowing for moments of tension to build gradually before releasing them in climactic scenes. These moments of release, or resolution, provide emotional catharsis for both the characters and the audience. In *The Phantom of the Opera*, the tension between the Phantom, Christine, and Raoul builds throughout the show, as the Phantom's obsession with Christine becomes increasingly dangerous. This tension reaches its peak in the final confrontation in the Phantom's lair, where Christine's compassion leads to a surprising resolution. The release of tension in this scene is heightened by the emotional intensity of the music and the stakes that have been established over the course of the musical.

Resolution in musicals doesn't always mean a happy ending, but it often provides closure to the central conflicts. In *Rent*, the characters face numerous personal and societal challenges, including illness, poverty, and loss. The resolution of the musical comes not from solving these problems but from the characters' reaffirmation of their bonds with each other and their commitment to living fully in the face of adversity. The song "Finale B," with its reprise of "Seasons of Love," offers a sense of emotional closure, reminding the audience that while the characters' struggles continue, they have found meaning and connection through their experiences.

In some cases, musicals leave certain conflicts unresolved, creating a more ambiguous or thought-provoking ending. In *Into the Woods*, the characters achieve their initial goals by the end of the first act, but the second act explores the consequences of their wishes, leading to new conflicts and moral dilemmas. The resolution is not neat or simple—while some characters find peace or reconciliation, others are left grappling with the aftermath of their actions. The final song, "No One Is Alone," suggests that while resolution may be elusive, the characters must continue to face their challenges together. This open-ended resolution invites the audience to reflect on the complexities of the characters' journeys and the themes of the musical.

The use of reprises is another effective way to highlight conflict and resolution in musicals. A reprise can remind the audience of earlier conflicts while showing how the characters have changed. In *Les Misérables*, the reprise of "Do You Hear the People Sing?" at the end of the musical takes on a new meaning, as the revolution has failed, but the hope for a better future lives on in the hearts of the survivors. The music is the same, but the context has shifted, providing a sense of resolution that acknowledges both the loss and the resilience of the characters.

In conclusion, building tension and resolving conflict are essential components of storytelling in a Broadway musical. Through the integration of script, music, and choreography, musicals create heightened emotional stakes that engage the audience and propel the narrative forward. The way a musical handles conflict—whether through interpersonal relationships, internal struggles, or external forces—shapes the dramatic arc of the story, creating moments of suspense, intensity, and emotional release. Ultimately, the resolution of these conflicts, whether triumphant, tragic, or bittersweet, provides the emotional catharsis that makes musicals such a powerful and unforgettable form of storytelling.

The Power of the Opening Number: Hooking Your Audience

The opening number of a Broadway musical is one of the most important moments in the entire production. It sets the tone, establishes the world of the show, introduces key characters, and lays the groundwork for the central themes. More than that, it must immediately engage the audience, capturing their attention and drawing them into the story. A powerful opening number can create a sense of anticipation and excitement, making the audience eager to follow the characters' journeys for the next two hours. Whether it's bold and energetic or subtle and mysterious, the opening number is the musical's first impression, and it must be carefully crafted to hook the audience from the start.

One of the primary functions of the opening number is to establish the world of the musical. This includes introducing the setting, tone, and atmosphere that will shape the rest of the production. For example, in *The Lion King*, the opening number "Circle of Life" immediately transports the audience to the African savannah. The iconic music, combined with the breathtaking visuals of the animal puppets and costumes, creates a sense of grandeur and wonder, immersing the audience in the world of the story from the very first note. The song also introduces the central themes of the musical, such as the cyclical nature of life and the connection between all living things, providing a thematic foundation that resonates throughout the show.

Similarly, *Hamilton* uses its opening number to set the stage for its unique blend of historical narrative and modern musical styles. The song "Alexander Hamilton" introduces the title character and his backstory, while also establishing the musical's fast-paced, hip-hop-infused sound. In just a few minutes, the audience is given an overview of Hamilton's early life and the challenges he will face, while also being introduced to the dynamic, innovative style that defines the musical. The energy and rhythm of the opening number grab the audience's attention immediately, signaling that this will be a fresh, modern take on the traditional Broadway format.

Another key function of the opening number is to introduce the main characters and hint at their central conflicts. A well-crafted opening number doesn't just introduce the world of the musical—it also gives the audience a sense of who the main players are and what they want. In *Wicked*, the opening number "No One Mourns the Wicked" sets the stage by introducing the world's perception of Elphaba as the "Wicked Witch of the West." The audience learns that Elphaba has died and that she was widely feared and reviled, creating an immediate sense of intrigue about her backstory. This opening number raises questions: Who was Elphaba really? Was she truly wicked, or was she misunderstood? By introducing these central conflicts right away, the opening number hooks the audience, making them eager to learn more about the character's journey.

In some cases, the opening number also serves to introduce the ensemble and establish their role in the story. In musicals where the community or group dynamic is important, the opening number often features the entire cast, giving the audience a sense of the collective world in which the story takes place. In *Les Misérables*, the opening number "Work Song" sets up the conflict between the oppressed workers and the powerful figures who control them. The ensemble's powerful chorus highlights the themes of poverty, injustice, and rebellion that will dominate the rest of the musical, while also introducing the character of Jean Valjean, who will carry the weight of these themes throughout his journey. The use of the ensemble in the opening number creates a sense of scope and scale, showing the audience that this is a story about more than just individual characters—it's about the struggle of an entire society.

Another important role of the opening number is to establish the musical's tone. Whether the show is a light-hearted comedy, a sweeping romance, or a dark drama, the opening number sets the emotional tone that will carry through the rest of the production. In comedies, the opening number often features humor and lightness, giving the audience permission to laugh and enjoy the show. In *The Book of Mormon*, the opening number "Hello!" introduces the audience to the quirky, over-the-top world of the Mormon missionaries, using humor and irony to establish the comedic tone that will define the musical. The cheerful, upbeat song contrasts with the often absurd situations the characters find themselves in, creating a satirical tone that lets the audience know they are in for a fun, irreverent ride.

In more serious musicals, the opening number may use music, lyrics, and staging to create a sense of tension or foreboding, signaling to the audience that they are entering a darker, more dramatic world. In *Sweeney Todd: The Demon Barber of Fleet Street*, the opening number "The Ballad of Sweeney Todd" immediately sets a macabre tone, with its ominous music and eerie lyrics. The ensemble's chant-like delivery of the song creates an unsettling atmosphere, letting the audience know that they are in for a story of vengeance, madness, and violence. By establishing this dark tone right away, the musical prepares the audience for the intense emotional and psychological journey they are about to experience.

The opening number is also a key moment for establishing musical motifs and themes that will recur throughout the show. Many successful musicals use motifs—recurring musical phrases or themes—that are introduced in the opening number and then repeated or varied later in the production. These motifs help create a sense of unity and continuity, reminding the audience of earlier moments or reinforcing key emotional beats. In *Into the Woods*, the opening number introduces several of the musical motifs that will recur throughout the show, including the "I Wish" theme that reflects the characters' desires and the "Into the Woods" theme that signifies their journey into the unknown. These motifs not only tie the musical together musically but also reinforce the central themes of desire, consequence, and the unexpected twists of life.

In addition to setting the tone and establishing the world, characters, and themes, the opening number must also create a sense of momentum that propels the story forward. It should generate excitement and anticipation, making the audience eager to see what happens next. A successful opening number leaves the audience hooked, not just because it's entertaining but because it promises an engaging story with characters worth investing in. This sense of forward momentum is often achieved through the pacing of the song, the build of the music, and the choreography or staging that accompanies it.

For instance, in *Annie*, the opening number "Maybe" introduces the title character's optimism and hope, despite her difficult circumstances. The simple, heartfelt melody and lyrics create an emotional connection between Annie and the audience, while also establishing the central conflict of her search for a family. As the song progresses, the music swells, and Annie's determination becomes clear. By the end of the number, the audience is rooting for her, invested in her journey, and eager to see how her story unfolds.

In contrast, *Chicago* opens with the dazzling "All That Jazz," a show-stopping number that immediately establishes the musical's glitzy, cynical tone. The fast-paced music, sultry choreography, and bold lyrics create a sense of excitement and spectacle, drawing the audience into the world of 1920s Chicago with its themes of fame, corruption, and manipulation. The number doesn't just introduce the world of the musical—it pulls the audience into it, creating a sense of energy and forward motion that carries through the rest of the show.

Finally, the opening number must leave a lasting impression. It should be memorable enough that the audience is thinking about it even as the show moves forward. A great opening number can set the stage for a musical to be unforgettable, giving the audience a reason to stay fully engaged for the duration of the performance. In *Rent*, the opening number "Rent" establishes the urgency and passion of the characters' lives, with its driving rock beat and lyrics about survival, art, and protest. The song's intensity and raw energy grab the audience's attention and refuse to let go, setting the tone for the rest of the musical's emotionally charged exploration of life, love, and loss.

In conclusion, the power of the opening number lies in its ability to hook the audience, establishing the world, characters, tone, and themes of the musical while creating a sense of momentum and excitement. A well-crafted opening number draws the audience into the story, setting the stage for the emotional journey ahead and ensuring that they are fully engaged from the very first note. Whether it's bold and energetic or quiet and introspective, the opening number is the musical's opportunity to make a lasting first impression, one that resonates throughout the rest of the production. When done effectively, it becomes a powerful narrative tool that captivates the audience and sets the tone for a memorable theatrical experience.

Emotional Climaxes: Crafting the Show-Stopping Moment

In every great Broadway musical, there is a moment when the emotional intensity reaches its peak, a moment when the story, characters, and music align to create a show-stopping experience that leaves the audience breathless. These emotional climaxes are the heart of the musical's dramatic arc, moments of catharsis that provide resolution to central conflicts or push characters into new emotional territory. Crafting these show-stopping moments requires a careful balance of music, performance, and narrative, as they must feel earned and serve as the culmination of everything that has come before. When done effectively, they become the moments that audiences remember long after the curtain falls.

An emotional climax in a musical is typically a pivotal moment of decision, realization, or transformation for a character. It often occurs at a critical point in the story when the character's internal or external conflict reaches its highest intensity. These moments of emotional release or discovery are often marked by a powerful song that captures the character's emotional journey, using music to heighten the stakes and provide insight into their state of mind.

One of the most iconic examples of an emotional climax is "Defying Gravity" from *Wicked*. This song serves as the turning point for Elphaba, as she fully embraces her power and rejects the forces that have tried to control her. Leading up to this moment, the musical builds tension as Elphaba grapples with her desire to do good, the betrayal of those she trusted, and the dawning realization that she must chart her own course. The soaring music, combined with the dramatic visuals of Elphaba rising into the air, creates a moment of pure theatrical magic. "Defying Gravity" isn't just a vocal showstopper—it's the emotional climax of Elphaba's arc, the moment when she takes control of her destiny and fully accepts the consequences of her choices. The music reflects her transformation, with its dynamic shifts and swelling crescendos, while the lyrics capture her newfound resolve and independence. The result is a moment that resonates deeply with the audience, both musically and emotionally.

Similarly, in *Les Misérables*, the song "One Day More" serves as a powerful emotional climax that unites multiple character arcs at a critical point in the story. As the characters prepare for the impending revolution, the song weaves together their individual hopes, fears, and conflicts into a single, swelling ensemble number. Each character's journey is reflected in their section of the song, whether it's Valjean's protective love for Cosette, Javert's unyielding pursuit of justice, or Marius's youthful passion for revolution and love. The music builds in intensity, with each voice adding to the tension and anticipation. By the end of the number, the audience feels the full weight of the impending battle and the emotional stakes for each character. "One Day More" is not only a musical high point but also a narrative climax that prepares the audience for the resolution of the characters' journeys.

Crafting an emotional climax in a musical requires careful pacing. The buildup to the climax must feel organic, with the character's emotional journey unfolding gradually so that the moment of release feels earned. In *Hamilton*, the song "It's Quiet Uptown" is a deeply emotional climax in Alexander Hamilton's personal journey, as he grapples with the death of his son Philip and attempts to find forgiveness from his wife Eliza. Leading up to this moment, the audience has witnessed Hamilton's relentless ambition, his personal mistakes, and the devastating consequences of his choices. By the time "It's Quiet Uptown" begins, the emotional weight of these events has been building steadily, making the song's quiet reflection all the more powerful. The music itself is restrained, with a gentle, repetitive melody that contrasts with the earlier, more frenetic numbers in the musical. This change in musical tone signals Hamilton's internal shift, as he confronts his grief and seeks redemption. The song's emotional impact comes not from a grand, showy performance but from its quiet, introspective power, making it one of the most poignant moments in the musical.

Another example of an emotional climax is "She Used to Be Mine" from *Waitress*. This song captures Jenna's moment of self-realization as she reflects on how her life has changed and how she has lost sight of the person she once was. The song is filled with raw emotion, as Jenna grapples with her feelings of regret, longing, and hope for a better future. Leading up to this moment, the audience has seen Jenna's struggles in her unhappy marriage and her attempts to find joy and meaning in her life. "She Used to Be Mine" serves as the emotional release for all of these pent-up feelings, with the music building gradually from a soft, introspective melody to a powerful, soaring climax. The simplicity of the piano accompaniment allows the emotional depth of the lyrics to shine, and the song's structure mirrors Jenna's emotional journey—from quiet resignation to a fierce determination to reclaim her life. The result is a show-stopping moment that resonates deeply with audiences, as Jenna's vulnerability and strength come to the forefront.

In many musicals, the emotional climax is tied to a character's decision or realization, a moment when they are forced to confront their deepest fears, desires, or flaws. In *Rent*, the song "I'll Cover You (Reprise)" serves as an emotional climax following the death of Angel, a beloved character whose love and generosity touched everyone around him. The reprise is a powerful moment of grief and remembrance, as Collins sings the same melody that was once a joyful expression of love, now transformed into a heartbreaking elegy. The juxtaposition of the original song's upbeat tempo with the mournful reprise creates an emotional contrast that heightens the sense of loss. The entire ensemble joins in, creating a sense of communal grief and solidarity that underscores the musical's themes of love, loss, and the resilience of the human spirit. The music builds to an intense emotional release, leaving the audience deeply moved.

For an emotional climax to truly resonate, the performance must match the intensity of the moment. In many cases, the show-stopping moment is not just about the music or the lyrics—it's about the actor's ability to fully inhabit the character's emotions and deliver a performance that feels raw, authentic, and powerful. A great example of this is "And I Am Telling You I'm Not Going" from *Dreamgirls*, which has become one of the most iconic show-stopping numbers in musical theater history. In this song, Effie White confronts her abandonment by the people she loves and refuses to give up without a fight. The emotional intensity of the song is matched by the powerhouse vocal performance, with the music building to an explosive climax that leaves both the character and the audience emotionally exhausted. The song's power lies not just in its soaring melody but in the raw emotion behind it—Effie's desperation, pain, and determination are palpable, making the moment unforgettable.

The visual and staging elements of a musical's emotional climax can also enhance its impact. In *The Phantom of the Opera*, the song "The Music of the Night" serves as an emotional and sensory climax, as the Phantom seduces Christine into his world of music and darkness. The staging of this moment, with the Phantom guiding Christine through his underground lair, combined with the lush, hypnotic music, creates an immersive experience that heightens the emotional tension. The song's slow, seductive build reflects the Phantom's control over Christine, and the staging reinforces the sense of entrapment and allure. This combination of music, performance, and visual spectacle makes "The Music of the Night" one of the most iconic and emotionally charged moments in the musical.

In conclusion, crafting an emotional climax in a musical is about more than just writing a powerful song—it's about building a moment that feels earned, authentic, and deeply connected to the characters' journeys. Whether the climax is a moment of triumph, heartbreak, or self-discovery, it must resonate both musically and emotionally with the audience. The best show-stopping moments are those that bring together music, performance, and narrative in a way that creates a lasting impact, leaving the audience with a sense of catharsis and connection. These climactic moments are the emotional high points of the musical, providing the audience with the release they've been waiting for and solidifying the show's place in their hearts long after the final curtain falls.

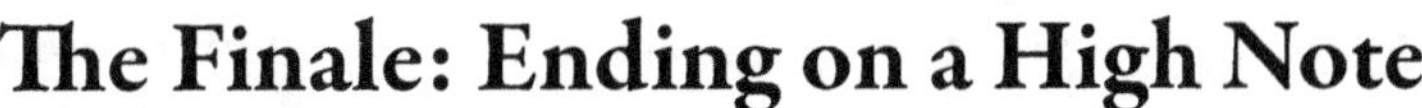

The Finale: Ending on a High Note

The finale of a Broadway musical is the last chance to leave a lasting impression on the audience. It brings the narrative to a close, resolves lingering conflicts, and delivers the emotional or thematic resolution that the show has been building toward. Whether the musical ends on a triumphant high note or a more reflective, bittersweet tone, the finale must offer closure while also capturing the essence of the story. A great finale ties together all the elements of the show—music, characters, and themes—and leaves the audience with a sense of fulfillment, often elevating the experience into something unforgettable.

One of the most important roles of a finale is to provide resolution. After the central conflicts of the musical have been explored, the finale is where the characters reach a point of resolution, whether through personal growth, reconciliation, or realization. In many cases, this resolution is reinforced through the music, with the finale reprising musical themes or motifs introduced earlier in the show. This creates a sense of continuity and cohesion, reminding the audience of the journey the characters have taken while bringing it to a satisfying conclusion.

In *Les Misérables*, the finale brings together the central themes of redemption, love, and sacrifice. After the death of Jean Valjean, the characters sing a reprise of "Do You Hear the People Sing?"—a powerful, unifying anthem that encapsulates the spirit of revolution and hope for a better future. The reprise of this melody, now sung by the full ensemble, creates a sense of emotional resolution. Valjean's personal journey toward redemption is complete, and the collective struggle of the people lives on in the form of hope and unity. The finale ties together the personal and political themes of the show, providing closure while also leaving the audience with a sense of upliftment and inspiration.

In many musicals, the finale brings the entire cast together in a final ensemble number, creating a sense of unity and celebration. This approach is particularly effective in musicals that emphasize community or collective experiences. In *Rent*, the finale reprises "Seasons of Love," bringing the surviving characters together to reaffirm their bond and their determination to live fully, despite the challenges they face. This song, which was introduced earlier in the musical as a meditation on time and the importance of love, now takes on a deeper meaning in light of the characters' experiences with loss, grief, and resilience. The ensemble performance gives the finale an emotional weight, reminding the audience that while some conflicts remain unresolved, the characters' commitment to each other and to living authentically endures. It leaves the audience with a sense of bittersweet hope.

Finales often reprise key musical themes, allowing the audience to revisit earlier moments in the show and see how the characters or circumstances have changed. Reprises are a common tool in musicals because they create a sense of musical and narrative closure, reinforcing key emotional beats and giving the audience a sense of satisfaction. In *The Sound of Music*, the finale reprises the song "Climb Ev'ry Mountain," which serves as both a motivational anthem and a thematic reminder of perseverance and faith. As the von Trapp family makes their escape across the mountains, the reprise of this song underscores their courage and determination, leaving the audience with a sense of triumph and emotional closure.

Sometimes, the finale offers a moment of reflection, allowing the audience to consider the broader themes of the musical or the impact of the characters' journeys. In *Wicked*, the finale brings Elphaba and Glinda's story full circle, with a reprise of "For Good." The song captures the emotional complexity of their relationship and the lasting impact they have had on each other. While their friendship has been strained by conflict and misunderstanding, the finale emphasizes that both characters have been changed "for good" by their experiences together. The reflective tone of the song provides emotional resolution, allowing the audience to feel the weight of their shared journey, even as the musical concludes on a bittersweet note.

In more lighthearted musicals, the finale serves as a moment of joyous celebration, sending the audience out on a high note. These finales often feature upbeat, energetic numbers that encapsulate the fun and excitement of the show. In *Hairspray*, the finale "You Can't Stop the Beat" is a high-energy, feel-good number that brings together the entire cast in a celebration of progress, acceptance, and self-expression. The infectious rhythm and uplifting lyrics create a sense of triumph and joy, leaving the audience energized and satisfied. The finale doesn't just tie up the storylines—it reinforces the show's central message of inclusivity and the unstoppable power of change, making the audience feel like they are part of the celebration.

In *Mamma Mia!*, the finale also ends on a high note, with a medley of ABBA songs that transforms the curtain call into a full-blown party. The characters and ensemble return to the stage for an encore performance, with the audience often clapping, dancing, and singing along. This type of finale is less about narrative closure and more about creating an unforgettable, joyful experience that sends the audience home in a celebratory mood. The musical numbers, while not directly related to the plot, capture the exuberant spirit of the show, making the finale a memorable, interactive experience.

Not all finales end on a purely happy note, however. Some musicals leave the audience with a more ambiguous or bittersweet resolution, reflecting the complexities of life. In *Into the Woods*, the finale is both reflective and somber, as the characters come to terms with the consequences of their actions. The song "No One Is Alone" provides a sense of comfort and unity, but the finale doesn't offer a simple, happy ending. The characters have faced loss and hardship, and their final moments reflect the idea that while they must continue to face challenges, they do so with the knowledge that they are not alone. This more nuanced approach to the finale leaves the audience with a deeper understanding of the show's themes, inviting reflection on the consequences of desire, choice, and responsibility.

Crafting a successful finale also involves ensuring that the emotional arc of the characters is fully realized by the end of the show. A finale should feel like the culmination of everything that has come before, with the characters reaching a point of closure or resolution in their personal journeys. In *Hamilton*, the finale focuses on the legacy Alexander Hamilton leaves behind, with Eliza's role in preserving his memory taking center stage. The song "Who Lives, Who Dies, Who Tells Your Story" reflects on the themes of history, memory, and legacy that have been woven throughout the musical. By shifting the focus to Eliza, the finale provides a poignant conclusion to Hamilton's story, while also reinforcing the idea that history is shaped by those who tell it. The finale leaves the audience with a sense of reflection, both on Hamilton's life and on the broader themes of the musical.

Staging and choreography play a crucial role in creating a dynamic and memorable finale. A visually impactful finale can elevate the emotional resonance of the music and performances, making the final moments of the show even more powerful. In *The Phantom of the Opera*, the finale is visually and emotionally intense, as the Phantom disappears into the shadows, leaving behind only his mask. This haunting image, combined with the dramatic orchestration, leaves the audience with a sense of mystery and unresolved tension, perfectly matching the darker, more gothic tone of the musical. The finale's visual elements enhance the emotional impact, making the ending unforgettable.

In conclusion, the finale of a Broadway musical is more than just the last song—it is the emotional and narrative culmination of the entire show. Whether it offers triumph, reflection, or bittersweet resolution, the finale must tie together the characters' journeys and reinforce the musical's central themes. Through a combination of music, performance, and visual spectacle, a great finale leaves the audience with a sense of closure and fulfillment, ensuring that the final moments of the show resonate long after the curtain falls. By ending on a high note—whether joyous or reflective—a well-crafted finale ensures that the musical's emotional impact stays with the audience, creating an unforgettable theatrical experience.

Incorporating Spectacle: Visual and Auditory Grandeur

Incorporating spectacle into a Broadway musical can elevate the audience's experience, creating moments of visual and auditory grandeur that leave lasting impressions. Spectacle in theater is not just about flashy effects or large-scale designs; it is about using visual and auditory elements to enhance the emotional and narrative depth of the story. Whether through stunning choreography, elaborate set designs, lighting, costumes, or soundscapes, spectacle creates a sense of wonder and immersion that transforms the musical into something truly magical.

The most successful uses of spectacle are those that complement the storytelling, serving as a natural extension of the musical's themes, characters, and emotional arcs. Rather than overpowering the narrative, spectacle in a well-crafted musical heightens the drama, making key moments more powerful and memorable. From awe-inspiring set pieces to dramatic lighting effects and intricate costume designs, spectacle can turn pivotal moments into show-stopping events that captivate the audience and bring the world of the musical to life.

One of the most iconic examples of spectacle in musical theater is *The Lion King*. The show's use of elaborate puppetry, costumes, and set design creates an immersive experience that transports the audience to the African savannah. The opening number, "Circle of Life," is a masterclass in how spectacle can enhance a musical. As the animals of the Pride Lands parade through the audience and ascend the stage, the combination of music, choreography, and visually stunning puppetry sets the tone for the entire production. The grandeur of the visual elements mirrors the thematic scope of the show—birth, death, and the cyclical nature of life. The spectacle of this opening number immediately hooks the audience and immerses them in the world of the story, making it an unforgettable moment in Broadway history.

Similarly, *Phantom of the Opera* uses spectacle to enhance its gothic, romantic atmosphere. The iconic chandelier crash is one of the most famous examples of visual spectacle on Broadway. The moment is not just a technical feat; it symbolizes the emotional and psychological tension that permeates the musical. The visual grandeur of the chandelier, combined with the swelling orchestration, heightens the drama and creates a visceral sense of danger and chaos. Other elements, such as the elaborate set designs of the opera house and the Phantom's underground lair, contribute to the sense of mystery and grandeur, making the audience feel as though they are part of a dark, romantic world that lies beneath the surface of reality.

Choreography is another key element in creating spectacle in a musical. Large ensemble numbers that incorporate intricate dance sequences can be visually stunning, adding energy and excitement to the production. In *West Side Story*, the choreography by Jerome Robbins serves as a form of visual spectacle that also deepens the emotional and thematic content of the musical. The famous "Dance at the Gym" and "America" sequences are not just impressive for their technical precision and high energy—they also reflect the social dynamics and cultural tensions of the characters. The spectacle of the dance is inseparable from the story, as the physical movements of the dancers mirror the conflicts and desires of the characters.

Lighting and special effects also play a crucial role in creating spectacle. Lighting can transform the atmosphere of a scene, heightening the emotional impact and drawing the audience's focus to key moments. In *Wicked*, the song "Defying Gravity" is a perfect example of how lighting and special effects can turn a powerful moment into a breathtaking spectacle. As Elphaba rises into the air, illuminated by a dramatic spotlight and surrounded by swirling lights, the visual grandeur of the moment mirrors her emotional transformation. The combination of lighting, flying effects, and powerful music creates a climactic, show-stopping scene that leaves the audience in awe.

Incorporating projection mapping and multimedia elements has become an increasingly popular way to create spectacle in modern musicals. Shows like *Dear Evan Hansen* use digital projections to enhance the storytelling in ways that traditional set designs cannot. In *Dear Evan Hansen*, the projections of social media feeds and online messages create a visual representation of the digital world that shapes the characters' lives. This use of multimedia not only adds a layer of visual complexity to the production but also reflects the themes of connection and isolation in the digital age. The spectacle of the projections becomes a storytelling tool, immersing the audience in the protagonist's internal struggles and the broader social context.

Sound design and auditory spectacle are just as important as visual elements in creating a sense of grandeur in a musical. A well-designed soundscape can transport the audience into the world of the musical, making them feel as though they are part of the action. In *The Phantom of the Opera*, the use of haunting organ music and the iconic Phantom theme creates an auditory spectacle that heightens the drama and tension. The music and sound effects in the show are as much a part of the spectacle as the visual elements, creating a fully immersive sensory experience. The grandeur of the score, combined with the atmospheric sound design, helps to create a sense of mystery, danger, and romance that defines the production.

Similarly, in *Hamilton*, the auditory spectacle comes from the innovative use of musical styles. The blending of hip-hop, R&B, and traditional musical theater creates a soundscape that is fresh, modern, and engaging. The rapid-fire lyrics, intricate rhymes, and rhythmic beats create an auditory spectacle that matches the intensity of the historical events being portrayed. The music itself becomes a form of spectacle, drawing the audience into the fast-paced world of Alexander Hamilton and the birth of the American nation. The innovative sound design, combined with the dynamic choreography and staging, creates a multi-sensory experience that leaves a lasting impact.

Costume design is another essential element of spectacle, particularly in musicals that feature fantasy, historical, or otherworldly settings. Elaborate costumes can instantly convey the time period, social status, or personality of a character while adding visual richness to the production. In *Wicked*, the contrasting costumes of Glinda and Elphaba visually represent their differing personalities and journeys—Glinda's sparkling, ethereal gowns reflect her popularity and outward charm, while Elphaba's dark, angular attire symbolizes her outsider status and internal struggles. The visual spectacle of the costumes helps to reinforce the musical's themes of identity, perception, and transformation.

In *Aladdin*, the lavish costumes and vibrant colors reflect the opulence and fantasy of the story's setting. The visual spectacle of the costumes is particularly evident in numbers like "Prince Ali," where the stage is filled with a parade of characters in elaborate, colorful outfits. The costumes contribute to the sense of grandeur and magic that defines the world of the musical, transporting the audience to the fantastical city of Agrabah. Costume design in this context is not just about visual appeal—it enhances the overall experience of the musical, making the world feel more alive and immersive.

Set design is often the foundation of visual spectacle in a musical. Large, dynamic sets that transform throughout the show can create a sense of scale and grandeur, making the world of the musical feel expansive and immersive. In *Les Misérables*, the use of the rotating stage is a perfect example of how set design can enhance the visual spectacle while also serving the story. The rotating stage allows for seamless transitions between scenes and creates a sense of constant movement, reflecting the ever-changing, tumultuous world of the characters. The set design, combined with the powerful music and ensemble performances, creates a sweeping sense of epic grandeur that matches the scale of the story.

Some musicals use spectacle to create moments of wonder or surprise that leave a lasting impression on the audience. In *Mary Poppins,* the character's flight across the stage is a moment of pure spectacle that delights and amazes the audience. The use of wire work and special effects allows Mary Poppins to soar above the stage, creating a magical moment that perfectly encapsulates the whimsical, fantastical tone of the musical. This use of spectacle is not just for show—it reinforces the idea that Mary Poppins is a magical, extraordinary figure, making the audience believe in the impossible.

In conclusion, incorporating spectacle into a Broadway musical is about more than just creating visually or auditorily impressive moments—it's about using those elements to enhance the storytelling and deepen the emotional impact of the production. Whether through elaborate set designs, stunning choreography, immersive soundscapes, or innovative lighting and special effects, spectacle serves to draw the audience into the world of the musical, making the story feel more immediate, immersive, and powerful. When done effectively, spectacle can turn a great musical into a transcendent theatrical experience, leaving the audience with a sense of wonder, excitement, and emotional resonance long after the final curtain falls.

Collaborative Genius: Working with a Creative Team

The creation of a Broadway musical is a highly collaborative process, requiring the combined efforts of many talented individuals, each contributing their unique skills and perspectives to bring the production to life. From the director and choreographer to the costume designer and lighting technician, a musical's success depends on the harmony and synergy of its creative team. These collaborators must work together seamlessly, aligning their creative visions and solving challenges in real time to ensure that every aspect of the production—from the music and dialogue to the visual design and technical elements—works cohesively to tell the story.

Collaboration in the theater is both an art and a science, requiring clear communication, flexibility, and a shared commitment to the larger vision. While each member of the creative team has their own specific role, they must also be able to adapt and contribute to the overall production. At the heart of a successful collaboration is mutual respect and trust, as the best ideas often emerge from open dialogue, brainstorming, and a willingness to experiment.

The director is often the leader of the creative team, serving as the central figure who guides the overall vision of the production. The director works closely with the writers, composers, and designers to ensure that every element of the musical supports the narrative and emotional arc of the show. A skilled director will listen to the input of each team member while also providing clear direction and maintaining a cohesive vision. The director is responsible for making sure that the story is told in the most effective way possible, overseeing everything from blocking and pacing to how the music and choreography enhance the characters' journeys.

For example, in *Hamilton*, director Thomas Kail worked closely with Lin-Manuel Miranda (the writer and composer) to ensure that the show's fast-paced, innovative style was reflected in every aspect of the production. Kail collaborated with the choreographer, set designer, lighting designer, and costume designer to create a dynamic, visually striking world that complemented Miranda's groundbreaking score. The result was a seamless integration of music, movement, and design, with each element enhancing the storytelling without overpowering the others.

Choreographers are another key part of the creative team, especially in musicals where dance plays a significant role. The choreographer's job is to translate the emotions, themes, and energy of the story into movement, creating dance sequences that are not just visually impressive but also meaningful within the context of the narrative. Collaborating with the director, the choreographer must ensure that the dance complements the story, whether it's adding to the spectacle of a large ensemble number or subtly underscoring a character's emotional journey through more intimate movement.

For instance, in *West Side Story*, Jerome Robbins' choreography is integral to the storytelling. The dance numbers, particularly the iconic "Dance at the Gym" and the "Rumble," reflect the tension and rivalry between the Jets and the Sharks, as well as the passion and danger that define the characters' lives. Robbins worked closely with the director and composers to ensure that the choreography was deeply embedded in the fabric of the musical, enhancing the emotional stakes and heightening the drama.

The music director and composer also play a crucial role in shaping the musical's sound and ensuring that the score aligns with the story. The music director works with the cast to teach vocal parts, arrange harmonies, and refine the musical performances. They collaborate closely with the composer to bring the score to life, ensuring that the musicality of the production supports the narrative. In some cases, the composer may also serve as the lyricist, working with the book writer to integrate the songs seamlessly into the dialogue and plot.

In *The Phantom of the Opera*, composer Andrew Lloyd Webber's iconic score is deeply intertwined with the musical's emotional arc. The music director ensures that the performances capture the operatic grandeur of the score while also drawing out the intimate, haunting emotions of the characters. Every musical number, from the haunting "Music of the Night" to the intense "Point of No Return," reflects the psychological and emotional complexity of the story, and the collaboration between the composer, music director, and performers is essential to making these moments resonate with the audience.

Designers are another vital part of the creative team, responsible for shaping the visual world of the musical. The set designer creates the physical environment in which the story unfolds, collaborating with the director to ensure that the set design supports the tone, style, and needs of the production. The costume designer works to define the characters visually, using clothing and accessories to reflect their personalities, status, and evolution throughout the story. Lighting designers play a crucial role in setting the mood and highlighting key moments through strategic use of light, color, and shadow. Sound designers ensure that the music, dialogue, and effects are balanced and clear, creating an immersive auditory experience.

The collaboration between these designers is crucial for creating a cohesive aesthetic. For example, in *Wicked*, the set, lighting, and costume design work together to create the magical, otherworldly atmosphere of Oz. The set's fantastical elements, such as the mechanical dragon and intricate gears, are complemented by lighting that shifts dramatically to reflect the changing moods and tones of the story. The costumes, particularly Elphaba's dark, angular wardrobe, highlight the contrast between the magical and political worlds of the story. Each designer must collaborate with the others to ensure that the visual elements feel unified, enhancing the overall storytelling without competing for attention.

One of the challenges of working with a creative team is the need for constant communication and problem-solving. Theater is a live art form, and unexpected challenges often arise during rehearsals and technical run-throughs. The creative team must be flexible and open to making adjustments, whether it's refining a piece of choreography, reworking a lighting cue, or adjusting the tempo of a song to better fit the staging. In these moments, the strength of the collaboration is tested, as team members must find solutions that maintain the integrity of the production while accommodating practical needs.

In the case of *Dear Evan Hansen*, the integration of projections and multimedia required close collaboration between the director, set designer, and projection designer. The projections, which represent social media interactions and the digital world that shapes the characters' lives, had to be carefully timed with the music and dialogue. The creative team worked together to ensure that the projections were not merely decorative but served as an integral part of the storytelling. This kind of collaboration requires trust and an understanding of how each element contributes to the overall vision of the show.

Trust and respect are at the core of any successful creative collaboration. Each member of the team brings their expertise, but they must also be willing to listen to and incorporate the ideas of others. The best creative teams are those where everyone feels empowered to contribute while also remaining open to feedback and new ideas. In some cases, the most innovative solutions or memorable moments emerge from collaborative brainstorming sessions, where different perspectives come together to solve a problem or explore a new idea.

For example, in *Rent*, the collaborative process between director Michael Greif, choreographer Marlies Yearby, and composer Jonathan Larson was key to creating the raw, authentic energy of the musical. Greif encouraged the cast and creative team to take risks and explore unconventional ideas, resulting in a production that broke new ground in musical theater with its rock-inspired score and gritty, contemporary subject matter. The success of *Rent* was a testament to the power of collaboration, as each team member contributed to the bold, revolutionary vision of the show.

Ultimately, the success of a Broadway musical depends on the ability of the creative team to work together toward a shared goal. Collaboration in theater is about finding the balance between individual creativity and collective vision, ensuring that every element of the production—music, choreography, design, and performance—works in harmony to tell a compelling story. When a creative team is truly aligned, the result is a production that feels cohesive, powerful, and emotionally resonant, leaving a lasting impact on the audience.

In conclusion, working with a creative team is both a challenge and an opportunity. It requires open communication, flexibility, and trust, as each member brings their expertise and perspective to the table. A successful collaboration is one where the director, writers, designers, and performers all contribute to the shared vision, creating a unified, immersive experience for the audience. The strength of this collaboration is often what makes a musical stand out, transforming it from a series of individual elements into a seamless, emotionally compelling work of art. When the creative team is truly in sync, the result is a Broadway musical that captivates, inspires, and resonates long after the final curtain falls.

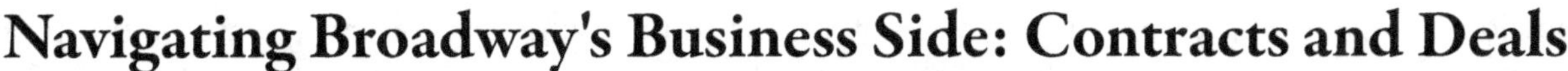

Navigating Broadway's Business Side: Contracts and Deals

Navigating the business side of Broadway is just as important as mastering the creative aspects of a musical. Behind the magic on stage is a complex world of contracts, deals, and negotiations that lay the foundation for a production's success. From securing rights and funding to handling agreements with key creative and production staff, understanding the business dynamics of Broadway is essential for ensuring a musical's smooth development and long-term viability. Contracts and deals protect the interests of everyone involved—from the producers and investors to the writers, actors, and creative team—and help mitigate risks while setting clear expectations for all parties.

At the heart of any Broadway production is the contract system, which defines the roles, responsibilities, and compensation for everyone involved in the musical. The types of contracts vary depending on the nature of the work, but they typically cover agreements with writers, composers, directors, designers, actors, producers, and investors. These contracts are not only legally binding but also essential for ensuring that the production runs smoothly from development to opening night and beyond.

One of the first business steps in launching a new Broadway musical is securing the rights to the material, especially if the story is based on pre-existing works. If a musical is adapted from a book, movie, or play, the producers must negotiate with the original rights holders to obtain the necessary permissions to create the musical. This usually involves a licensing agreement, which outlines the scope of the adaptation, the compensation for the original creators, and any conditions they may impose. For instance, the adaptation of *Les Misérables* required negotiations with the estate of Victor Hugo, as well as with the original French creators of the musical. These licensing deals are critical, as they form the foundation for the entire production and determine how the adaptation can proceed.

Once the rights are secured, producers typically work to assemble a team of investors who will finance the production. Producing a Broadway musical is an expensive venture, with budgets often running into the millions of dollars. Investors, sometimes called "angels," provide the capital needed for everything from pre-production development to set construction, marketing, and day-to-day operations. In return, investors receive a percentage of the profits if the show becomes successful. The financial agreements with investors are detailed in production contracts, which clearly outline how profits will be divided, how expenses will be handled, and what recourse investors have if the show does not succeed. A key part of this process involves drafting a "recoupment schedule," which estimates how long it will take for the production to break even and start generating profit, based on projected ticket sales.

The producers are responsible for overseeing these financial aspects and managing the risks associated with Broadway productions. They must balance the creative vision with practical concerns such as budget limits, ticket pricing, and audience demand. A well-drafted contract with investors ensures that everyone is clear on their financial commitments and expectations, helping to avoid conflicts later on.

ANOTHER KEY ELEMENT in the business of Broadway is the contract with the creative team. Writers, composers, lyricists, and directors often work under commission agreements, which specify their roles in developing the musical and how they will be compensated. These contracts usually include royalty arrangements, where the creators receive a percentage of the gross profits, in addition to any upfront fees. The royalty structure can be complicated, with different percentages allocated to various parties, including the book writer, composer, lyricist, and director. In the case of *Hamilton*, for example, Lin-Manuel Miranda, as the writer, composer, and lyricist, would have received a substantial share of the royalties, while the director, Thomas Kail, would have also earned a percentage based on his contributions to the show's success.

In addition to royalties, creators may also negotiate for points, which represent a share of the production's ownership. Points allow creators to benefit financially from long-term successes, such as national tours, merchandise sales, and film adaptations. For example, the creators of *The Phantom of the Opera* continue to earn royalties and points decades after the show's debut, due to its enduring popularity and various international productions. These financial arrangements ensure that creators are fairly compensated for their work and have a vested interest in the success of the show.

Contracts with actors are another crucial part of Broadway's business framework. Actors are usually employed under the guidelines of the Actors' Equity Association (AEA), the union that represents theater actors and stage managers. Equity contracts establish minimum pay rates, working conditions, and benefits such as health insurance and pension contributions. Depending on the actor's role and experience, contracts may also include clauses for additional compensation, such as bonuses for extraordinary performance, profit-sharing, or guaranteed roles in future productions or tours. High-profile stars, in particular, often negotiate custom contracts that include higher salaries, housing allowances, or special performance schedules.

Rehearsal periods, performance schedules, and termination clauses are also typically included in actor contracts. These agreements ensure that both the production and the actors are protected in case of unforeseen events, such as injury, illness, or creative differences. For example, an actor may have a "run of show" clause that guarantees them a role for the entire run of the production unless they voluntarily leave or breach their contract. These clauses provide security for actors, while also giving the production team a clear understanding of their responsibilities and contingencies.

Directors, designers, and choreographers also operate under specific contracts, which outline their creative responsibilities and compensation. These agreements often include provisions for collaboration with the rest of the creative team, timelines for delivering work, and bonuses for exceptional success, such as a Tony Award win or a long-running hit. Directors and choreographers may also negotiate royalties, particularly if their contributions are critical to the show's identity. For example, Jerome Robbins' choreography for *West Side Story* became iconic, and he received royalties for his work long after the show's original run.

The legal framework of contracts also covers the technical staff, including stage managers, lighting designers, sound engineers, and set designers. These behind-the-scenes roles are essential for the smooth running of any Broadway production, and their contracts ensure fair compensation and set expectations for working hours, responsibilities, and conditions. Many of these workers are also represented by unions, such as the International Alliance of Theatrical Stage Employees (IATSE), which negotiates wages and working conditions on their behalf.

In addition to individual contracts, Broadway productions must also navigate collective bargaining agreements with unions that represent the various workers involved in the show. These agreements ensure standardized pay and conditions for union members, protecting their rights while also helping producers maintain a clear understanding of labor costs. Key unions include Actors' Equity (for performers and stage managers), IATSE (for technical crew), and the American Federation of Musicians (for orchestra members). Producers must adhere to the rules and guidelines set by these unions, and failure to do so can result in costly disputes, work stoppages, or even strikes.

Promotion and marketing deals are another important aspect of Broadway's business side. Producers work with publicists, marketers, and advertising agencies to create buzz around the show and sell tickets. Contracts with these parties specify the scope of promotional activities, from online marketing and social media campaigns to traditional advertising in newspapers, magazines, and television. These deals are crucial to building the show's brand, reaching potential audiences, and driving ticket sales. Successful marketing campaigns can make the difference between a long-running hit and a show that struggles to fill seats.

Ticketing deals are also part of the business landscape, as producers negotiate with theaters and ticketing platforms to sell tickets. Producers may strike deals with discount ticket platforms like TodayTix or TKTS to offer last-minute or discounted tickets to boost attendance during slower times. These arrangements help fill seats while also generating revenue and maintaining the show's visibility.

In conclusion, navigating Broadway's business side is a complex and critical part of producing a successful musical. Contracts and deals form the backbone of this process, ensuring that every party involved—whether creative talent, technical staff, or investors—understands their roles, responsibilities, and compensation. From securing the rights to the material and raising funds to negotiating fair pay for the creative and technical teams, Broadway's business side requires careful planning, negotiation, and legal expertise. When handled effectively, these agreements create a strong foundation for a musical's success, allowing the creative magic to unfold on stage while protecting the interests of everyone behind the scenes.

Filling Seats: Building an Audience for Your Show

Building an audience for a Broadway show is essential to its long-term success. While a show's quality—its script, music, performances, and production design—are crucial, they are only part of the equation. A well-crafted audience-building strategy ensures that people not only know about the show but are motivated to buy tickets and spread the word. This requires a multifaceted approach that includes marketing, public relations, social media engagement, partnerships, and word-of-mouth. The goal is to create excitement and anticipation for the production, turning it into a must-see event that fills seats and generates momentum for a long run.

The first step in building an audience for a show is identifying its target demographic. Every Broadway musical appeals to a different audience, depending on its themes, genre, and style. For example, a family-friendly show like *The Lion King* or *Aladdin* will naturally appeal to parents and children, while a more contemporary or edgy production like *Dear Evan Hansen* may attract younger adults and teens. Understanding who the show is likely to resonate with allows producers and marketers to tailor their efforts, ensuring they reach the right people in the most effective way.

Once the target audience has been identified, the next step is developing a marketing strategy that highlights the unique selling points of the show. This includes crafting key messages that communicate what makes the musical special—whether it's the star power of the cast, the originality of the music, the emotional impact of the story, or the spectacle of the production. These messages are then used across all marketing materials, including posters, trailers, advertisements, and social media campaigns.

A strong visual identity is critical in building awareness for the show. This includes the logo, poster design, and other branding elements that represent the musical. The visual branding should capture the essence of the show, making it instantly recognizable and memorable. For instance, *Wicked* has an iconic logo featuring the green face of Elphaba and the silhouette of Glinda, which communicates the magical and mysterious tone of the musical. The branding is consistent across all platforms, helping the show stand out and stick in the minds of potential audience members.

Trailers and teaser videos are effective tools for building excitement and giving audiences a taste of the show. A well-produced trailer can showcase the best aspects of a musical—its music, cast, and visual style—while also creating intrigue. For example, *Hamilton* used teaser videos and performance clips to build anticipation before its Broadway debut, showcasing Lin-Manuel Miranda's innovative blend of history and hip-hop to create buzz. These short, shareable videos can be distributed on social media, websites, and through email campaigns, reaching a wide audience and generating excitement.

Public relations (PR) is another crucial aspect of building an audience for a Broadway show. Getting press coverage in key publications, such as *The New York Times*, *Variety*, *Playbill*, or theater blogs, helps establish credibility and visibility for the production. Producers typically work with PR agencies or in-house publicists to secure interviews with the cast and creative team, feature articles, and reviews. Press releases announcing important milestones—such as casting news, opening night, or award nominations—can also help keep the show in the public eye.

For instance, when *The Phantom of the Opera* celebrated its record-breaking run as the longest-running Broadway show, the PR campaign capitalized on this milestone by generating extensive media coverage, creating renewed interest in the production. PR efforts can also be targeted toward securing television appearances, radio interviews, and podcasts to reach broader audiences and bring the show to the attention of people who may not normally follow Broadway.

Word of mouth is one of the most powerful tools for filling seats. Once a show opens, audience members who love the production become its best ambassadors, sharing their experiences with friends, family, and online networks. Social media plays a significant role in amplifying word-of-mouth, as audience members post about the show on platforms like Instagram, Twitter, Facebook, and TikTok. Encouraging audience engagement through official hashtags, interactive posts, and user-generated content campaigns can help build a buzz that spreads organically.

For example, *Dear Evan Hansen* cleverly leveraged social media to build a devoted fanbase. The musical's themes of social media, anxiety, and connection resonated with young audiences, who actively engaged with the show's message online. The production created hashtag campaigns and encouraged fans to share their personal stories, which not only promoted the show but also fostered a sense of community. As fans shared their emotional responses to the musical, the show's reach grew, filling seats through the power of personal recommendations.

Social media influencers and theater bloggers can also play a role in generating buzz for a show. Inviting influencers to see the production and share their experiences online can help reach new audiences, especially younger demographics. Theater bloggers, YouTubers, and Instagram influencers who post reviews, backstage content, or interviews with the cast help spread the word to their followers, building anticipation and drawing more people to the theater.

Discounts and promotions are another effective way to attract audiences, particularly during a show's early run when it may not yet have established its reputation. Partnering with discount ticket platforms like TodayTix, TKTS, or Goldstar can help fill seats, especially during slower performances or previews. Offering rush tickets or lotteries for affordable seats, as *Hamilton* did with its "Ham4Ham" lottery, can generate excitement and make the show accessible to a wider audience. These promotions not only help fill the theater but also create a sense of urgency and exclusivity, making people feel like they're getting a special deal.

Strategic partnerships can also expand the reach of a Broadway show. Collaborating with corporate sponsors, tourism boards, or major brands can help reach new audiences and build visibility. For example, *The Lion King* partnered with Disney's marketing machinery, leveraging its global brand to promote the musical. These kinds of partnerships often include cross-promotion in other media, such as advertisements on television networks, theme parks, or digital streaming platforms, which can introduce the musical to audiences who may not typically follow theater.

Additionally, Broadway producers often collaborate with hotels, restaurants, and tourism companies to create special packages that bundle tickets with dining or accommodation options. This is especially effective in attracting tourists to Broadway, who may be looking for a full "Broadway experience." These packages can be advertised on travel websites or through tour operators, making it easy for visitors to plan a night out at the theater.

Email marketing remains a tried-and-true method for building and maintaining an audience. Producers can build email lists through the show's website or ticketing platforms, sending out regular newsletters with updates, behind-the-scenes content, ticket offers, and exclusive promotions. Personalized email campaigns can help keep potential audience members engaged, reminding them of upcoming performances or special events, and offering them incentives to buy tickets.

Television and radio advertising are still valuable tools for reaching a broad audience. TV commercials, especially during peak viewing hours or major events, can showcase the spectacle, stars, and music of a Broadway show, giving potential ticket buyers a glimpse of the experience. Radio spots, especially on local New York stations or nationally syndicated shows, can also drive awareness and attract listeners who may not be actively searching for theater tickets but could be swayed by a compelling ad.

Finally, awards recognition plays a critical role in building an audience for a Broadway show. Winning prestigious awards, such as the Tony Awards, can boost ticket sales and cement a show's reputation as a must-see event. A Tony win, especially for Best Musical, often leads to a surge in demand, with audiences eager to experience the show that critics and voters have deemed the best. Shows like *Hamilton*, *Dear Evan Hansen*, and *The Book of Mormon* saw dramatic increases in ticket sales after their Tony victories, with their award recognition serving as a powerful marketing tool.

In conclusion, filling seats for a Broadway show involves a combination of smart marketing, PR, social media engagement, promotions, and partnerships. By understanding the target audience and leveraging a variety of tools to reach them, producers can build anticipation and create a buzz that drives ticket sales. From crafting a strong visual identity and engaging in targeted marketing campaigns to building a community of devoted fans online, the key to success lies in creating a sense of excitement and urgency around the show. When all these elements come together, they not only help fill the theater but also create a lasting connection between the production and its audience, ensuring that the show enjoys a long and successful run.

Cultural Impact: Creating a Show That Resonates with the Times

Creating a Broadway show that resonates with the cultural and social climate of its time is a powerful way to ensure its relevance, longevity, and deep connection with audiences. A musical that captures the spirit of the moment can transcend the theater, becoming more than just entertainment—it can reflect, challenge, and even shape societal conversations. Achieving this kind of cultural impact requires a deep understanding of the current zeitgeist, the ability to address themes that matter to people, and a creative vision that pushes boundaries while remaining accessible to a wide audience. Musicals that successfully tap into the cultural pulse often become landmark productions that continue to influence both the theater world and broader popular culture.

One of the most notable examples of a Broadway show that achieved significant cultural impact is *Hamilton*. Lin-Manuel Miranda's groundbreaking musical not only reimagined American history through a contemporary lens but also did so in a way that spoke directly to the modern American experience. By casting actors of color in the roles of America's founding fathers and using hip-hop and R&B as the musical's core language, *Hamilton* created a powerful commentary on the idea of who gets to write history and what it means to be an American. Its exploration of ambition, immigration, legacy, and political idealism resonated with audiences at a time when issues of race, identity, and the American Dream were at the forefront of national discussions.

Moreover, *Hamilton* capitalized on the rise of social media and digital platforms, which allowed its themes and music to spread far beyond the theater. It became a cultural phenomenon, with its songs quoted, remixed, and shared across various platforms, and its performances inspiring passionate conversations about history, representation, and social justice. The show's relevance to the moment—combined with its innovative approach to storytelling—turned it into not just a Broadway success but a cultural milestone.

Another example is *Rent*, which premiered in the mid-1990s and captured the struggles and hopes of a generation grappling with the AIDS crisis, poverty, and the search for identity and community. Jonathan Larson's rock musical was revolutionary in the way it portrayed marginalized characters—artists, LGBTQ+ individuals, and people living with HIV/AIDS—and addressed issues like love, loss, and survival in an unapologetically raw and real way. The musical resonated deeply with young audiences, many of whom saw their own struggles reflected on stage for the first time.

The cultural impact of *Rent* extended far beyond the theater. Its message of "no day but today" became a rallying cry for a generation confronting issues of mortality, activism, and self-expression. The show's themes of community and resilience in the face of adversity were deeply relevant to the cultural moment, and *Rent* helped break down barriers in how Broadway portrayed diversity and social issues. Its legacy continues to influence musicals today, particularly in how it opened the door for more inclusive storytelling on stage.

For a Broadway show to resonate with the times, it must engage with themes that reflect the current social, political, or cultural climate. This often means addressing issues that are relevant to audiences in a meaningful, thought-provoking way. *Dear Evan Hansen*, for instance, struck a chord with contemporary audiences by exploring themes of mental health, anxiety, loneliness, and social media's role in shaping identity and connection. At a time when conversations about mental health and the pressures of living in a digitally connected world were gaining prominence, the musical tapped into those emotions with authenticity and empathy.

The character of Evan Hansen—a socially awkward teen who struggles to fit in and feels invisible in a hyper-connected world—resonated with audiences, particularly younger generations who saw themselves in his struggles. The musical's portrayal of social media as both a tool for connection and a source of isolation mirrored real-life debates about the impact of the digital age on mental health. *Dear Evan Hansen* became not only a critical and commercial success but also a cultural touchstone for a generation grappling with these issues.

To create a show that resonates culturally, it's essential for writers, composers, and directors to be attuned to the current social landscape and to understand how their work can reflect or respond to it. This doesn't always mean directly addressing political issues or taking a stance on current events, but it does mean creating stories and characters that feel relevant, urgent, and meaningful to the audience's experience of the world. In some cases, shows become culturally resonant by pushing the boundaries of what is expected on stage, challenging norms, and offering new perspectives on familiar topics.

For example, *A Chorus Line* premiered in 1975 and broke new ground by focusing on the lives of dancers auditioning for a Broadway show. The musical didn't just showcase the talent and spectacle of Broadway—it peeled back the curtain to reveal the personal stories, struggles, and dreams of the performers themselves. At a time when America was experiencing social and cultural upheaval, with growing conversations around identity, individualism, and the pursuit of the American Dream, *A Chorus Line* spoke to audiences in a deeply personal way. Its exploration of ambition, rejection, and the need for validation resonated with a society questioning traditional paths to success.

A Chorus Line also introduced a more realistic, documentary-style approach to storytelling on Broadway, rejecting elaborate sets and traditional narratives in favor of a raw, honest portrayal of the dancers' lives. This innovative approach helped the musical resonate with audiences as a reflection of the changing cultural landscape, making it a landmark production that continues to influence theater today.

Another important aspect of creating cultural impact is diversity and representation. Shows that reflect the diverse experiences and voices of society often have a stronger cultural resonance because they speak to underrepresented or marginalized groups. *Fun Home*, based on Alison Bechdel's graphic memoir, broke new ground in Broadway representation by telling the story of a young woman coming to terms with her sexuality and her relationship with her closeted father. The show was one of the first Broadway musicals to focus on a lesbian protagonist, and its intimate, personal storytelling resonated with LGBTQ+ audiences who saw their experiences reflected on stage in a way that hadn't been done before.

The musical's exploration of identity, family, and self-acceptance, set against the backdrop of a more conservative era, created a dialogue between the past and present. *Fun Home* became a critical success not only because of its innovative structure and music but because it filled a cultural gap in Broadway storytelling, offering representation for audiences who had long been left out of mainstream narratives.

Timing is also critical when it comes to a show's cultural resonance. Some musicals arrive at exactly the right moment, capturing the public's imagination by reflecting the concerns or aspirations of the time. *The Book of Mormon*, with its satirical take on religion and missionary culture, arrived at a moment when religious satire was gaining popularity in media, and conversations around the role of religion in modern society were increasingly visible. The irreverence and humor of the show resonated with audiences who were looking for entertainment that challenged traditional institutions while still being hilarious and entertaining.

In creating a show that resonates with the times, it's also important to ensure that the production remains adaptable. Social and cultural climates can shift quickly, and a show's relevance may change as new issues or events come to the forefront. Some productions have successfully adapted to changing cultural landscapes by reinterpreting or reimagining their themes. For example, revivals of *West Side Story* have updated the musical's portrayal of race and immigration to align with contemporary conversations about these issues, making the show feel fresh and relevant for new generations of theatergoers.

In conclusion, creating a Broadway show that resonates with the times involves more than simply entertaining the audience—it requires engaging with the cultural moment in a way that feels relevant, meaningful, and thought-provoking. Whether by addressing pressing social issues, offering representation for marginalized voices, or innovating in form and content, musicals that connect with the zeitgeist often become culturally significant works that extend beyond the theater. Shows like *Hamilton*, *Rent*, *Dear Evan Hansen*, and *Fun Home* demonstrate the power of theater to reflect and shape society, creating lasting cultural impact by telling stories that resonate deeply with their audiences. When a musical captures the spirit of its time, it becomes more than a performance—it becomes a cultural milestone that endures for generations.

Revivals and Reinventions: Breathing New Life into Classic Musicals

Revivals and reinventions of classic musicals are an integral part of Broadway, allowing new audiences to experience beloved shows while giving creative teams the opportunity to bring fresh perspectives to time-honored works. While classic musicals often hold a cherished place in the theater canon, revivals breathe new life into these productions by reinterpreting them for modern times. Successful revivals honor the original work's legacy while updating elements—such as casting, design, direction, and choreography—to reflect contemporary cultural sensibilities or explore new thematic depths. Reinventions go even further, transforming a show's tone, presentation, or message, offering a bold reimagining that can resonate differently with modern audiences.

Revivals typically follow two approaches: a faithful reproduction of the original production or a reimagined version that makes bold choices in direction, casting, or staging. Both approaches have their merits and can achieve significant cultural and artistic impact, but successful revivals always maintain a deep respect for the source material, ensuring that the core of the musical remains intact.

One of the key aspects of reviving a classic musical is considering how the show's themes resonate with modern audiences. Many of Broadway's most beloved musicals—like *West Side Story*, *Fiddler on the Roof*, or *Oklahoma!*—were written decades ago, during different social and cultural contexts. While their core stories and themes often remain timeless, revivals offer an opportunity to explore these works through a modern lens, reflecting changes in society's attitudes toward issues like race, gender, identity, and power.

For example, when *Oklahoma!* was revived in 2019, director Daniel Fish took a radically different approach to the classic Rodgers and Hammerstein musical. While the original *Oklahoma!* is often remembered for its sunny optimism and sweeping romanticism, the 2019 revival presented a darker, more complex interpretation. Fish emphasized the show's underlying tensions about land, justice, and violence, using minimalist staging, modern costumes, and moody lighting to create a sense of intimacy and urgency. This reimagining resonated with modern audiences who were eager to explore the complexities of American history and identity, making the revival both relevant and fresh.

Similarly, the 2020 Broadway revival of *West Side Story*, directed by Ivo van Hove, sought to update the classic musical's portrayal of race, immigration, and violence. While maintaining the core story of the tragic rivalry between two gangs, the production incorporated multimedia elements, including live video projections, to heighten the sense of immediacy and chaos. The revival also featured contemporary choreography by Anne Teresa De Keersmaeker, replacing Jerome Robbins' iconic dance sequences with movement that reflected the visceral intensity of modern street life. These choices brought new energy to the musical, making it resonate with a contemporary audience grappling with ongoing issues of racial tension and social injustice.

Casting decisions in revivals are often a key way to update classic musicals for modern times. In recent years, more diverse and inclusive casting has become a hallmark of successful Broadway revivals, reflecting the changing demographics of audiences and the industry's growing commitment to representation. Casting actors of color in roles that were traditionally played by white actors can bring new layers of meaning to a story, offering fresh perspectives on classic characters and their struggles.

For example, in 2018, the Broadway revival of *Carousel* cast Black actor Joshua Henry as Billy Bigelow, a role that had historically been played by white actors. Henry's portrayal brought a new dimension to Billy's struggles with violence, poverty, and redemption, offering audiences a fresh interpretation of the character's emotional journey. By casting actors who reflect the diversity of contemporary society, revivals can make classic stories feel more inclusive and relevant, giving them new life and meaning.

Revivals also offer opportunities to reexamine and update problematic elements in older musicals. Many classic works contain outdated representations of gender, race, or class that may no longer align with modern values. In these cases, directors and creative teams must decide how to handle these elements—whether to preserve them as historical artifacts, reframe them in a new context, or modify them to align with contemporary sensibilities.

For example, the 2018 revival of *My Fair Lady*, directed by Bartlett Sher, made subtle yet significant changes to the ending, which had long been a source of debate among audiences and critics. In the original production, Eliza Doolittle returns to Professor Henry Higgins after their tumultuous relationship, reinforcing traditional gender dynamics of the time. In Sher's revival, however, Eliza walks away from Higgins in the final scene, suggesting a more empowered, independent future for her character. This reinterpretation resonated with modern audiences who were attuned to issues of female agency and autonomy, making the revival feel fresh and relevant while still honoring the original work.

In some cases, revivals go beyond subtle updates and embrace full-scale reinventions, transforming the original musical into something entirely new. These productions often take bold risks with staging, tone, and even the narrative structure, offering a radical reimagining that can provoke fresh insights or challenge the audience's expectations. Reinventions can breathe new life into classic material by pushing boundaries and inviting the audience to see familiar stories in a completely different light.

One of the most famous examples of a reinvention is the 1996 revival of *Chicago*, directed by Walter Bobbie. The original *Chicago*, which debuted in 1975, was a moderate success but never reached the heights of other Broadway hits. However, the 1996 revival stripped down the production to its core elements, emphasizing a minimalist, vaudeville-inspired aesthetic that focused on the cynical, satirical tone of the show. By removing elaborate sets and focusing on the sharp, biting choreography of Bob Fosse, the revival reinvented *Chicago* as a commentary on media sensationalism, celebrity culture, and the corrupting power of fame. The revival became a massive hit, running for decades and inspiring a successful film adaptation, proving that reinvention can lead to renewed commercial and artistic success.

Another striking example of reinvention is the 2015 Broadway revival of *The Color Purple*, directed by John Doyle. This production took a minimalist approach, stripping away the lush sets and elaborate costumes of the original 2005 production and instead focusing on the emotional depth of the characters and the power of the music. With a bare stage, simple costumes, and a strong emphasis on the actors' performances, the revival highlighted the raw emotional journey of Celie, the show's protagonist. The result was a more intimate, powerful production that resonated deeply with audiences and critics alike, earning multiple Tony Awards, including Best Revival of a Musical. The success of this reinvention demonstrated how a pared-down, focused approach could reveal new layers of meaning in a classic work.

Revivals also play an important role in preserving the legacy of classic musicals. By bringing these works back to the stage, revivals introduce them to new generations of theatergoers, ensuring that their cultural and artistic contributions continue to be celebrated. Classic musicals like *Fiddler on the Roof, Cabaret,* and *Hello, Dolly!* are regularly revived because they offer timeless stories, beloved music, and universal themes that resonate across generations. These revivals not only honor the original productions but also create opportunities for contemporary artists to bring their own interpretations to the material.

For instance, the 2015 revival of *Fiddler on the Roof,* directed by Bartlett Sher, maintained the traditional staging and design of the original production while emphasizing the themes of displacement and cultural survival in ways that spoke to modern audiences. The story of Tevye and his family's struggle to maintain their traditions in the face of societal change resonated with contemporary issues of migration, identity, and resilience, making the revival feel fresh and relevant despite its traditional approach.

In conclusion, revivals and reinventions offer Broadway the opportunity to keep classic musicals alive and thriving, while also adapting them for modern audiences. Whether through subtle updates, diverse casting, or radical reimaginings, revivals breathe new life into beloved works, allowing them to remain relevant and impactful in changing cultural landscapes. By balancing respect for the original material with a willingness to explore new interpretations, revivals can both honor the legacy of the past and create exciting, innovative theater for the future. Whether faithfully recreating a beloved classic or boldly transforming it, the art of revival ensures that Broadway's rich history continues to evolve and inspire new generations of theatregoers.

The Role of Critics: How to Handle Feedback and Reviews

Critics and reviews play a significant role in shaping the success of a Broadway musical. Positive reviews can generate excitement, boost ticket sales, and enhance a show's reputation, while negative feedback can pose challenges for a production's commercial viability. Whether the feedback is glowing or harsh, learning how to handle criticism effectively is crucial for the longevity and overall success of a Broadway show. Producers, directors, writers, and performers must navigate the world of critical reviews with both professionalism and resilience, using feedback constructively without allowing it to undermine their creative vision.

The role of critics in Broadway theater has evolved over time, but their influence remains substantial. A favorable review from a prestigious critic or publication can elevate a show's status almost overnight, helping it reach new audiences and secure a long run. For example, rave reviews from *The New York Times* or *Variety* can validate a production and lend it credibility, often leading to a surge in ticket sales. Conversely, a negative review—especially from a high-profile critic—can make it harder for a show to gain traction, particularly if audiences are uncertain about whether to invest in a ticket.

Critics serve as cultural gatekeepers who provide an informed, often analytical perspective on the production, evaluating everything from the script and performances to the staging, music, and design. While their opinions are subjective, critics aim to offer an assessment that helps potential audiences decide whether a show is worth seeing. Reviews can spark conversations about a musical's themes, creative choices, and relevance, contributing to the larger cultural dialogue around theater. For many theatergoers, critics are a trusted source of guidance, and their reviews can shape public perception of a show.

Handling positive reviews is generally the easier task, but even praise requires careful management. Producers can capitalize on glowing feedback by incorporating excerpts from positive reviews into marketing materials, trailers, and advertisements. Phrases like "critically acclaimed" or "a must-see" can be powerful endorsements that attract theatergoers who might otherwise be undecided. This was particularly evident with shows like *Hamilton* and *The Book of Mormon*, where overwhelmingly positive critical reception played a significant role in building buzz and filling seats.

However, it's important to avoid complacency even in the face of rave reviews. Positive feedback can be energizing and affirming, but the creative team must continue striving for excellence in every performance. Consistency is key to maintaining the momentum that good reviews generate, as audiences will come with heightened expectations based on critical praise. Keeping the cast, crew, and creative team motivated and focused ensures that the show continues to deliver high-quality performances long after opening night.

Negative reviews, on the other hand, present a more delicate challenge. When faced with criticism, it's essential for the creative team to remain composed and professional, resisting the temptation to respond emotionally. Theater, like all art, is subjective, and even the best productions may receive mixed or critical reviews. Rather than viewing criticism as a personal attack, it's important to treat it as a learning opportunity. In some cases, reviews can highlight areas for improvement that the creative team may not have noticed during rehearsals or previews.

For example, a critic might point out that a particular scene drags in pace, that the character development feels incomplete, or that the choreography doesn't fully align with the musical's tone. If multiple reviews mention similar concerns, it could be a sign that adjustments need to be made. Many successful shows have undergone revisions after receiving critical feedback, with directors tightening pacing, reworking scenes, or refining performances to address concerns. *The Phantom of the Opera*, during its early stages, faced criticism for pacing issues, and the creative team made adjustments that ultimately contributed to the show's legendary success.

At the same time, it's important not to overreact to every piece of criticism. Not all feedback requires changes, and creative teams must discern when to take reviews to heart and when to stand by their artistic vision. Some shows, especially those that push boundaries or take risks, may polarize critics, and that's not necessarily a bad thing. *Rent*, for instance, received mixed reviews when it first premiered, with some critics questioning its raw, unpolished style. However, the musical's authenticity and emotional intensity resonated with audiences, ultimately leading to its critical and commercial success. In these cases, staying true to the original vision can be more important than making changes based on critical feedback.

One of the most effective ways to handle criticism is to maintain a long-term perspective. A single review, whether positive or negative, doesn't define a show's overall success. While opening night reviews are influential, they are not the final word on a production. Some shows, like *Wicked*, initially received mixed reviews but went on to become massive hits due to word of mouth and audience support. Over time, audiences may develop a deeper appreciation for a show, regardless of its early critical reception. Consistent, high-quality performances, strong audience engagement, and positive word-of-mouth can help a show overcome early criticism.

In recent years, social media has added another layer to the world of feedback and reviews. While traditional critics remain influential, audience members now have the ability to share their thoughts and opinions instantly via platforms like Twitter, Instagram, and TikTok. These platforms democratize the process of reviewing theater, allowing anyone who sees a show to share their experience. In some cases, audience reactions on social media can have as much impact as a traditional review, especially if a show develops a strong fan following.

For example, *Six: The Musical* gained momentum largely through social media buzz, with fans sharing clips of performances, posting reactions, and engaging in discussions about the show's themes of female empowerment and historical reimagining. This grassroots enthusiasm helped drive ticket sales and build a loyal audience, even before the show received major critical recognition. Similarly, musicals like *Hadestown* and *Dear Evan Hansen* benefited from social media engagement, where passionate fans helped spread the word about their emotional impact and innovative storytelling.

Handling social media feedback requires a similar approach to traditional reviews. It's important for the creative team to monitor audience reactions online, engaging positively with fans and taking note of any recurring themes in the feedback. However, it's also crucial to avoid getting bogged down by individual negative comments, as social media can sometimes amplify criticism in unconstructive ways. Focusing on the broader conversation and identifying patterns in feedback can help the creative team gauge how the show is resonating with audiences while maintaining a balanced perspective.

In cases where negative reviews or feedback threaten to overshadow a show's potential, producers may take proactive steps to manage public perception. This can include launching new marketing campaigns that highlight the show's strengths, offering discounts or promotions to attract new audiences, or leveraging positive audience reviews to counterbalance critical negativity. Inviting influencers, theater bloggers, or social media personalities to experience the show can also help generate positive buzz, especially if they have a large following that trusts their opinions.

Ultimately, handling feedback and reviews is about maintaining a sense of balance and resilience. While reviews are important, they are just one aspect of a show's overall success. Broadway is a collaborative art form, and a production's journey involves many stages of development, performance, and refinement. By approaching criticism with an open mind, taking constructive feedback to heart, and staying committed to the creative vision, the team can ensure that their show continues to grow and evolve, regardless of critical reception.

In conclusion, the role of critics in Broadway theater is significant, but it's not the sole determinant of a show's success. Positive reviews can boost a show's visibility and credibility, while negative feedback can provide opportunities for growth and improvement. Navigating the world of reviews requires professionalism, openness to constructive criticism, and a long-term perspective. By engaging thoughtfully with feedback—whether from critics or audiences—producers, directors, and creative teams can ensure that their show remains dynamic, responsive, and impactful.

Word of Mouth: Cultivating Buzz and Momentum

Word of mouth is one of the most powerful forces in driving the success of a Broadway musical. While marketing campaigns, critical reviews, and social media engagement all play important roles in promoting a show, it is often the organic buzz generated by audiences that truly sustains momentum and keeps a show running long after its initial opening. When people leave the theater excited and eager to share their experience, they become ambassadors for the production, encouraging friends, family, and colleagues to see it for themselves. Cultivating word of mouth can turn a promising show into a runaway hit, and understanding how to foster and sustain that buzz is essential for long-term success on Broadway.

Word of mouth is particularly powerful because it is based on personal recommendations, which audiences often trust more than traditional advertising or even critical reviews. When someone raves about a show to their friends or posts about it on social media, they're sharing their authentic, personal reaction. This kind of enthusiasm is contagious and can motivate others to buy tickets, especially when recommendations come from people whose opinions they value. For a Broadway show, this can translate into sold-out performances, repeat attendees, and a growing sense of excitement that fuels continued success.

To cultivate strong word of mouth, the most important factor is delivering a show that leaves a lasting impression on audiences. While this might seem obvious, it's crucial to understand that audiences don't just respond to high-quality performances—they respond to moments that move them, surprise them, or create a sense of awe. The best word-of-mouth campaigns stem from shows that create unforgettable experiences, whether through emotional storytelling, groundbreaking music, innovative staging, or jaw-dropping spectacle.

Shows like *Hamilton*, *Dear Evan Hansen*, and *Hadestown* were all able to generate intense word of mouth because they offered something that felt fresh and meaningful to their audiences. *Hamilton* combined the historical narrative of the American Revolution with contemporary hip-hop and R&B, offering a unique and exhilarating experience that audiences couldn't stop talking about. The emotional impact of *Dear Evan Hansen*'s exploration of loneliness and social anxiety resonated deeply with audiences, leading to passionate discussions and recommendations. Similarly, *Hadestown*'s blend of myth, folk music, and visually striking staging created a deeply immersive experience that audiences wanted to share with others.

Creating memorable moments in a show is key to generating buzz. Whether it's a show-stopping musical number, a powerful emotional scene, or a surprising plot twist, these moments give audiences something to talk about after the curtain falls. These "watercooler moments" are what people will recount to their friends or post about on social media, helping to create excitement and intrigue around the show. Producers and directors should think carefully about how to craft these moments in their productions, ensuring that the audience leaves with something to rave about.

Beyond creating an impactful show, there are several strategies producers and marketing teams can use to help cultivate and amplify word of mouth. One of the most effective ways is through targeted audience engagement. This can begin even before the show opens, with early previews, invitations to influencers, and fan engagement campaigns. Offering preview performances to select audiences, such as theater enthusiasts, influencers, and bloggers, can help generate early buzz. These audiences are often eager to share their thoughts and experiences, creating a groundswell of excitement before the official opening.

For example, *Six: The Musical* was able to build significant buzz before its Broadway debut through early performances and strong social media engagement. The musical's unique concept—a modern retelling of the lives of Henry VIII's wives through pop music—captured the attention of young, digitally savvy audiences who were quick to share their excitement online. By engaging with fans early and offering sneak peeks into the show's music and performances, *Six* cultivated a dedicated following that helped propel its success once it officially opened.

Social media plays a crucial role in amplifying word of mouth in the digital age. Platforms like Twitter, Instagram, TikTok, and Facebook allow audiences to share their reactions instantly, often while they are still riding the high of the show. Encouraging audience members to post about their experience, share photos from the theater, or use specific hashtags can help build momentum and create a sense of community around the show. When done effectively, social media campaigns can spread far beyond the immediate theater-going community, reaching new potential audience members who may not have heard about the show otherwise.

Creating shareable content is another way to drive online word of mouth. This can include behind-the-scenes videos, cast interviews, performance clips, and other digital content that fans can repost and discuss. *Hamilton* was especially successful at leveraging online buzz, in part because Lin-Manuel Miranda and the cast actively engaged with fans on Twitter and other platforms. This level of engagement helped create a sense of intimacy and excitement around the show, making fans feel like they were part of a larger cultural moment.

The *Ham4Ham* lottery, which offered $10 tickets to lucky fans and included impromptu sidewalk performances by the cast, became an innovative way to build word of mouth. By making the show more accessible to fans who might not otherwise afford Broadway tickets and creating mini-events around the performances, *Hamilton* generated even more buzz and goodwill, which translated into long-term momentum.

Another key factor in cultivating word of mouth is creating opportunities for audiences to connect with the show on a personal level. This can include hosting talkbacks or Q&A sessions with the cast and creative team, where audience members get to interact with the people behind the production. This kind of direct engagement helps foster a sense of connection between the show and its fans, making them more likely to recommend it to others.

Word of mouth is also driven by the communal experience of theater, and producers can create opportunities for audiences to share their excitement together. Post-show events, such as meet-and-greets, themed nights, or social events, can extend the theater experience and encourage audience members to discuss the show with others. When people are able to bond over a shared experience, it strengthens their connection to the show and increases the likelihood that they will talk about it with others.

Discounts and promotions can also be an effective way to encourage word of mouth, particularly in the early stages of a show's run. Offering rush tickets, lotteries, or group discounts helps fill seats and ensures that more people have the opportunity to see the show. When audiences feel like they've gotten a great deal, they are more likely to spread the word to friends and family, encouraging others to take advantage of the offer. Additionally, special promotions or themed events, such as sing-alongs or costume nights, can create unique experiences that people want to share with others.

It's important to note that word of mouth can be a double-edged sword. Just as positive buzz can boost a show's success, negative word of mouth can spread quickly and damage a production's prospects. To mitigate this, producers should focus on maintaining high-quality performances and addressing any issues that arise in previews or early performances. Listening to audience feedback and making adjustments when necessary can help ensure that word of mouth remains positive. Consistency in the quality of the show is essential, as a single disappointing performance can lead to negative reviews and a decline in momentum.

Finally, word of mouth is often sustained by cultivating a dedicated fan base. Some shows develop "superfans" who see the production multiple times, bring friends, and actively promote the show online and in their communities. Encouraging and rewarding this kind of loyalty can help create a long-term following that keeps the show running.

Offering exclusive merchandise, fan events, or access to special content can strengthen the connection between the show and its most devoted fans, turning them into lifelong advocates.

In conclusion, cultivating word of mouth is essential for building momentum and sustaining a Broadway musical's success. By delivering a memorable, impactful show and engaging with audiences both in person and online, producers can create the kind of buzz that drives ticket sales and keeps people talking long after they leave the theater. Whether through social media campaigns, early audience engagement, special events, or personal connections, word of mouth is one of the most powerful tools in ensuring that a show thrives on Broadway. When done effectively, it can turn a great production into a cultural phenomenon that audiences can't stop recommending to everyone they know.

Touring and Expanding Your Show Beyond Broadway

Touring and expanding a Broadway musical beyond its original New York run is a critical step in maximizing a show's reach and financial success. Once a show has established itself on Broadway, whether through critical acclaim, strong word of mouth, or awards recognition, the next phase often involves taking the production on the road. This can include national and international tours, as well as licensed productions in regional theaters, West End transfers, and other commercial ventures. Expanding a show beyond Broadway allows it to reach new audiences, grow its fan base, and generate additional revenue streams, all while maintaining the momentum of its success.

The process of touring a Broadway show requires careful planning and adaptation to ensure that the production can travel smoothly while still maintaining its artistic integrity. Touring a Broadway musical is about more than just replicating the New York production—it involves tailoring the show to different venues, audiences, and logistical challenges. Producers, directors, and creative teams must collaborate to ensure that the heart of the show remains intact while adapting it to the realities of a touring production.

1. Preparing for the Tour

Before a show can go on tour, the production team must make key logistical and creative decisions about how to adapt the show for the road. This often begins with adjustments to the set, lighting, and technical elements. Touring productions must be designed to fit a variety of theaters, which can vary in size, stage dimensions, and technical capabilities. Sets may need to be scaled down or modular to accommodate different venues, while lighting and sound designs may be simplified to ensure quick load-ins and efficient travel between locations.

For example, large-scale shows like *The Lion King* and *Wicked* had to adapt their elaborate sets for touring without losing the spectacle and magic that made the original Broadway productions so successful. This often involved creating more portable versions of key set pieces and using technology like projections or LED screens to replicate certain effects in a way that could be easily transported. In some cases, adjustments to the choreography, blocking, or special effects may also be necessary to account for different stage configurations.

Another important aspect of preparing for a tour is casting. While some Broadway stars may continue with the production on tour, touring casts are often assembled specifically for the road. It's essential to find talented performers who can bring the same energy and emotional depth to the roles, even if they are new to the production. Touring casts need to be adaptable and resilient, as the demands of life on the road—constant travel, new venues, and different audiences—can be more physically and mentally taxing than a stationary Broadway run.

The production team must also consider the size and scope of the tour. Some shows launch national tours that visit major cities across the U.S., while others may start with more limited runs in key regional markets. Expanding internationally, such as launching a tour in the UK, Europe, or Asia, requires additional logistical planning, including navigating language barriers, cultural differences, and international labor laws. Shows like *Les Misérables* and *Hamilton* successfully expanded their reach through international tours and licensed productions, creating global fan bases that helped sustain their popularity for years.

2. Marketing and Promoting a Touring Production

Just as with the original Broadway production, marketing is a crucial element in the success of a touring show. However, the strategies for marketing a tour differ from those used on Broadway. When a show is on tour, the production must promote itself to new audiences in each city, many of whom may not be as familiar with the show as New York theatergoers. The marketing team must create campaigns that highlight the show's appeal and build excitement in each new location.

Promoting a touring production often involves heavy collaboration with local venues and media outlets in each city. Local marketing efforts may include partnerships with regional theaters, promotions through local radio and television stations, interviews with cast members, and collaborations with tourism boards to encourage visitors to attend the show. Digital marketing campaigns—using targeted ads on social media platforms, search engines, and email newsletters—are also important tools for reaching potential audiences in different cities.

Word of mouth remains a powerful driver of ticket sales for touring productions, so creating buzz in each new location is key. Producers may work with influencers, bloggers, and local media to generate early excitement and encourage audiences to share their experiences. Special events, such as press previews, charity performances, or behind-the-scenes tours, can help build interest and generate positive press in new cities.

Touring shows often rely on advance ticket sales, so building anticipation early is important. Offering pre-sale opportunities, discounts for groups, and promotional events can help create urgency and encourage early ticket purchases. Additionally, partnerships with local businesses, such as restaurants, hotels, and transportation services, can help create a complete experience for theatergoers, particularly for visitors traveling to see the show from neighboring cities.

3. Licensing and Regional Productions

In addition to launching a touring production, many Broadway shows expand their reach through licensed productions in regional theaters, community theaters, and schools. Licensing a musical allows other theater companies to perform the show while paying royalties to the creators and producers. This is a significant revenue stream for successful Broadway musicals and helps keep the show's legacy alive long after the original run ends.

For example, musicals like *Les Misérables*, *Rent*, and *Chicago* have all been performed in countless regional and community theaters, making them accessible to audiences who may never have the opportunity to see the Broadway or touring versions. These productions help build new generations of fans, ensuring that the show's music, themes, and messages continue to resonate across different communities.

Licensing agreements typically outline the terms of the production, including the required royalty payments, restrictions on changes to the script or score, and guidelines for how the show should be staged. Producers often work with licensing companies, such as Music Theatre International (MTI) or Samuel French, to manage these agreements and ensure that the show is performed according to the creators' vision.

Schools, in particular, play a major role in expanding a show's cultural reach. High school and college productions of musicals like *Grease*, *The Sound of Music*, and *Into the Woods* have introduced young audiences to the magic of Broadway, sparking a lifelong love of theater. These productions not only generate revenue through licensing fees but also ensure that the musical remains a part of the cultural fabric for years to come.

4. International Expansions: West End and Beyond

For many Broadway shows, a natural next step after a successful run in New York is to transfer to London's West End, the UK's equivalent of Broadway. The West End is one of the most prestigious theater markets in the world, and a successful transfer can help solidify a show's international reputation. Shows like *Hamilton*, *The Phantom of the Opera*, *Wicked*, and *The Lion King* have all enjoyed long-running West End productions that rival their Broadway success.

Expanding internationally requires careful adaptation to local markets, including considerations around cultural nuances, language differences, and ticket pricing. For English-language shows, transfers to English-speaking countries like the UK, Australia, or Canada are relatively straightforward, but expanding to non-English-speaking countries often involves translating the show's dialogue and lyrics. This process can be complex, as it requires preserving the original meaning and emotional impact of the songs while ensuring that the translation resonates with local audiences.

Beyond the West End, many Broadway shows expand to other international markets, including Europe, Asia, and South America. Productions like *The Lion King* have toured in countries as diverse as Japan, South Africa, and Brazil, building a global fan base. These international expansions often involve partnerships with local producers and theater companies who understand the regional market and can help adapt the production to local tastes.

5. Additional Revenue Streams: Merchandise, Cast Albums, and Film Adaptations

Touring and expanding a Broadway musical also creates opportunities for additional revenue streams beyond ticket sales. Merchandise, such as T-shirts, posters, programs, and cast recordings, can be sold at performances and online, creating lasting memorabilia for fans and boosting profits. Popular shows like *Wicked*, *The Phantom of the Opera*, and *Hamilton* have all built successful merchandise empires that continue to generate revenue long after the show's initial run.

Cast albums are another important revenue stream. Recording and releasing a cast album allows fans to relive their favorite moments from the show and introduces the music to new audiences who may not have seen the production live. Successful cast albums can become cultural phenomena in their own right, as evidenced by the cast recording of *Hamilton*, which became a best-seller and earned numerous awards, including a Grammy.

Film adaptations are another way to expand a Broadway musical's reach and bring it to a global audience. Musicals like *Les Misérables*, *Chicago*, *Rent*, and *In the Heights* have all been adapted into successful films, further solidifying their cultural impact and generating new revenue streams through box office sales, streaming platforms, and home video releases. A successful film adaptation can introduce a Broadway musical to millions of people who may never have seen it on stage, ensuring that the show's legacy endures for years to come.

Touring and expanding a Broadway show beyond New York is a vital part of ensuring the long-term success and cultural impact of a musical. Through national and international tours, regional productions, and licensing agreements, Broadway shows can reach new audiences, generate additional revenue, and build global fan bases. The process requires careful planning, adaptation, and marketing to ensure that each production maintains the quality and spirit of the original while resonating with diverse audiences around the world. By expanding beyond Broadway, musicals can evolve from local successes into global phenomena, leaving a lasting legacy that continues to inspire and entertain.

The Role of Social Media in Promoting Broadway Musicals

Social media has transformed the way Broadway musicals are promoted, offering unprecedented opportunities to engage with audiences, build fan communities, and create buzz before, during, and after a show's run. While traditional marketing efforts—like billboards, print ads, and TV spots—still play a role in Broadway promotion, social media has emerged as one of the most powerful tools for reaching potential ticket buyers, especially younger, digitally savvy theatergoers. Platforms like Twitter, Instagram, Facebook, TikTok, and YouTube allow Broadway producers to reach a global audience, create viral moments, and foster direct engagement with fans in ways that were previously impossible.

The role of social media in promoting Broadway musicals is multifaceted, as it enables theaters and productions to create a dynamic and interactive presence online. By harnessing the reach of social media, shows can connect with fans, share behind-the-scenes content, showcase key moments, and keep the momentum going long after the initial buzz of opening night. The ability to interact directly with the audience allows producers to cultivate excitement, drive ticket sales, and ensure a lasting cultural impact for the production.

1. Creating a Buzz Before Opening

One of the most important uses of social media in promoting a Broadway musical is creating buzz before the show even opens. This phase of the promotion helps build anticipation and excitement, introducing the show to potential audiences and encouraging people to start talking about it.

Early on, social media campaigns typically involve sharing teaser content, such as short video clips, cast announcements, rehearsal footage, and behind-the-scenes photos. These posts help generate interest in the production by offering glimpses into the creative process and allowing fans to feel like they're part of the journey from the very beginning. For example, the musical *Six* created excitement by releasing snippets of its pop-driven songs, showcasing its energetic cast, and posting rehearsal videos on Instagram and Twitter long before its official Broadway opening. This early content helped to build a dedicated fan base that eagerly awaited the show's debut.

Cast announcements are particularly effective in building pre-opening buzz, especially if the show features well-known actors or rising stars. Sharing these announcements on social media can quickly generate excitement as fans of the actors spread the word, drawing attention to the production. Platforms like Instagram and Twitter allow for real-time engagement, as fans can like, share, and comment on the announcements, further amplifying the reach of the news.

Trailers and promotional videos are also key tools in the pre-opening phase. Short trailers that showcase the show's music, performances, or visual elements can go viral on platforms like YouTube, Instagram, and TikTok. These trailers are often shared across multiple platforms, giving potential audience members a taste of the production and encouraging them to share the excitement with their networks. *Hamilton*, for example, used short clips of Lin-Manuel Miranda performing songs like "My Shot" to build anticipation before the musical's Broadway debut, creating a viral sensation that helped turn the show into a cultural phenomenon.

2. Engaging Fans with Interactive Content

Social media thrives on interaction, and Broadway musicals can leverage this by creating engaging, interactive content that encourages fans to participate in the conversation. Interactive campaigns foster a sense of community among fans, making them feel more invested in the show and more likely to promote it through word of mouth.

Hashtag campaigns are one of the most effective ways to encourage audience participation. By creating a unique, catchy hashtag that fans can use to tag their posts, producers can track and amplify fan-generated content. For example, *Dear Evan Hansen* used the hashtag #YouWillBeFound to encourage fans to share their own stories of hope, resilience, and overcoming challenges—resonating deeply with the musical's themes of mental health and connection. This campaign not only helped promote the show but also created a powerful emotional bond between the musical and its audience, fostering a sense of community.

Contests and giveaways are another interactive tool. Offering fans a chance to win free tickets, exclusive merchandise, or backstage tours in exchange for sharing posts, tagging friends, or creating their own content can generate significant engagement. These promotions increase visibility for the show while incentivizing fans to spread the word. Social media influencers, particularly those with a passion for theater, can also be invited to participate in these contests, further boosting the show's reach to their followers.

Polls and questions on Instagram Stories or Twitter are a fun way to engage with audiences, giving them a chance to share their opinions or vote on aspects of the show, such as favorite characters or songs. This type of content encourages interaction and creates an ongoing dialogue with fans. The show *Beetlejuice*, for example, regularly interacted with fans on Twitter, running polls and responding to comments in a witty, humorous tone that matched the musical's irreverent style. This not only kept fans engaged but also built the musical's online persona, making the digital experience feel like an extension of the show itself.

3. Amplifying the Show with User-Generated Content

User-generated content (UGC) is one of the most powerful ways to spread the word about a Broadway musical. When fans post about their experience seeing a show, share videos of themselves singing along to the soundtrack, or recreate moments from the production, it serves as free, authentic advertising that can reach a wide audience. UGC often feels more trustworthy and genuine than traditional marketing, as it comes from real fans who are excited about the show.

Encouraging fans to share their experiences on social media can be as simple as creating a designated photo area in the theater, where audience members can snap pictures and post them on Instagram with a branded hashtag. Some shows, like *Hadestown*, feature a photo op in front of a backdrop with the show's logo, encouraging fans to document their night at the theater and share it with their followers. By making it easy and fun for fans to share their experiences, producers can turn audience members into brand ambassadors who help spread the word to their friends and networks.

Musicals like *Hamilton* and *Wicked* have successfully leveraged UGC to create viral moments. Fans of *Hamilton* frequently posted videos of themselves performing covers of the musical's songs, which were often reshared by the official *Hamilton* accounts, amplifying the reach of these fan performances. This kind of two-way engagement between the production and the audience not only builds a sense of community but also keeps the show in the social media spotlight.

TikTok, in particular, has become a major platform for fan-generated content. Fans post clips of themselves lip-syncing, dancing, or reenacting scenes from their favorite musicals, and these videos can quickly go viral. Shows like *Six* and *Beetlejuice* saw significant boosts in popularity due to the viral nature of TikTok challenges and fan creations. TikTok's short-form video format is ideal for sharing clips of catchy songs, high-energy dance numbers, and memorable moments, all of which are crucial for spreading excitement about a musical.

4. Keeping Momentum with Ongoing Content

Once a show has opened, maintaining momentum on social media is crucial to keeping it top of mind for potential theatergoers. Ongoing content helps keep the conversation alive and sustains excitement even after the initial buzz of the premiere has passed. This includes posting regular updates, sharing new behind-the-scenes content, and engaging directly with fans through comments, retweets, and replies.

Behind-the-scenes content remains one of the most effective ways to keep fans engaged. Sharing backstage tours, interviews with cast members, rehearsal footage, and blooper reels gives audiences a glimpse into the inner workings of the production, creating a deeper connection to the show. Audiences love to see how the magic happens, and social media provides the perfect platform for offering these insider looks.

Engaging with fans directly by liking, commenting, and resharing their posts helps build a loyal fan base. When productions respond to fans on Twitter, Instagram, or TikTok, it makes fans feel valued and part of the show's community. Shows like *Beetlejuice* and *Mean Girls* built strong online communities by regularly interacting with fans in a playful, humorous way that matched the tone of the productions.

To sustain long-term momentum, social media campaigns should evolve over time, introducing new content and keeping up with trends. Incorporating social media trends, such as TikTok challenges, meme formats, or popular hashtags, helps keep a show relevant and ensures that it stays in the cultural conversation. A show's digital presence should feel dynamic and responsive to current events and fan interests.

5. Influencer Partnerships and Collaborations

Collaborating with influencers can significantly amplify the reach of a Broadway musical, especially among younger audiences. Theater influencers, lifestyle bloggers, and even celebrities with large followings can help promote a show by sharing their experiences, reviewing the production, or posting about exclusive behind-the-scenes access. By inviting influencers to press nights, special events, or backstage tours, producers can generate buzz and introduce the show to new audiences.

TikTok influencers, in particular, have become an important part of Broadway's promotional strategies. Short, engaging videos that feature influencers attending a show, meeting the cast, or participating in a viral dance challenge can quickly reach millions of viewers. These collaborations help introduce Broadway to younger audiences who might not be regular theatergoers but are active on platforms like TikTok and Instagram.

Social media has become an indispensable tool in promoting Broadway musicals, offering new ways to engage with audiences, build excitement, and create lasting cultural impact. From creating pre-opening buzz to fostering fan communities and amplifying user-generated content, social media allows Broadway shows to reach far beyond the traditional theater-going demographic. The interactive, visual, and viral nature of platforms like Instagram, Twitter, TikTok, and YouTube offers unique opportunities to connect with audiences on a personal level, turning fans into advocates who help spread the word. By leveraging the full power of social media, Broadway musicals can cultivate a global following, ensuring that their impact endures long after the final curtain call.

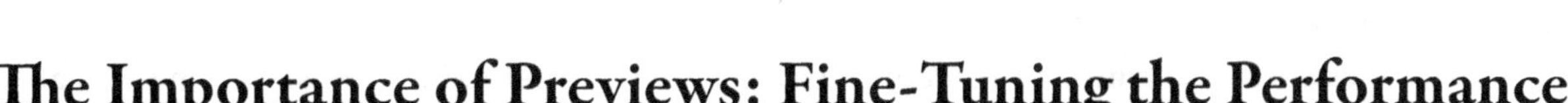

The Importance of Previews: Fine-Tuning the Performance

Previews are a critical phase in the production of a Broadway musical, providing the creative team with the opportunity to fine-tune the performance before the official opening night. This period, typically lasting several weeks, allows the cast, crew, and creative team to gauge audience reactions, make adjustments to the show's pacing, dialogue, choreography, and technical elements, and address any issues that arise during live performances. Previews are essential for ensuring that a Broadway show is in peak condition for its opening, providing valuable insight that can make the difference between a good show and a great one.

While previews are open to paying audiences, they are distinct from the official run of the show. During this period, the production is still considered a work in progress, and changes can be made from night to night based on audience feedback and the observations of the creative team. These tweaks can range from minor adjustments—such as tightening transitions between scenes—to major rewrites of songs or dialogue. The purpose of previews is to identify what works, what doesn't, and how to improve the overall flow and impact of the show before critics attend and the reviews are published.

1. Gauging Audience Reactions

One of the primary functions of previews is to observe how audiences respond to the show in real-time. While rehearsals allow the cast and creative team to perfect their performances, there's no substitute for the energy and feedback of a live audience. During previews, the creative team pays close attention to how the audience reacts to key moments in the show—such as dramatic scenes, comedic bits, or musical numbers.

If a scene that was expected to get big laughs falls flat, or if a dramatic moment doesn't land emotionally, the team can take that as a cue to reassess the material. Conversely, if an unexpected moment generates an enthusiastic response, it might be worth expanding or emphasizing. Audience reactions also help the creative team assess the pacing of the show. If parts of the musical feel sluggish or overly long, they can be trimmed or adjusted to maintain momentum and keep the audience engaged.

For example, during the preview period of *Hamilton*, the creative team made several changes to the show based on audience feedback. The pacing of certain scenes was adjusted, and small tweaks were made to ensure the show's intricate blend of history, music, and emotion resonated with viewers. The preview process allowed *Hamilton* to refine its storytelling and deliver the high-energy, tightly constructed show that went on to become a Broadway sensation.

2. Testing the Timing of Humor and Drama

The timing of both comedic and dramatic elements is essential in a Broadway musical. What may feel perfectly timed in rehearsals can play differently in front of an audience, and previews offer the chance to test and refine this timing. Comedy, in particular, depends heavily on audience reaction, and the preview period allows performers to adjust their delivery based on how the audience responds. If a joke consistently lands awkwardly or fails to get laughs, the writers and director may consider rewriting the line, altering the delivery, or even cutting it entirely.

Likewise, dramatic moments benefit from the preview process. If a scene that is meant to evoke strong emotional reactions doesn't resonate as expected, the creative team can examine what might be missing—whether it's a matter of dialogue, music, or staging. Previews offer a valuable opportunity to fine-tune these moments so that they have the desired impact.

For instance, in the original previews of *Rent*, the production team realized that certain emotional beats in the show weren't connecting with audiences as strongly as intended. This led to adjustments in staging and pacing that ultimately heightened the impact of the show's key emotional moments, helping it resonate deeply with audiences by the time of its official opening.

3. Fine-Tuning Technical Elements

Previews are also essential for refining the technical aspects of the production. Broadway musicals are complex, multi-layered productions that rely on precise coordination between lighting, sound, sets, costumes, and special effects. During previews, the technical team can identify any issues with these elements and make necessary adjustments to ensure everything runs smoothly during the official run.

For example, sound balance is often a key focus during previews. Ensuring that the orchestra doesn't overpower the singers, that dialogue is clearly heard, and that sound effects are timed correctly are all critical to creating a polished production. Lighting cues, set changes, and costume transitions are similarly refined during previews, ensuring that each technical element supports the show without distracting from the performances.

In musicals with elaborate special effects, such as *The Phantom of the Opera* or *Wicked*, the preview period is especially important for testing how these effects play in front of a live audience. Timing, safety, and the overall impact of the effects must be perfected during previews to ensure they add to the show's spectacle without causing disruptions.

4. Making Adjustments to Pacing and Flow

One of the most common changes made during previews involves the pacing and flow of the show. A musical's pacing is crucial to maintaining audience engagement and emotional investment. If the show feels too slow, audiences may lose interest; if it feels rushed, key moments may not have the emotional weight they need. Previews give the creative team the opportunity to observe the rhythm of the show in real time and make adjustments where necessary.

Pacing adjustments might involve cutting or condensing scenes, reordering songs, or adding transitions to improve the flow between scenes. Sometimes entire musical numbers are added, cut, or replaced based on how they fit into the overall structure of the show. For example, the original Broadway production of *Wicked* made significant changes during its preview period, including cutting a song and rewriting parts of the script to improve the pacing and enhance the relationship between the two lead characters, Elphaba and Glinda. These changes ultimately contributed to the show's lasting success.

5. Addressing Performer Needs

Previews also provide valuable insight into the needs of the performers. Performing in front of an audience reveals how the cast is handling the physical and emotional demands of the show. If certain parts of the show are too taxing, adjustments may be made to ensure that performers can consistently deliver high-quality performances without overextending themselves.

For instance, if a musical number is particularly physically demanding, the director may decide to make slight changes to the choreography to reduce the risk of injury or fatigue. Alternatively, if a performer struggles with quick costume changes or transitions between scenes, additional time may be built into the show to allow for smoother transitions. Previews are the ideal time to address these challenges, ensuring that performers feel comfortable and confident when the show officially opens.

6. Reworking and Refining the Book and Score

The preview period often includes adjustments to the book (the script) and score (the music) to improve the overall narrative and emotional arc of the show. It's not uncommon for songs to be reworked or replaced entirely based on how they play in front of an audience. In some cases, entire scenes may be rewritten to improve character development or clarify the plot.

For example, during the previews of *Les Misérables*, the creative team made numerous changes to the show's book and score, including altering the order of songs and making cuts to streamline the story. These changes were based on how the show was received during previews and ultimately contributed to the musical's success as a long-running hit.

7. Preparing for Critics and the Official Opening

One of the main reasons previews are so important is that they allow the creative team to perfect the show before critics attend and reviews are published. Critics typically attend a performance during the final week of previews, just before opening night. The feedback from critics can significantly impact the show's reception and long-term success, so it's essential that the production is in the best possible shape by the time reviews are written.

Previews give the production team the time to ensure that every element of the show—from performances to technical elements—is polished and ready for critical scrutiny. By addressing any issues that arise during previews, the team can minimize the risk of negative reviews and increase the chances of receiving positive press that will drive ticket sales and build momentum for the show.

Previews play a vital role in the success of a Broadway musical, providing the creative team with invaluable feedback and the opportunity to refine the show before its official opening. By observing audience reactions, adjusting pacing and timing, fine-tuning technical elements, and addressing performer needs, the production can ensure that every aspect of the show is in top form. This period of trial and adjustment helps ensure that by the time critics arrive and the curtain rises on opening night, the show is as polished, engaging, and powerful as possible.

Bringing in the Investors: Pitching Your Show for Financing

Securing financing is one of the most crucial steps in getting a Broadway musical off the ground, and it requires convincing investors that the show is not only artistically sound but also a financially viable venture. While Broadway musicals are often driven by creativity and artistic vision, they are also significant business investments. Investors need to feel confident that a show has the potential to be profitable, and pitching your musical effectively is key to attracting the financial backing needed to bring the production to life.

A successful pitch combines both passion and practicality, offering potential investors a clear understanding of the show's creative strengths, its commercial appeal, and the strategy for recouping their investment. From discussing the concept and creative team to laying out a solid business plan, pitching a Broadway musical for financing is about balancing artistry with financial responsibility.

1. Crafting a Compelling Story

The first step in pitching your Broadway musical is crafting a compelling story—both in terms of the show's narrative and the journey of the production itself. Investors are more likely to get behind a project if they are captivated by its concept and can see its potential to engage audiences.

Begin by explaining the central idea of the musical, including its plot, characters, and themes. What makes the story unique or particularly relevant? Why will audiences be drawn to this show? Investors want to know that the musical has broad appeal or speaks to a specific niche audience with passion. A well-told story that resonates with current social, cultural, or emotional themes can make your show stand out.

For example, when *Hamilton* was pitched, Lin-Manuel Miranda emphasized its unique concept—recasting the story of America's founding fathers with a diverse cast and setting it to contemporary hip-hop music. This innovative approach immediately set *Hamilton* apart and showed investors that it had the potential to capture the imagination of a wide audience, including those who might not normally attend Broadway shows.

When pitching your musical, it's important to highlight why now is the right time for this show. Is it addressing a timely social issue? Does it offer a fresh take on a classic story or tap into current cultural trends? Positioning your musical as relevant and necessary in today's theater landscape can help investors see the opportunity for success.

2. Introducing the Creative Team

A strong creative team is one of the most important factors in attracting investors. Potential backers want to know that the people responsible for bringing the show to life have the experience, talent, and vision to make it a success. Your pitch should introduce the key members of the creative team, including the writer, composer, lyricist, director, choreographer, and producer.

Highlight the team's previous successes, especially if they have worked on other profitable or critically acclaimed productions. Even if some members are new to Broadway, emphasize their unique skills or innovative approaches that make them a valuable part of the team. For example, if the director has a background in film or television, point out how their visual storytelling techniques will enhance the theatrical experience.

Investors are often more comfortable backing a project if they have confidence in the creative team's ability to deliver a high-quality production. If your team includes notable names in the industry, their involvement can lend credibility to the project and reassure investors that the show has the talent to succeed.

3. Presenting the Business Plan

While the creative vision is critical, investors need to see a solid business plan that outlines how the show will be produced, marketed, and ultimately turn a profit. This section of the pitch is where you must demonstrate financial transparency and a clear understanding of the costs involved in bringing the musical to Broadway.

Start by outlining the estimated production budget, which includes costs for sets, costumes, lighting, sound, cast salaries, theater rental, marketing, and other expenses. Broadway musicals can cost anywhere from several million dollars for smaller productions to tens of millions for large-scale spectacles. It's important to provide a detailed breakdown of these costs to show investors exactly where their money will be going.

Next, outline the strategy for recouping the investment. This involves estimating ticket sales, pricing strategies, and projected weekly grosses. Investors want to know how long it will take to recoup their initial investment (known as the "recoupment period") and how profits will be distributed once the show becomes profitable. Typically, investors receive a percentage of the profits proportional to their investment, but it's important to clearly explain the financial structure in the pitch.

It's also valuable to provide case studies of similar shows in terms of genre, style, or audience appeal that have succeeded financially. If your musical is a family-friendly production like *The Lion King*, point to the long-running success of similar shows to demonstrate the potential for longevity and profitability. If your show targets a niche market, such as fans of contemporary music or social justice themes, show how similar productions have captured that audience and turned a profit.

Additionally, discuss any ancillary revenue streams, such as cast recordings, merchandise, touring productions, and film or TV adaptations. These revenue streams can provide investors with long-term financial returns beyond the Broadway run.

4. IDENTIFYING THE Target Audience

One of the key elements of any Broadway pitch is identifying the target audience. Investors need to know who is most likely to buy tickets and why the show will appeal to them. Be specific about the demographics you are targeting—whether it's families, young adults, theater aficionados, tourists, or fans of a particular genre (such as musical theater enthusiasts or fans of rock music, for example).

Present market research that supports your claims about the target audience. For instance, if your show is aimed at younger audiences, highlight the growing trend of younger theatergoers attending Broadway productions or cite successful shows that have captured the same demographic. If your show has crossover appeal, explain how it will attract both traditional theater audiences and new segments.

Investors want to know that your show has broad enough appeal to fill seats consistently, and showing that you understand your target audience and have a plan for reaching them will instill confidence.

5. Marketing and Promotion Strategy

Along with identifying the target audience, it's important to outline the marketing and promotion strategy that will drive ticket sales. Investors need to see that there is a clear plan for generating buzz, attracting attention, and keeping the show in the public eye.

Discuss how you plan to use traditional marketing methods such as print ads, television commercials, and billboards, as well as digital marketing strategies that leverage social media, online ads, and influencer collaborations. Social media is an increasingly important tool in promoting Broadway musicals, so be sure to include strategies for engaging with potential audiences through platforms like Instagram, Twitter, TikTok, and YouTube.

Highlight any unique marketing opportunities that align with the show's concept. For example, if the musical has a strong musical component, discuss how cast recordings or performances on platforms like YouTube can create viral moments that drive ticket sales. If the show has strong visual elements, discuss how teaser trailers or behind-the-scenes footage can generate online buzz.

Finally, explain how the show will continue to promote itself after opening night. Long-running Broadway shows require sustained marketing efforts to maintain audience interest, and investors will want to see that you have a plan for keeping the momentum going.

6. Showing the Financial Projections

While it's important to inspire confidence in the artistic vision, investors ultimately want to know what kind of return they can expect. Providing clear financial projections is essential to showing that the musical is a viable investment. These projections should include estimated weekly grosses, break-even points, and expected profits once the show starts to recoup its initial investment.

Be realistic in your projections, and consider different scenarios—such as best-case and worst-case outcomes—based on the potential performance of the show. If the musical is a hit and runs for years, how much profit can investors expect? If the show closes early, how quickly will they be able to recoup their investment? Transparency is key in this section, as investors need to feel confident that they understand both the risks and rewards of the project.

7. Addressing the Risks

While no investor expects a guarantee of success, acknowledging the risks involved and explaining how you plan to mitigate them is an important part of any pitch. Be honest about the challenges, whether it's the competitive nature of Broadway, the high costs of production, or the potential for negative reviews. Investors appreciate honesty and are more likely to trust a producer who is upfront about the risks while demonstrating a plan to navigate them.

For example, discuss contingency plans for slower ticket sales, such as offering discounts or promotions to boost attendance. Show that you have strategies for maintaining audience interest beyond the initial opening and can adjust marketing efforts or ticket pricing if necessary. Addressing these risks proactively reassures investors that you are prepared to handle challenges and maximize the show's potential for success.

8. Creating Excitement and Confidence

At the end of the day, pitching your Broadway musical to investors is about creating excitement and confidence. Investors want to feel passionate about the project, and your pitch should convey your enthusiasm, creativity, and belief in the show. Use storytelling to make the investors feel emotionally connected to the project, while providing the financial data and business strategy that assures them they are making a sound investment.

Encourage questions and dialogue during your pitch to show that you are open to feedback and willing to address any concerns investors may have. The more confident and prepared you appear, the more likely investors are to get on board.

Bringing in investors for a Broadway musical requires a well-balanced pitch that combines creative passion with a solid business plan. By presenting a compelling story, introducing a talented creative team, offering clear financial projections, and addressing potential risks, you can inspire confidence in your project and secure the financial backing needed to bring your musical to life. A successful pitch demonstrates both the artistic merit and commercial viability of the show, ensuring that investors see its potential for success on the Great White Way.

Handling Success: Managing a Hit Show's Ongoing Production

Managing the ongoing production of a hit Broadway show presents both exciting opportunities and unique challenges. Once a musical becomes a hit, the focus shifts from getting it off the ground to sustaining its success over the long term. A hit show often runs for years, possibly expanding into tours, international productions, and even other media formats. To handle the success of a hit show, producers, directors, and the creative team must balance maintaining the high quality of the performance, keeping the show fresh for audiences, managing the cast and crew, and maximizing the show's financial success through smart business decisions.

A hit show is a dynamic entity, and even after its initial success, careful attention is needed to keep it running smoothly and ensure that the excitement and energy remain strong throughout its run. Proper management of resources, personnel, and marketing is essential for ensuring that the show's momentum continues for as long as possible.

1. Maintaining Performance Quality

One of the most important aspects of managing a hit Broadway show is maintaining the performance quality over time. Audiences who attend the show a year into its run expect the same level of energy, professionalism, and spectacle as those who saw it during the first few weeks. Ensuring that the cast and crew continue to deliver high-quality performances is essential to preserving the show's reputation and keeping ticket sales strong.

To achieve this, producers and directors need to provide ongoing support to the cast and crew. Regular rehearsals, even after the show has been running for a while, are crucial for keeping the cast sharp and addressing any areas where performance quality might have slipped. Directors often come back periodically to observe performances, provide feedback, and ensure that the actors stay true to the original vision of the show.

Additionally, the cast and crew need to be supported emotionally and physically. Long-running shows can lead to burnout or fatigue, especially for actors performing demanding roles. It's important to monitor the health and well-being of the cast and crew, making adjustments to the schedule or offering rest days when needed. Producers and stage managers should foster a positive working environment to keep morale high, which in turn helps maintain performance quality.

2. Managing Cast Changes

In a long-running show, it's inevitable that some cast members will eventually leave, whether due to other career opportunities, personal reasons, or the physical demands of the role. Managing cast changes while maintaining the integrity of the production is a key challenge for hit shows. New cast members must be seamlessly integrated into the production without disrupting the rhythm of the show or disappointing audiences who have high expectations.

Casting replacements requires finding performers who can bring their own unique energy to the role while still staying true to the character and the production's overall tone. Producers often look for actors who can embody the essence of the original performance but also bring something fresh to the role to keep the production from becoming stale. In some cases, big-name actors may be brought in to play leading roles, which can generate renewed interest in the show and drive ticket sales.

A strong understudy system is essential for handling unexpected absences due to illness or injury. Understudies and swings (actors who can cover multiple roles) must be well-prepared to step into the spotlight at a moment's notice, ensuring that the show can continue without interruption. Regular rehearsals with understudies and swings help ensure that they are always ready to perform at the same high standard as the principal cast members.

3. Keeping the Show Fresh

Even a hit show needs to stay fresh to avoid feeling repetitive or formulaic, both for the performers and the audience. Over time, the creative team may make subtle adjustments to the show to keep it engaging while maintaining the core elements that made it successful. This could include fine-tuning the pacing, updating choreography, or refreshing certain visual elements such as costumes or sets.

For example, shows like *The Phantom of the Opera* and *Wicked* have incorporated small changes over the years to keep their long-running productions exciting. While the essence of the shows remains the same, these adjustments help prevent the production from feeling dated and encourage repeat audience members to return for a slightly new experience.

Bringing in new creative team members or consulting with the original creative team can also help keep the show dynamic. Directors, choreographers, and designers might collaborate on ways to update or enhance certain aspects of the show while preserving its original appeal. The goal is to maintain the spirit of the hit production while ensuring that it continues to evolve.

4. Expanding the Brand: Tours, International Productions, and Licensing

Once a show becomes a hit on Broadway, there are numerous opportunities to expand its reach beyond New York. Launching a national tour, opening a production in London's West End, or licensing the show for regional and international performances are all ways to capitalize on the success of the original production.

National tours allow the show to reach audiences across the country who may not have the opportunity to see it on Broadway. These tours are often scaled-down versions of the Broadway production, with adjustments made to sets, lighting, and choreography to accommodate different venues. Producers must ensure that the quality of the touring production matches the original, as the reputation of the show is tied to the entire brand, not just the Broadway performance.

International productions, particularly in the West End or in major cities like Tokyo, Sydney, or Toronto, offer the chance to bring the show to new markets. These productions may involve translating the show into different languages or adjusting certain cultural references to better resonate with local audiences. Successful international productions can significantly extend the life of a hit show and generate additional revenue through ticket sales and merchandise.

Licensing the show for regional theater productions, school performances, and community theaters is another important way to expand the brand. Licensing deals allow smaller theaters to perform the musical while paying royalties to the original creators and producers. This not only provides a steady stream of income but also keeps the musical in the cultural consciousness long after its Broadway run ends.

5. Managing Merchandise and Ancillary Revenue

Hit shows often generate significant revenue through merchandise sales, including cast recordings, T-shirts, posters, programs, and other memorabilia. Managing this ancillary revenue is an important aspect of handling a successful Broadway show. Cast recordings, in particular, can become cultural phenomena in their own right, as was the case with *Hamilton*, *Rent*, and *The Book of Mormon*. A well-produced cast album helps extend the reach of the show and keeps its music in the public ear.

Beyond traditional merchandise, producers may explore opportunities for additional revenue streams through branded partnerships, special events, or even theme park attractions. Shows like *The Lion King* and *Frozen* have successfully expanded their brands through Disney's vast entertainment network, with merchandise, films, and theme park shows contributing to the financial success of the original Broadway production.

Film adaptations are another lucrative option for hit Broadway shows. Musicals like *Les Misérables*, *Chicago*, *Cats*, and *In the Heights* have been adapted into successful films that brought the story and music to a global audience. A well-executed film adaptation can introduce the musical to millions of people who may never have seen it on stage, creating new fans and increasing demand for the live production.

6. Marketing a Long-Running Show

Sustaining the marketing momentum of a hit show requires a different approach than launching a new production. While the initial marketing campaign may have focused on building buzz and selling out early performances, a long-running show needs ongoing marketing efforts to attract new audiences and keep the show in the public eye.

One strategy for maintaining interest in a long-running show is to leverage cast changes or special events. For example, bringing in a well-known actor for a limited engagement can generate new interest and boost ticket sales. Special anniversary performances, charity events, or themed nights can also help keep the show relevant and exciting.

Social media continues to play a key role in keeping the show connected to its fan base. Engaging with fans through platforms like Instagram, Twitter, TikTok, and YouTube helps keep the show top of mind, especially among younger audiences. Creating content around the cast, behind-the-scenes moments, and audience reactions can foster a sense of community and encourage fans to promote the show to their networks.

Additionally, targeted marketing campaigns aimed at tourists can help sustain long-running shows. Broadway is a major draw for visitors to New York City, and many hit shows, like *The Lion King* and *Phantom of the Opera*, rely heavily on tourists to fill seats. Marketing efforts that target visitors—through travel websites, hotel partnerships, and discount packages—can help ensure that the show continues to attract new audiences.

7. Financial Management and Profitability

Managing the financial aspects of a hit show is crucial to its ongoing success. Once a show recoups its initial investment, the focus shifts to maximizing profits while controlling costs. Long-running shows can be expensive to maintain, with ongoing expenses for theater rental, cast and crew salaries, marketing, and technical upkeep.

Producers must regularly assess the show's financial health, adjusting budgets as needed to ensure profitability. For example, if ticket sales begin to decline, the production may implement cost-cutting measures, such as scaling back on marketing or reducing performance schedules. At the same time, producers must balance cost-saving measures with the need to maintain the quality of the production, as any noticeable decline in quality could lead to further drops in ticket sales.

Dynamic pricing, where ticket prices fluctuate based on demand, can help maximize revenue. During peak seasons or when demand is high, ticket prices can be raised, while discounts and promotions can be offered during slower periods to encourage sales. Managing this balance between supply and demand helps ensure that the show remains profitable while still attracting a wide range of theatergoers.

Handling the success of a hit Broadway show requires careful management, both artistically and financially. Producers and creative teams must focus on maintaining performance quality, managing cast changes, and keeping the show fresh for both performers and audiences. At the same time, opportunities for expanding the brand—through tours, international productions, merchandise, and film adaptations—can help extend the show's reach and maximize profitability.

Sustaining the marketing momentum, managing ancillary revenue streams, and controlling production costs are all critical to ensuring the long-term success of the show. A hit Broadway musical is not just a one-time achievement—it's an ongoing process of refinement, adaptation, and smart business decisions that keep the production thriving and culturally relevant for years to come.

The Long Road: The Journey from Workshop to Opening Night

The journey from a workshop to a Broadway opening night is an intricate and often lengthy process that requires a blend of creativity, perseverance, collaboration, and business savvy. Creating a Broadway musical involves more than just writing songs and a script—it's a multi-stage process of development, refinement, testing, and adaptation that can take years to come to fruition. From the initial concept and writing phases to workshops, readings, previews, and finally, opening night, each step is crucial in transforming an idea into a fully realized production that's ready for the Broadway stage.

The "long road" to Broadway is marked by many milestones and challenges, with each phase designed to shape the show into its best possible version before it meets a paying audience and, ultimately, the scrutiny of critics and theatergoers. Understanding the key stages in this journey helps explain why some shows become long-running hits while others never make it past the early stages.

1. Conceptualization and Writing

Every Broadway musical begins with a concept, whether it's an original story, an adaptation of a book or film, or a historical event reimagined through song and dance. The conceptualization stage involves creating the basic idea of the show, its themes, and its overall tone. At this stage, the writers—whether a single person or a team of composer, lyricist, and book writer—begin developing the characters, plot, and music that will form the foundation of the production.

For some musicals, this process starts with a single song or character that sparks the development of the entire show. For example, Lin-Manuel Miranda began writing *Hamilton* after reading Ron Chernow's biography of Alexander Hamilton, starting with the song "Alexander Hamilton" and expanding the concept into a full musical. The initial writing phase can take months or even years, as writers work on perfecting the script (the book), the lyrics, and the score.

Collaboration is key during this stage, especially when multiple creatives are involved. Writers must ensure that the music, lyrics, and dialogue align to create a cohesive narrative, and that each element of the show serves the overall story. The characters' motivations, the emotional arc of the plot, and the pacing of the musical numbers all need to be carefully constructed to engage the audience and deliver a satisfying experience.

2. Workshops and Readings

Once the initial draft of the musical is completed, the next step is often a workshop or reading. These early-stage performances are not full productions but rather an opportunity for the creative team to hear the material performed aloud, often for the first time, and to gather feedback from actors, peers, and industry insiders.

A reading typically involves the cast reading through the script and performing the songs without full staging or costumes. It's a stripped-down version of the show, designed to focus on the writing and character development. Readings allow the writers to see how the dialogue flows, whether the pacing works, and how the audience responds to the characters and story.

Workshops are more involved than readings, usually incorporating some basic staging, choreography, and technical elements, though still far from a full production. Workshops allow the creative team to experiment with how the show will look and feel on stage. They are particularly useful for musicals with complex choreography, large casts, or intricate technical needs. The cast performs the show with minimal costumes and sets, and the creative team gets a chance to see how the music, movement, and dialogue come together.

Both readings and workshops are essential for refining the material. Writers often make significant revisions based on the feedback they receive during these early performances. Songs may be rewritten, dialogue may be cut, and entire scenes may be reworked to improve the show's structure, pacing, or emotional impact.

Many iconic musicals underwent multiple workshops before reaching Broadway. For example, *Rent* went through numerous workshops where creator Jonathan Larson made changes based on feedback, including cutting songs and refining the relationships between characters. These workshops were instrumental in shaping the final version of the show.

3. Raising Funds and Securing Producers

While the creative team is focused on developing the show, the business side of Broadway requires securing the financial resources to bring the musical to life. Producing a Broadway show is an expensive endeavor, with costs for sets, costumes, lighting, actors, theater rental, marketing, and more. Musicals typically require millions of dollars in upfront investment, and raising these funds is often a long and difficult process.

Producers play a key role in shepherding the musical from workshop to Broadway, acting as both the financial backers and the project managers. They are responsible for assembling investors, negotiating contracts, and managing the budget throughout the production process. Many musicals will partner with a lead producer who takes charge of the fundraising efforts, pitching the show to potential investors and explaining how the show will turn a profit.

At this stage, producers may host additional readings or workshops to attract investors. These performances allow potential backers to see the material in action and decide whether they want to invest in the project. The success of this stage hinges on the producers' ability to convince investors that the show has commercial potential and that it can recoup its investment on Broadway.

In some cases, producers will seek out theater owners early in the process to secure a venue for the show. Broadway theaters are limited in number, and securing a prime location is critical for the success of a show. The availability of a theater can also influence the timing of the production, determining when the show will premiere.

4. Out-of-Town Tryouts

Before a musical opens on Broadway, it often undergoes an out-of-town tryout, where the show is performed in another city to test how it plays with live audiences in a lower-stakes environment. These tryouts give the creative team valuable insight into how real theatergoers respond to the material, and they provide an opportunity to refine the show based on feedback before bringing it to the intense scrutiny of the Broadway stage.

Cities like Chicago, San Francisco, Boston, and Washington, D.C., are popular locations for out-of-town tryouts. During this phase, the full production is staged, including sets, costumes, choreography, and technical effects. The goal is to replicate the experience of a Broadway performance as closely as possible, allowing the creative team to make final adjustments based on audience reactions.

Out-of-town tryouts are crucial for identifying any weaknesses in the show and addressing them before the Broadway opening. For instance, the musical *Wicked* had its tryout in San Francisco, where several major changes were made to the script, songs, and character development. A song called "Which Way's the Party?" was cut, and the relationship between Elphaba and Glinda was reworked to heighten the emotional stakes. These changes were instrumental in refining the show into the version that eventually became a Broadway hit.

Sometimes, out-of-town tryouts can lead to more dramatic overhauls. A show that doesn't resonate with audiences may undergo significant rewrites, song replacements, or even changes in cast and creative team members. The goal is to ensure that by the time the show reaches Broadway, it is polished, cohesive, and ready to shine.

5. Previews

After the out-of-town tryouts, the musical moves to Broadway for a period of previews before its official opening night. Previews are public performances, but the show is still considered to be in development. This period allows the creative team to continue making adjustments based on how Broadway audiences respond to the material. Previews are especially valuable for fine-tuning the technical elements of the production, such as lighting, sound, and special effects, as well as for pacing and transitions.

Previews also offer the opportunity to see how different audiences react on various nights, helping the team identify patterns and make decisions about what to change or keep. During this time, songs may still be cut or added, dialogue may be tweaked, and performances may be adjusted. For example, during the previews of *The Book of Mormon*, several changes were made to refine comedic timing and ensure that the humor landed consistently with audiences.

The preview period is the final step before the show opens to critics, so the creative team uses this time to make the production as tight and polished as possible.

6. Opening Night

After months or even years of development, opening night marks the official debut of the musical on Broadway. By this point, the show should be fully realized, with all creative and technical elements locked in place. Critics attend the performances leading up to opening night, and their reviews will play a significant role in shaping the show's future.

A strong critical reception can propel a musical into long-term success, while negative reviews can be challenging to overcome. Regardless of the reviews, opening night is a major milestone for the cast, crew, and creative team, signifying the culmination of their hard work and dedication.

The road from workshop to opening night is a long and winding journey filled with creative evolution, financial challenges, and ongoing refinement. Every step of the process—from the initial concept and writing to workshops, out-of-town tryouts, and previews—plays a critical role in shaping the final production that audiences see on Broadway. Managing this process requires a blend of artistic vision and practical decision-making, ensuring that the musical not only captivates audiences but also has the potential for commercial success. For those that make it through this long road, the reward is seeing their work come to life in one of the most iconic and revered theater venues in the world: Broadway.

Iconic Imagery: Designing Posters and Programs That Stand Out

Designing iconic posters and programs for a Broadway musical is a vital part of its marketing strategy, as these visual elements serve as the first impression for potential audience members. A well-designed poster can capture the essence of a show, create intrigue, and even become an emblem of the production that stays in the public consciousness long after the curtain falls. Similarly, programs are not just informative—they offer an opportunity to enhance the audience's experience by deepening their connection to the show through visual storytelling. Both posters and programs need to convey the musical's tone, themes, and identity while standing out in a crowded market.

The design of posters and programs requires collaboration between the creative team and marketing professionals. Striking the right balance between artistic expression and commercial appeal is key, as these visual assets must not only reflect the spirit of the musical but also attract attention and drive ticket sales.

1. Capturing the Essence of the Show

At the heart of any great poster or program design is the ability to capture the essence of the musical. Whether it's a family-friendly show, a dark drama, a comedy, or a groundbreaking work that defies genre, the visual design must communicate the show's core message and tone in a single glance. The design should evoke the emotions and ideas the show is built around, instantly connecting with potential theatregoers.

For example, the iconic poster for *Les Misérables* features a simple yet striking image of young Cosette, taken from an illustration by Émile Bayard from the original Victor Hugo novel. Her solemn face against a stark background conveys the tone of revolution, suffering, and hope central to the musical. The imagery is both evocative and timeless, immediately signaling the emotional gravity of the story to potential audiences.

In contrast, *The Lion King* poster design features the stylized face of a lion, evoking the African-inspired aesthetics of the show and signaling the adventurous, majestic tone of the musical. The bold, graphic design is instantly recognizable and hints at the visual spectacle audiences will experience.

When designing a poster, it's important to focus on the core elements of the show that need to be conveyed. Is it a character-driven story? Then a central image of a character may work best. Is the setting or world of the musical a major draw? Then design elements that hint at the environment or mood, such as color schemes or stylized landscapes, may be more effective. The key is to give potential theatergoers a taste of the show's world while leaving enough mystery to spark their curiosity.

2. CREATING A VISUAL Identity

A Broadway musical's poster and program design are part of a larger visual identity that encompasses all of its marketing materials. This visual identity must be consistent across platforms, from social media posts to billboards, to build recognition and trust with potential audiences. The poster design serves as the foundation of this visual identity, which can be expanded upon in other promotional materials.

Typography, color schemes, and imagery all play a significant role in establishing this visual identity. For instance, *Wicked*'s poster features the iconic image of the Wicked Witch whispering into Glinda's ear, with a dark green and black color palette that signals the show's magical and mysterious themes. This visual identity extends into all aspects of the show's branding, from merchandise to theater decorations, reinforcing the association between the imagery and the musical.

Typography is particularly important in creating a memorable visual identity. The font style used in the poster or program design should reflect the show's personality. A modern, sleek font might work well for a contemporary or edgy musical, while a more traditional or decorative font might suit a period piece or a classic story. The typography used for *Hamilton* is a great example—it's bold, clear, and slightly vintage, suggesting both historical importance and revolutionary energy, perfectly capturing the essence of the show.

3. Evoking Emotion Through Color and Imagery

Color is one of the most powerful tools in design, as it can evoke specific emotions and set the tone for the musical. The colors used in posters and programs should reflect the mood and themes of the show. For example, a dark, moody musical might use deep blues, blacks, or grays to signal its tone, while a vibrant, energetic show might use bright reds, yellows, or oranges to convey excitement and joy.

In *Chicago*, for example, the bold red and black color scheme is used throughout the poster and program design, evoking a sense of danger, intrigue, and seduction that matches the musical's themes of crime and scandal. The imagery of the lead characters striking glamorous poses further reinforces the musical's tone, suggesting a mix of dark humor and razzle-dazzle.

The imagery chosen for the poster should be bold and memorable, providing a visual anchor for the show's marketing. A well-chosen image, whether it's a close-up of a key character, a symbolic object, or a scene from the show, can create an emotional connection with the audience. For instance, the poster for *The Phantom of the Opera* features the iconic white mask and rose, instantly conjuring feelings of mystery, romance, and obsession. This simple yet evocative imagery has made it one of the most enduring and recognizable posters in Broadway history.

4. ENSURING READABILITY and Clarity

While artistic expression is essential, a Broadway poster or program also needs to convey essential information clearly. Potential theatergoers need to be able to quickly understand the name of the show, the venue, and perhaps a tagline or critical acclaim, depending on the design.

A cluttered design with too many competing elements can overwhelm the viewer and dilute the impact of the imagery. Designers should aim for clarity, ensuring that the most important information—such as the show's title and tagline—is prominently displayed. The *Hamilton* poster, for example, is highly effective because of its simplicity: the title, the star logo, and a tagline all fit together in a way that's easy to read yet visually striking.

Balancing artistic creativity with practical readability is key. While an abstract or avant-garde poster may grab attention, if the name of the show is obscured or difficult to read, it may confuse potential audiences. Clear hierarchy in the design ensures that the viewer's eye is drawn to the most important elements first.

5. Designing Programs That Enhance the Experience

Programs serve a dual purpose: they inform the audience about the cast, creative team, and production details, while also enhancing the audience's connection to the musical through visual and written storytelling. Like posters, programs should align with the show's visual identity and further immerse the audience in the world of the musical.

Programs often include cast biographies, behind-the-scenes insights, production notes, and photographs, all of which should be presented in a visually engaging way. The design should reflect the show's aesthetic while making it easy for audience members to find the information they're looking for.

For example, *Wicked*'s program not only provides the usual cast and crew information but also features lush green and black imagery, reinforcing the magical and darkly whimsical tone of the musical. Programs can also serve as a keepsake for audience members, and a well-designed program adds value to their experience by making it visually appealing and informative.

Programs can also include additional elements, such as interviews with the cast or creative team, background on the story's inspiration, or insights into the musical's development. These extras give audience members a deeper understanding of the show, making the program a meaningful part of their theater experience.

6. Becoming Iconic: How Design Creates Longevity

Some Broadway musicals become defined, in part, by their visual branding. A truly iconic poster design can become synonymous with the show itself, transcending the theater and becoming a part of pop culture. This is the goal of any marketing design for a Broadway musical: to create a visual identity so memorable that it becomes instantly recognizable.

The *Cats* poster is a perfect example of this. Its simple design, featuring the yellow, cat-like eyes against a black background, became a cultural icon that lasted well beyond the show's original run. Even those who hadn't seen the musical could recognize the poster, making it an enduring image in Broadway history.

To achieve this kind of longevity, designers need to think beyond the immediate needs of the production and consider how the design can evolve and adapt over time. Posters and programs that tap into universal emotions, timeless imagery, or bold, unique designs are more likely to become iconic.

Designing posters and programs that stand out is a crucial part of promoting a Broadway musical and creating a lasting visual identity. The design must capture the essence of the show, evoke emotion, and provide essential information in a clear and engaging way. A well-designed poster can become an iconic symbol of the musical, drawing audiences in and contributing to the show's long-term success. Programs, too, play a vital role in enhancing the audience's experience, serving as both an informative guide and a visual extension of the show's world. Together, these elements help define a Broadway musical's identity and contribute to its cultural impact.

Leaving a Legacy: Creating a Musical That Lasts Beyond Broadway

Creating a musical that lasts beyond Broadway is the ultimate goal for many theater creators, as it signifies that the show has made a lasting cultural impact, transcending the theater world to become a permanent part of the artistic landscape. While achieving success on Broadway is a remarkable accomplishment, leaving a legacy means that the musical continues to resonate with audiences long after its original run, whether through tours, revivals, cast recordings, film adaptations, or even cultural references in other media. Longevity in the world of musical theater is about more than box office sales—it's about creating something that touches audiences on a deep level, that is relevant across time, and that inspires future generations.

To create a musical that leaves a legacy, the creative team must consider several factors, from crafting a universally resonant story to building a strong and adaptable brand that can evolve with the times. While many elements go into the making of a hit musical, certain key aspects contribute to ensuring that a show remains relevant and beloved long after its Broadway debut.

1. Universal Themes and Emotional Resonance

One of the most important factors in creating a musical that lasts beyond Broadway is the universality of its themes. Audiences are drawn to stories that speak to universal human experiences—love, loss, ambition, hope, fear, and redemption. A musical with themes that transcend time and place is more likely to remain relevant, as future audiences will continue to connect with its core message.

For example, *Les Misérables* explores themes of justice, love, sacrifice, and redemption, all set against the backdrop of political upheaval and revolution. These themes are timeless, which is why *Les Misérables* has resonated with audiences for decades across the globe. Its emotional depth and universal appeal have ensured that it endures through numerous revivals, international productions, and film adaptations.

Similarly, *Hamilton* taps into themes of ambition, legacy, and the quest for freedom—ideas that are as relevant today as they were during the American Revolution. By blending history with modern music and casting choices, *Hamilton* bridges the gap between the past and the present, creating a story that resonates across generations.

To leave a lasting legacy, a musical should aim to explore themes that connect deeply with audiences on an emotional level. When people see themselves in the characters or relate to the experiences portrayed on stage, they are more likely to carry that connection with them, ensuring that the musical stays relevant long after its initial run.

2. MEMORABLE MUSIC and Lyrics

The music and lyrics of a Broadway musical are often what audiences remember long after the final curtain falls. Songs that capture the emotional highs and lows of the story, that express the characters' inner thoughts and desires, and that are simply enjoyable to listen to, help ensure that a musical continues to thrive.

Iconic musicals like *The Phantom of the Opera*, *Wicked*, and *The Sound of Music* are known for their unforgettable scores. Songs like "Music of the Night," "Defying Gravity," and "My Favorite Things" have become standards not only in musical theater but in popular culture as well. These songs are performed in concerts, featured in commercials, and sung by fans around the world, extending the life of the musical beyond the stage.

To create a musical that lasts, the music needs to be both emotionally powerful and musically compelling. Catchy melodies, intricate harmonies, and clever lyrics that enhance the storytelling all contribute to a score that audiences will want to listen to again and again. A cast recording that becomes a best-seller or earns critical acclaim can help cement the musical's place in the cultural canon, ensuring that its songs are remembered and loved for years to come.

3. Strong Character Development and Relatable Heroes

Another important element in creating a lasting musical is strong character development. Audiences are drawn to characters who feel real, who face relatable struggles, and who grow throughout the course of the story. Memorable protagonists, as well as compelling villains and side characters, help ensure that a musical stays in the hearts and minds of audiences long after the show ends.

A character like Elphaba in *Wicked* has become iconic because of her complexity and emotional depth. Audiences relate to her feelings of being misunderstood and her journey from outsider to powerful, self-assured figure. Characters like Jean Valjean in *Les Misérables* or Alexander Hamilton in *Hamilton* similarly capture the audience's attention with their ambition, personal growth, and moral struggles. These characters are not only well-drawn but also deeply human, making them relatable to audiences across time.

A show with memorable characters is more likely to be revived, adapted, or performed in schools and regional theaters, as people are drawn to the emotional journeys and personal growth depicted in the musical.

4. Building a Strong and Adaptable Brand

Creating a musical that lasts beyond Broadway also requires building a strong brand that can adapt to new formats, technologies, and trends. Shows that leave a legacy often expand beyond the Broadway stage, with touring productions, film or TV adaptations, licensed productions in schools and regional theaters, merchandise, and even theme park attractions.

A strong visual identity, recognizable logo, and consistent marketing help establish a show's brand. For example, the *Wicked* logo featuring the silhouette of the Wicked Witch of the West and Glinda is instantly recognizable and has become synonymous with the musical. Similarly, the *Hamilton* star logo with the silhouette of Alexander Hamilton raising his arm has become an iconic image that represents the show across all platforms.

An adaptable brand means that the musical can evolve to stay relevant. Shows like *The Lion King* and *Frozen* have successfully expanded their brands through Disney's global entertainment network, with adaptations in different languages, regional productions, and spin-off media like films and animated series. The ability to adapt to new formats allows these musicals to reach wider audiences and remain culturally significant for generations.

5. Touring, Revivals, and Licensing

One of the key ways a musical can leave a legacy is through touring productions, revivals, and licensing agreements. Once a Broadway show closes, its life can continue through national and international tours that bring the musical to audiences around the world. Successful touring productions ensure that the show reaches new markets and stays relevant, even after its Broadway run has ended.

For example, *Rent* and *The Book of Mormon* both experienced significant success through national and international tours that expanded their reach and solidified their place in musical theater history. International productions in London's West End, Europe, Asia, and other regions also contribute to a musical's legacy, allowing it to cross cultural and linguistic boundaries.

Reviving a show on Broadway or in major cities is another way to ensure that a musical remains part of the theatrical landscape. Musicals like *Chicago, Fiddler on the Roof,* and *A Chorus Line* have all enjoyed successful revivals that introduced the shows to new generations of theatergoers. Revivals give creative teams the chance to reimagine or update the production while preserving the core elements that made the show a hit.

Licensing agreements for regional theaters, schools, and community productions help further extend a musical's legacy. Shows like *The Sound of Music, Grease,* and *Annie* have become staples in school and community theater productions, ensuring that their stories and songs are performed and celebrated for years to come. Licensing helps keep the musical in the public consciousness and introduces it to young performers and audiences who may go on to love the show for the rest of their lives.

6. Film Adaptations and Cultural Impact

Film adaptations of Broadway musicals can significantly enhance a show's legacy by bringing it to a much larger audience. Musicals like *Les Misérables, Chicago, The Phantom of the Opera,* and *Hairspray* have all enjoyed successful film adaptations that helped introduce their stories and songs to millions of viewers worldwide. A well-executed film version can ensure that a musical remains culturally relevant and continues to inspire new fans.

Some musicals also leave a legacy by becoming part of the broader cultural conversation. When a show introduces new ideas, breaks boundaries, or reflects societal shifts, it can have a lasting impact that goes beyond the theater. *Hamilton,* for example, has had a profound influence on both musical theater and American culture, blending hip-hop with traditional musical forms, reimagining history, and sparking conversations about race, identity, and the American narrative.

7. Creating a Lasting Emotional Experience

Ultimately, a musical's legacy is determined by the emotional experience it creates for its audiences. Musicals that leave a lasting impact are those that move, inspire, or challenge viewers, creating memories that stay with them long after they leave the theater. Whether through powerful performances, evocative music, or resonant themes, a show that touches the audience deeply is more likely to endure.

For example, *Dear Evan Hansen* resonated with audiences because of its raw portrayal of mental health, loneliness, and connection in the digital age. Audiences were moved by the emotional depth of the characters and the honesty of the storytelling, helping the show leave a lasting impact on those who saw it.

Creating a musical that leaves a legacy is about creating an experience that audiences carry with them, inspiring conversations, repeat viewings, and emotional reflection.

Leaving a legacy in musical theater involves more than just a successful Broadway run—it's about creating a show that resonates with audiences on a deep emotional level, offers memorable music and characters, and adapts to new platforms and cultural contexts. By focusing on universal themes, crafting iconic music and visuals, building a strong brand, and expanding through tours, revivals, licensing, and film adaptations, a musical can achieve longevity and cultural relevance far beyond its original Broadway debut. When a musical becomes part of the fabric of popular culture, it not only leaves a legacy but continues to inspire and entertain for generations to come.

Lessons from the Great Shows: The Phantom of the Opera

The Phantom of the Opera provides an insightful look into one of the most iconic and beloved musicals in theatrical history. Andrew Lloyd Webber's **The Phantom of the Opera**, based on the novel by Gaston Leroux, has captivated audiences since its debut in 1986, becoming the longest-running show in Broadway history. Its sweeping romance, lush score, and haunting atmosphere create a story that transcends time. However, beneath its spectacle, **The Phantom of the Opera** offers valuable lessons for storytellers, directors, and screenwriters, particularly in crafting compelling characters, themes, and emotional depth.

In this chapter, we will explore the essential storytelling techniques that make *The Phantom of the Opera* a timeless piece of art. We'll look at how the musical balances complex characters with universal themes, how it uses music and atmosphere to enhance emotional resonance, and what lessons writers can draw from its masterful blend of love, obsession, and tragedy.

Complex Characters and Sympathetic Antagonists

One of the most compelling aspects of *The Phantom of the Opera* is its portrayal of the **Phantom**, a character who serves as both antagonist and tragic hero. The Phantom is not a typical villain—his tortured past, his unrequited love for Christine, and his desire for acceptance make him a deeply **sympathetic antagonist**. This complexity allows the audience to feel both fear and pity for him, blurring the lines between hero and villain.

The lesson here is the power of creating **multi-dimensional characters**, particularly antagonists who evoke empathy. The Phantom's disfigurement and isolation make him an outsider, and his longing for love and understanding is something that resonates universally. His darker impulses—kidnapping Christine, manipulating her, and terrorizing the opera house—stem from his inability to be loved, not from pure malice. By giving the Phantom a tragic backstory, the musical allows the audience to see him not just as a monster but as a deeply flawed and lonely individual.

This approach encourages writers to avoid one-dimensional villains. By giving antagonists relatable motivations and emotional depth, you create more nuanced conflicts. In *The Phantom of the Opera*, the audience is torn between rooting for Christine's escape and feeling sympathy for the Phantom's plight, which adds layers of tension and emotional complexity.

Themes of Obsession and Unrequited Love

The central themes of **obsession** and **unrequited love** run deeply through *The Phantom of the Opera*. The Phantom's love for Christine is not a healthy one—it is possessive and controlling. He becomes obsessed with Christine, seeing her as the key to his redemption and happiness. However, his obsession blinds him to the reality that love cannot be forced, and his inability to accept this truth drives much of the tragedy.

Christine, on the other hand, is torn between two men: Raoul, her childhood love, and the Phantom, her enigmatic teacher. Her relationship with the Phantom represents the allure of the unknown, the dangerous pull of someone who offers her musical genius but also entraps her. Meanwhile, Raoul represents safety, familiarity, and genuine affection.

The juxtaposition between these two men—one offering a destructive, all-consuming love, and the other offering a more grounded, selfless affection—creates a compelling emotional triangle. This dynamic highlights the danger of **obsessive love**, which focuses on possession and control rather than mutual respect and care.

Writers can take inspiration from how *The Phantom of the Opera* handles these themes, showing how obsession, when unchecked, can lead to destructive consequences. The tension between love and obsession adds depth to relationships and can be a powerful engine for both plot and character development.

Emotional Resonance through Music and Atmosphere

Music is the lifeblood of **The Phantom of the Opera**, and it serves as a tool for expressing the inner emotions of its characters. **Andrew Lloyd Webber's score** enhances the emotional impact of the story, using recurring musical themes to reinforce the connections between characters and their emotional journeys. The haunting "Music of the Night," the soaring "All I Ask of You," and the dramatic "The Point of No Return" each reflect key emotional beats in the narrative.

The lesson here is that **music and atmosphere** can be used to underscore emotional stakes, even in non-musical storytelling. Writers and directors can create atmospheres that enhance the audience's emotional engagement, whether through evocative descriptions, carefully chosen settings, or soundscapes in film and television. Just as the music in *The Phantom of the Opera* heightens the intensity of each scene, a story's atmosphere should work in tandem with the plot to evoke the right emotions—be it tension, romance, or fear.

For example, the Phantom's lair beneath the opera house is not just a physical setting but a reflection of his inner darkness, his isolation, and his separation from the world above. The setting amplifies his mystery and danger while also symbolizing his emotional imprisonment. Writers can use settings in a similar way to reflect the inner lives of their characters and enhance the story's emotional resonance.

The Beauty and Tragedy of the Outsider

At its core, **The Phantom of the Opera** is a story about an **outsider**, someone who exists on the fringes of society and craves acceptance. The Phantom's deformity has made him a pariah, and he lives in the shadows, manipulating events from behind the scenes because he believes that no one could ever love him if they saw him for who he truly is.

The tragedy of the Phantom lies in his belief that his deformity defines him, preventing him from finding love and acceptance. His fate is sealed not because of his physical appearance but because of his inability to connect with others on a deeper, more human level. He tries to force Christine to love him, believing that his musical genius can make up for his physical disfigurement, but this only drives her further away.

This theme resonates with audiences because it taps into the universal fear of rejection and the longing for acceptance. The Phantom's story is a reminder of the power of compassion and the consequences of isolation. It also highlights how **appearances** can be deceiving—beneath the Phantom's terrifying mask is a vulnerable, deeply wounded man.

For writers, the lesson is to explore the beauty and tragedy of characters who exist on the margins, those who feel alienated from society but still yearn for connection. These characters often resonate deeply with audiences, as they reflect the universal desire for understanding and acceptance.

Creating a Sense of Mystery and Suspense

The Phantom of the Opera expertly uses **mystery and suspense** to keep the audience engaged. From the opening moments, when the chandelier is raised and the story shifts back in time, the show builds an aura of mystery around the Phantom. His presence is felt long before he is seen, and his manipulation of the opera house staff, the mysterious notes, and his haunting voice create a sense of dread and anticipation.

This sense of mystery is crucial to the show's atmosphere. The audience is intrigued by the Phantom's abilities, his hidden identity, and the tension between him and the other characters. The gradual unveiling of his past and his deeper motivations keeps the audience hooked, wanting to know more.

Writers can apply this technique by **withholding key information** to create suspense and build tension. The Phantom's gradual reveal as both a villain and a tragic figure is an effective way of keeping the audience engaged.

Creating a character who operates from the shadows, whose true nature is slowly uncovered, can add layers of intrigue to any story.

Tragic Endings and the Power of Redemption

The conclusion of *The Phantom of the Opera* is bittersweet and tragic. The Phantom, after kidnapping Christine and attempting to force her to stay with him, is finally confronted with the reality of his actions. Christine's kiss—an act of compassion rather than love—forces him to realize that his obsessive behavior has only driven her away. In the end, the Phantom lets Christine go, choosing her happiness over his own desires.

This act of selflessness, though it comes too late to redeem the Phantom fully, adds a layer of **tragedy** to the ending. He has finally learned the difference between love and possession, but it is a lesson that comes at great personal cost. The final scene, where the Phantom disappears, leaving behind only his mask, symbolizes the end of his reign of terror and his retreat into the shadows, forever an outsider.

The lesson here is that **tragic endings** can be powerful and emotionally resonant when they reflect the character's internal growth or failure to achieve redemption. The Phantom's tragedy is that he learns too late that love cannot be forced, and his inability to change earlier in the story leads to his ultimate downfall. For writers, this kind of ending can be deeply moving, especially when it reflects a character's internal journey and the consequences of their actions.

Lessons from The Phantom of the Opera offer valuable insights for writers and creators seeking to craft stories with emotional depth, complex characters, and powerful themes. Through its sympathetic portrayal of a tragic antagonist, its exploration of obsessive love, and its use of music and atmosphere to heighten emotional stakes, *The Phantom of the Opera* has remained a timeless piece of storytelling.

Writers can draw inspiration from its multi-dimensional characters, its exploration of themes like isolation and redemption, and its masterful use of suspense and tragedy. By creating characters who evoke empathy, exploring the darker sides of love and obsession, and delivering emotional payoffs that reflect the characters' internal journeys, storytellers can craft narratives that resonate with audiences long after the final curtain falls.

Lessons from the Great Shows: Chicago

Chicago explores the enduring appeal of one of Broadway's most iconic musicals, *Chicago*. With its biting satire, dark humor, and commentary on fame, corruption, and justice, *Chicago* has captivated audiences since its 1975 debut. Written by John Kander, Fred Ebb, and Bob Fosse, the show takes place in the Roaring Twenties and follows two women, Roxie Hart and Velma Kelly, as they navigate the corrupt world of the Chicago criminal justice system to achieve fame and freedom after committing murder.

What makes *Chicago* stand out is its unique blend of vaudeville style, social commentary, and character-driven storytelling. Beneath the glitz and glamor, it offers a sharp critique of celebrity culture, media manipulation, and the fickle nature of public attention. In this chapter, we'll explore the storytelling techniques that make *Chicago* such a powerful and enduring show, including its use of satire, morally ambiguous characters, and the interplay between spectacle and substance. These lessons can serve as valuable tools for writers, directors, and storytellers looking to create narratives that resonate with contemporary audiences while offering deeper social and cultural insights.

Satire as Social Commentary

One of the most powerful tools *Chicago* employs is **satire**, using humor and exaggeration to critique serious issues like corruption, the media, and the justice system. The entire premise of *Chicago* is built around the idea that murderers, through clever manipulation of the press and public opinion, can be turned into celebrities, effectively buying their way out of punishment.

This satirical lens allows the show to explore how easily the public can be swayed by sensationalism and how the justice system can be exploited by those with enough charm, money, or media attention. The musical numbers themselves often serve as commentary, like "All I Care About," where Billy Flynn, the slick lawyer, declares his "altruistic" intentions to help his clients while really only caring about fame and fortune. In songs like "Razzle Dazzle," Billy's strategy of distracting the jury with spectacle highlights the absurdity of a legal system more focused on theatrics than truth.

For writers, the lesson here is the power of **satire as a narrative device**. By using humor, irony, and exaggeration, *Chicago* exposes the flaws in societal systems, making a sharp statement about fame and justice while still entertaining the audience. Satire allows for a deeper commentary on important issues without being heavy-handed, and it encourages audiences to question the world around them. For those creating stories, especially in genres like comedy or drama, satire can be a powerful way to engage audiences while delivering a critique of cultural or political systems.

Morally Ambiguous Characters

One of the defining features of *Chicago* is its cast of **morally ambiguous characters**. Neither Roxie Hart nor Velma Kelly, the two main protagonists, can be considered traditional heroes. Both are murderers who show little remorse for their crimes, and both are driven primarily by their desire for fame and fortune rather than any sense of justice or morality. Billy Flynn, their lawyer, is equally unscrupulous, concerned only with how much money he can make off his clients and how much fame he can attain.

Despite their flaws, these characters are deeply compelling. Audiences are drawn to Roxie and Velma not because they are morally righteous but because they are human, ambitious, and relatable in their quest for survival and success. Their moral ambiguity makes them more complex, as they navigate a world where right and wrong are less important than winning the court of public opinion.

The key lesson for writers is that **flawed, morally ambiguous characters** can be just as, if not more, compelling than traditional heroes. Audiences are often more interested in characters who struggle with their darker impulses, who are driven by ambition or self-interest, and who reflect the moral complexities of real life. By allowing characters to be morally ambiguous, writers can create richer, more nuanced narratives that challenge the audience's expectations and provoke deeper engagement with the story.

The Power of Media Manipulation

A central theme in *Chicago* is the **power of the media** and its role in shaping public perception. Roxie and Velma's success in avoiding conviction hinges not on their innocence but on their ability to manipulate the press, turning their criminal trials into media spectacles. Billy Flynn understands this perfectly, and his primary role as a lawyer is to craft narratives that play well in the press, shifting public opinion in favor of his clients.

Through numbers like "We Both Reached for the Gun," where Billy literally acts as a ventriloquist while Roxie mouths his carefully crafted statements to the press, *Chicago* highlights the ease with which the media can be manipulated. The song makes it clear that truth is irrelevant; what matters is the story that sells. The press, eager for scandal and sensation, is complicit in this manipulation, eagerly turning murderers into stars and feeding the public's appetite for entertainment.

For storytellers, this offers a valuable lesson in how **media and perception** can play a critical role in shaping narrative outcomes. In a world saturated with information, the way a story is told often matters more than the truth itself. Writers can explore how characters use media to their advantage, shaping public perception to suit their needs, or they can highlight the dangers of a society where sensationalism trumps reality. This theme is particularly relevant in today's media-driven world, where truth is often overshadowed by spectacle.

The Allure and Danger of Fame

Another important theme in *Chicago* is the **allure of fame** and the lengths to which people will go to achieve it. Both Roxie and Velma see their criminal trials not as tragedies but as opportunities to become famous. Fame is portrayed as the ultimate goal, more valuable than justice, love, or even personal safety. This obsession with celebrity mirrors society's fascination with fame and the often toxic consequences of seeking it at any cost.

The musical critiques the idea that fame can erase one's past sins, as long as the public remains entertained. Roxie's dream sequence, "Roxie," reveals her fantasies of stardom, showing how deeply she craves the spotlight, regardless of the moral compromises she must make to get there. Velma, too, is driven by a desire to reclaim her fading fame, and both women are willing to lie, cheat, and manipulate their way back into the public eye.

For writers, this theme offers rich material for exploring characters' motivations and the darker side of ambition. The desire for fame can be a powerful motivator, but it can also lead characters down destructive paths. By showing both the allure and the **danger of fame**, storytellers can tap into a universal theme that resonates across genres. Fame, in the world of *Chicago*, is fleeting and often empty, leaving characters to grapple with the consequences of their pursuit once the spotlight fades.

The Role of Spectacle

Chicago is known for its use of **spectacle**, both in its vaudeville-inspired musical numbers and its overall aesthetic. The show presents itself as a series of performances within a performance, with characters frequently breaking the fourth wall to address the audience directly. This self-awareness adds to the satirical nature of the show, emphasizing that everything—whether it's a courtroom or a media interview—is a performance designed to entertain and manipulate.

The use of spectacle is particularly evident in numbers like "Razzle Dazzle," where Billy Flynn explains how to distract the jury with theatrics and charm rather than facts. The song's choreography and staging mirror the idea of courtroom trials as theatrical productions, complete with glittering lights and dazzling distractions. The audience is reminded that what they are watching is, in many ways, a reflection of how society consumes entertainment, whether it be in the form of news, trials, or celebrity gossip.

For writers, the lesson here is that **spectacle can serve a deeper narrative purpose**. It's not just about creating visually striking moments but about using spectacle to reflect the themes and tone of the story. In *Chicago*, the glitzy, exaggerated performances are a direct commentary on the superficiality of the justice system and the media. When used thoughtfully, spectacle can enhance the story's message, making the audience aware of the larger societal commentary at play.

The Fluidity of Morality

In *Chicago*, morality is fluid, and the lines between right and wrong are constantly blurred. The show doesn't offer clear heroes or villains, and its moral ambiguity invites the audience to question their own values. The legal system is portrayed as corrupt, and characters like Billy Flynn succeed not because they seek justice but because they know how to manipulate it.

This **fluidity of morality** allows the show to explore themes of survival, power, and the corrupting influence of ambition. Roxie and Velma aren't punished for their crimes; instead, they become stars, celebrated for their ability to navigate the system. The show doesn't offer a moral lesson in the traditional sense; rather, it forces the audience to confront the uncomfortable reality that in a world driven by spectacle and media, justice is often secondary to entertainment.

For writers, this fluidity of morality can be a powerful tool for creating complex narratives. Stories that challenge traditional notions of right and wrong often resonate more deeply because they reflect the complexities of real life. By allowing characters to operate in morally gray areas, writers can explore the tension between personal ambition and ethical compromise, creating richer, more thought-provoking stories.

Lessons from *Chicago* offer valuable insights into how storytelling can combine spectacle with substance, satire with social commentary, and moral ambiguity with character-driven narratives. Through its biting critique of fame, justice, and the media, *Chicago* reveals the darker side of human ambition and the lengths people will go to achieve success.

Writers and storytellers can draw inspiration from *Chicago*'s use of satire, its morally complex characters, and its exploration of media manipulation. By embracing these elements, creators can craft stories that not only entertain but also provoke thought, challenging audiences to question the systems and values that shape our world. Like *Chicago*, the most memorable stories are those that hold a mirror to society, revealing the flaws, contradictions, and truths that lie beneath the surface.

Lessons from the Great Shows: The Lion King

The Lion King explores the remarkable storytelling and thematic depth of one of the most beloved and successful musicals of all time. Based on the 1994 Disney animated film, *The Lion King* premiered on Broadway in 1997, with direction and design by Julie Taymor. The show's unforgettable blend of breathtaking visuals, innovative puppetry, a powerful score by Elton John and Tim Rice, and a universal story of responsibility, identity, and family has captivated audiences for decades.

At its heart, *The Lion King* is a coming-of-age tale set against the backdrop of the African savannah, following the young lion prince, Simba, as he grows from a carefree cub to a responsible king. The musical adds new layers to the film's already rich story, enhancing its emotional depth and cultural resonance. In this chapter, we'll explore the essential storytelling techniques that make *The Lion King* a standout production, including its use of universal themes, symbolism, music, and visual spectacle. We'll also look at the lessons that writers and creators can learn from the show's masterful blend of tradition, innovation, and emotional storytelling.

Universal Themes: Responsibility, Identity, and the Circle of Life

One of the most powerful aspects of *The Lion King* is its exploration of **universal themes** that resonate with audiences across cultures and generations. At its core, the story is about **responsibility** and **identity**—the journey of a young lion prince, Simba, who must confront his past and embrace his role as king in order to restore balance to the Pride Lands. This theme of growing up and accepting responsibility for one's actions is relatable to audiences of all ages, making *The Lion King* a timeless story.

The idea of **the "Circle of Life"** is a central theme that runs throughout the show, symbolizing the interconnectedness of all living things. Mufasa's lesson to Simba about the balance between predators and prey, life and death, reflects the broader theme of harmony in nature and the responsibility that comes with leadership. The Circle of Life is both a literal and metaphorical framework, underscoring the cyclical nature of life, death, and renewal, as well as the importance of each generation fulfilling its role in preserving that balance.

For storytellers, the lesson here is the power of **universal themes** that tap into fundamental human experiences. Themes like responsibility, the search for identity, and the idea of renewal through nature create emotional connections with the audience. By weaving these themes into the fabric of the narrative, *The Lion King* creates a story that feels both personal and epic, speaking to individual struggles while also addressing larger philosophical questions about life and leadership.

Character Arcs: Simba's Hero's Journey

Simba's journey follows the classic **hero's journey** or monomyth structure, a storytelling framework identified by Joseph Campbell. His path from innocence to experience, from exile to return, mirrors the arc of many traditional heroic narratives. In *The Lion King*, this journey is beautifully rendered, with each stage of Simba's development—his fall from grace, his time in exile, and his eventual return to reclaim his place as king—representing key moments of transformation.

Simba's character arc is particularly powerful because it is rooted in **personal growth and self-discovery**. At the beginning of the story, Simba is a carefree cub who dreams of becoming king without fully understanding the weight of that responsibility. His father, Mufasa, tries to teach him about the duties that come with leadership, but it isn't until Simba experiences tragedy—the death of his father and his own exile—that he begins to understand the importance of these lessons.

Simba's **internal conflict** is central to his journey. After his father's death, he is consumed by guilt and shame, manipulated by his uncle Scar into believing that he is responsible for the tragedy. This sense of guilt drives him to abandon his identity and live a carefree life in the jungle, avoiding his responsibilities. His eventual return to the Pride Lands, after being reminded of his true identity by Rafiki and Mufasa's spirit, marks the resolution of his internal conflict as he finally accepts his place in the circle of life.

For writers, the lesson from Simba's journey is the importance of **character arcs** that reflect meaningful internal growth. The external conflicts in the story—Scar's rise to power, the desolation of the Pride Lands—are important, but it is Simba's internal journey of self-acceptance and responsibility that gives the story its emotional weight. A well-crafted character arc allows the audience to connect with the protagonist on a deeper level, making the hero's triumph feel earned and resonant.

Symbolism and Cultural Resonance

The Lion King is filled with **symbolism** that adds layers of meaning to the story. One of the most prominent symbols is the **sunrise** that opens the musical, representing the beginning of a new life cycle and the birth of a future king. The recurring image of the sun rising and setting throughout the show mirrors the cyclical nature of the Circle of Life, with each new dawn bringing hope and renewal.

Mufasa's presence as a **spiritual guide** is another important symbol. After his death, Mufasa continues to influence Simba's life, appearing in the stars and in Simba's memories. His line, "Remember who you are," serves as a reminder of Simba's heritage and his role in the Circle of Life. Mufasa's appearance in the sky during a pivotal moment in the story reinforces the idea that ancestors and the past are always with us, guiding us toward our destiny.

The show also incorporates **African cultural elements**, blending storytelling traditions from the continent with Western theatrical forms. Julie Taymor's direction and design embrace African aesthetics through the use of masks, puppetry, and costume design that reflect the natural world and the cultural roots of the story. The use of the Zulu language in songs like "Circle of Life" and "He Lives in You" adds authenticity and depth, connecting the audience with the spiritual and cultural significance of the story.

For writers, the lesson here is the power of **symbolism and cultural resonance**. Symbols can serve as visual and thematic touchstones that reinforce the deeper meaning of the story. By drawing on cultural traditions and universal symbols, *The Lion King* creates a narrative that feels both specific to its setting and universally relatable. Writers can use symbolism to add depth and meaning to their stories, allowing audiences to engage with the narrative on multiple levels.

The Role of Music in Storytelling

Music plays a central role in *The Lion King*, not just as entertainment but as a tool for **emotional storytelling**. Elton John and Tim Rice's score, along with additional music by Hans Zimmer and Lebo M, elevates the story's emotional beats and deepens the audience's connection to the characters and themes. Songs like "Circle of Life," "Can You Feel the Love Tonight," and "He Lives in You" resonate not only because of their melodies but because of how they reflect the emotional and thematic core of the story.

For example, "Circle of Life" introduces the audience to the central theme of the story—the cyclical nature of life and the interconnectedness of all living things. This song sets the tone for the entire show, framing Simba's journey as part of something much larger than himself. "He Lives in You," which appears in the stage musical but not the original film, reinforces the idea that Mufasa's spirit lives on in Simba and within the Circle of Life, providing an emotional turning point in Simba's journey.

The lesson for storytellers is that **music can be a powerful tool for enhancing emotional and thematic resonance**. In *The Lion King*, the songs are not simply added to entertain but are integral to the narrative. They help convey the emotional stakes, highlight the central themes, and provide insight into the characters' inner lives. In any form of storytelling, music—or its narrative equivalent, such as internal monologue or symbolic imagery—can be used to reinforce the emotional core of the story.

Visual Spectacle and Innovation

One of the most memorable aspects of *The Lion King* is its **visual spectacle**. Julie Taymor's groundbreaking use of **puppetry, masks, and elaborate set design** creates a visually stunning experience that immerses the audience in the African savannah. From the opening number, where the animals gather to witness Simba's presentation, to the stampede scene that leads to Mufasa's death, the show's visual elements are integral to its storytelling.

The use of **puppetry and masks** allows the actors to embody animals in a way that feels both abstract and lifelike, adding a layer of artistry to the performance. The visual design of the show reflects the natural beauty of the savannah while also symbolizing the characters' inner worlds. For example, the larger-than-life puppet for Mufasa symbolizes his wisdom and strength, while Scar's angular, sharp design reflects his deceitful and dangerous nature.

The lesson here is the importance of **innovation in storytelling**. While *The Lion King* could have relied on traditional theatrical methods, it chose to push the boundaries of what was possible on stage, creating an immersive and unique experience. For writers and creators, this serves as a reminder to think outside the box and explore new ways of telling stories. Whether through visual design, narrative structure, or thematic exploration, innovation can set a story apart and create a lasting impact on the audience.

Redemption and the Importance of the Past

A key element of Simba's journey is the theme of **redemption** and the role of the past in shaping the future. Simba's exile is driven by his guilt over Mufasa's death, and his eventual return to the Pride Lands represents his redemption. However, in order to redeem himself, Simba must confront his past and accept responsibility for his actions.

The lesson Mufasa imparts to Simba—that the past is always with us but should not control our future—is central to Simba's growth. This message, delivered through the line "Remember who you are," encourages Simba to embrace both his past and his future, reclaiming his identity as the rightful king. The redemption arc in *The Lion King* reflects the broader theme of the Circle of Life, showing that renewal and growth are only possible when we acknowledge and learn from the past.

For storytellers, the theme of **redemption** can provide powerful emotional depth to a narrative. Characters who confront their past mistakes and seek redemption often resonate deeply with audiences, as their struggles mirror the human desire for forgiveness and growth. By incorporating themes of redemption and renewal, writers can create stories that offer both personal and universal insights into the human experience.

Lessons from *The Lion King* reveal the power of storytelling that is both universal and deeply personal. Through its exploration of themes like responsibility, identity, and the Circle of Life, *The Lion King* resonates with audiences on a profound emotional level. Its use of symbolism, music, visual spectacle, and character arcs enhances the storytelling, creating a rich and immersive experience that has captivated generations.

Writers and creators can learn from *The Lion King*'s ability to balance tradition with innovation, its masterful use of character development, and its exploration of timeless themes. By weaving together personal journeys with universal truths, storytellers can craft narratives that resonate deeply with audiences, just as *The Lion King* continues to do. The show's success lies not only in its spectacle but in its emotional and thematic richness, reminding us that the most powerful stories are those that speak to the core of the human experience.

Lessons from the Great Shows: Wicked

Wicked examines the storytelling brilliance behind one of Broadway's most iconic and beloved musicals. *Wicked*, with music and lyrics by Stephen Schwartz and a book by Winnie Holzman, first premiered in 2003 and quickly became a cultural phenomenon. Based on Gregory Maguire's novel *Wicked: The Life and Times of the Wicked Witch of the West*, the musical reimagines the world of *The Wizard of Oz* by focusing on the untold story of Elphaba, the Wicked Witch of the West, and her complex friendship with Glinda, the Good Witch. Through its exploration of identity, friendship, power, and destiny, *Wicked* offers a rich tapestry of themes and characters that resonate with audiences on a profound emotional level.

The show's success lies not only in its lush musical score and stunning visual design but in its ability to reframe a well-known story from a new perspective. *Wicked* asks audiences to reconsider what they think they know about good and evil, to question societal norms, and to empathize with misunderstood characters. In this chapter, we'll explore the key storytelling techniques that make *Wicked* a standout production and what lessons writers can draw from its complex characters, redefined narratives, and universal themes of friendship, identity, and moral ambiguity.

Reimagining a Classic Story from a New Perspective

One of the most remarkable aspects of *Wicked* is how it **reframes a classic story**—*The Wizard of Oz*—by shifting the focus from the familiar characters of Dorothy, the Scarecrow, and the Tin Man to the so-called "Wicked" Witch, Elphaba. In doing so, the show encourages the audience to question the traditional black-and-white depictions of good and evil. The Wicked Witch, a figure previously defined by her malevolence, becomes a sympathetic, misunderstood character, while characters previously seen as good, like the Wizard and even Glinda, are shown to have moral complexities.

By telling the story from Elphaba's perspective, *Wicked* challenges the audience's assumptions about right and wrong, demonstrating how **perspective shapes narrative**. Elphaba's journey—from an ostracized, green-skinned outsider to a powerful yet demonized figure—highlights how society often unfairly labels those who are different. The show explores how Elphaba's actions, viewed from another angle, are driven by courage, integrity, and a desire for justice, even though she is ultimately branded as "wicked."

For writers, the lesson here is the power of **reimagining familiar stories** from new perspectives. Taking a well-known narrative and examining it through the eyes of an antagonist or side character can provide fresh insights and create compelling new stories. By reframing the narrative, *Wicked* taps into universal themes of prejudice, power, and the complexity of human motivations, showing that no one is purely good or evil. Writers can explore the gray areas of morality by shifting focus in similar ways, offering audiences a deeper, more nuanced understanding of characters and situations.

COMPLEX AND SYMPATHETIC Characters

At the heart of *Wicked* are its two protagonists, **Elphaba** and **Glinda**, whose evolving relationship drives much of the story's emotional depth. Both characters are richly complex, with strengths, flaws, and moments of vulnerability. Elphaba is portrayed as intelligent, principled, and brave, yet also struggling with self-doubt and feelings of rejection.

Glinda, on the surface, is bubbly and popular, but she, too, faces her own internal struggles with insecurity, ambition, and the need for approval.

Their friendship forms the emotional core of the musical, and the show's greatest strength is how it allows these two women to grow and change over time. Neither Elphaba nor Glinda is perfect, and both make mistakes. However, their dynamic shows the importance of empathy, forgiveness, and understanding in relationships, and it also highlights the complexity of female friendship in a way that's rarely explored in musical theater.

The depth of Elphaba and Glinda's characterization is a reminder that **flawed and multifaceted characters** are often the most compelling. Elphaba is not simply a misunderstood hero; she is someone who grapples with her choices and is forced to make difficult moral decisions. Glinda, while initially vain and self-absorbed, shows growth throughout the show, ultimately realizing the costs of her ambition and her complicity in the political corruption of Oz.

For writers, the lesson is to **embrace complexity** in character development. Characters who are morally ambiguous, who struggle with internal conflicts, and who evolve over the course of the story feel more authentic and relatable to the audience. Elphaba and Glinda's friendship is so powerful because it is layered with tension, growth, and deep emotional connection. Writing characters who are both flawed and capable of change creates a dynamic narrative that resonates with audiences.

Thematic Depth: Power, Prejudice, and Identity

Wicked explores **power, prejudice, and identity** in profound ways, making it more than just a story about witches and magic. Elphaba's green skin serves as a metaphor for **otherness**, and her struggles with discrimination reflect broader societal issues about how people who are different are often marginalized or feared. Throughout the show, Elphaba's identity as an outsider shapes her worldview and motivates her actions, as she seeks both acceptance and justice in a world that is stacked against her.

The show also critiques the **corruption of power**, particularly through the character of the Wizard, who uses lies and propaganda to maintain control over the citizens of Oz. The Wizard's manipulation of public perception, branding Elphaba as the "Wicked Witch," serves as a commentary on how those in power can distort the truth to serve their own ends. This theme of power and control resonates with contemporary audiences, making *Wicked* relevant in discussions of politics, media, and the way marginalized voices are silenced.

Another central theme is the exploration of **identity** and self-acceptance. Elphaba's journey is not only about fighting external oppression but also about coming to terms with who she is and embracing her own power. Her iconic song, "Defying Gravity," is a turning point in the musical, where she rejects the expectations placed on her and decides to forge her own path, no matter the consequences. This moment is a declaration of independence and self-empowerment, making it one of the most emotionally resonant moments in the show.

For writers, *Wicked* offers lessons in how to weave **thematic depth** into a story. By addressing issues like power dynamics, prejudice, and identity, the musical speaks to universal concerns while also allowing for personal reflection. Writers can create stories with greater impact by exploring how societal forces shape individual lives and how characters grapple with their sense of self in a world that seeks to define them.

Moral Ambiguity and the Complexity of Good vs. Evil

One of the most significant lessons from *Wicked* is its exploration of **moral ambiguity** and the complexity of good versus evil. The musical asks the audience to reconsider what it means to be "good" or "wicked," showing that the labels we place on people are often a reflection of societal bias rather than objective truth. Elphaba is seen as "wicked" not because of her actions but because she refuses to conform to the expectations of those in power. Meanwhile, characters like the Wizard, who appears charming and benevolent, are revealed to be morally corrupt and self-serving.

This **subversion of traditional hero-villain dynamics** allows *Wicked* to delve into the gray areas of morality, where characters must navigate difficult ethical dilemmas and the consequences of their choices. The show does not offer easy answers—Elphaba's rebellion against the Wizard's regime is justifiable, but her methods are sometimes extreme. Glinda, while more complicit in the status quo, is not evil, but rather misguided by her own desire for popularity and power. This moral complexity invites the audience to engage with the story on a deeper level, encouraging them to think critically about the nature of justice, power, and individual responsibility.

For writers, the lesson is that **moral ambiguity** can lead to richer storytelling. Characters who exist in the gray areas of morality—who struggle with ethical dilemmas and whose actions are motivated by complex, sometimes conflicting, values—are often the most interesting and relatable. By avoiding clear-cut definitions of good and evil, writers can create narratives that challenge the audience's perceptions and provoke thoughtful reflection on human nature.

The Role of Music in Emotional Storytelling

Wicked's score, composed by Stephen Schwartz, plays a crucial role in conveying the emotional journey of its characters. Songs like "Defying Gravity," "For Good," and "Popular" are not just musical interludes but key moments that express the characters' inner turmoil, desires, and transformations. Music in *Wicked* serves as an emotional guide, helping the audience connect with the characters on a deeper level.

For example, "Defying Gravity" is not only a musical showstopper but also a pivotal moment in Elphaba's character arc. It is the point where she decides to embrace her identity and reject societal expectations, marking her transition from outcast to self-determined rebel. The song's soaring melody and powerful lyrics encapsulate Elphaba's emotional release, making it one of the most memorable and moving moments in the show. Similarly, "For Good," the duet between Elphaba and Glinda, provides emotional closure to their friendship. The song reflects on how their relationship has changed them both for the better, despite their differences and the paths they have chosen. The lyrics, which emphasize gratitude and forgiveness, add emotional depth to the show's ending, leaving the audience with a sense of bittersweet resolution. The lesson for writers is that **music (or its narrative equivalent, such as dialogue or imagery)** can enhance the emotional impact of a story. In *Wicked*, the music doesn't just support the narrative—it is an integral part of the storytelling, helping to communicate the characters' emotions and drive key plot points. Writers can achieve similar emotional resonance by carefully crafting key moments where characters reveal their inner selves, whether through song, monologue, or symbolic action.

The Importance of Visual Spectacle

In addition to its emotional and thematic depth, *Wicked* is known for its **visual spectacle**. The show's elaborate set designs, lighting, and special effects—such as Elphaba's flight during "Defying Gravity"—create a sense of wonder and immersion for the audience. Julie Taymor's imaginative staging, combined with the intricate costumes and magical elements, helps to transport the audience to the fantastical world of Oz while also reflecting the inner lives of the characters. The visual elements in *Wicked* are not just for show; they serve to enhance the themes and emotions of the story. For instance, the contrasting visual styles of Elphaba and Glinda—Elphaba's dark, sharp-edged costumes versus Glinda's light, shimmering gowns—reflect their different approaches to life and power. The set design, with its towering gears and clock motifs, symbolizes the mechanical and often heartless nature of the political system in Oz, further reinforcing the show's critique of corruption and control. For storytellers, the lesson here is the **importance of visual storytelling**. Whether in theater, film, or literature, the way a story looks can reinforce its themes and character arcs. Visual elements—whether it's a setting, costume, or symbol—can add layers of meaning to the narrative, helping to create a more immersive and emotionally resonant experience for the audience.

Lessons from *Wicked* offer invaluable insights into how to craft complex characters, explore moral ambiguity, and reimagine familiar stories in fresh and compelling ways. Through its rich character development, thematic depth, and stunning visual and musical storytelling, *Wicked* has become a timeless narrative that resonates with audiences on both an emotional and intellectual level. Writers and creators can draw inspiration from *Wicked*'s ability to challenge traditional narratives, its exploration of power and identity, and its nuanced portrayal of friendship and moral complexity. By embracing these storytelling techniques, creators can craft narratives that not only entertain but also provoke thought, encourage empathy, and leave a lasting impact on their audience. Like *Wicked*, the most powerful stories are those that dare to defy convention, question societal norms, and explore the full spectrum of human experience.

Lessons from the Great Shows: Rent

Rent delves into the ground-breaking impact and enduring appeal of one of the most influential musicals in modern theater. *Rent*, with music, lyrics, and book by Jonathan Larson, premiered in 1996 and revolutionized Broadway with its raw, contemporary approach to storytelling. The show, loosely based on Giacomo Puccini's opera *La Bohème*, follows a group of young artists in New York City's East Village as they navigate love, friendship, poverty, and the AIDS crisis in the late 1980s and early 1990s. With its themes of community, survival, and the fleeting nature of life, *Rent* captured the struggles and hopes of a generation and became an instant cultural phenomenon.

What makes *Rent* stand out is its ability to address serious social issues while celebrating the power of love, art, and resilience. Its use of rock music, its diverse and complex characters, and its unapologetic portrayal of real-world struggles set it apart from traditional Broadway fare. In this chapter, we'll explore the storytelling techniques that make *Rent* a timeless and emotionally resonant show, including its exploration of love and loss, its use of music as a narrative tool, and its message of community and living in the moment. These lessons provide valuable insights for writers and creators seeking to tell authentic, emotionally charged stories that resonate across generations.

Addressing Social Issues with Honesty and Compassion

One of the most significant aspects of *Rent* is its ability to **address pressing social issues**—specifically poverty, addiction, the AIDS crisis, and the LGBTQ+ experience—without sugarcoating or simplifying these struggles. Jonathan Larson's portrayal of characters living with HIV/AIDS, struggling with addiction, and dealing with the harsh realities of homelessness and financial instability was revolutionary for its time, particularly on Broadway, where such themes were rarely depicted with this level of honesty.

What makes *Rent* so impactful is that it approaches these issues with **compassion and empathy**. Characters like Angel and Collins, who are dealing with AIDS, are not defined by their illness. Instead, they are portrayed as vibrant, loving, and full of life, showing that even in the face of mortality, there is beauty, love, and connection. Similarly, characters like Roger, who struggles with addiction, and Mimi, who battles her own demons, are given complexity and depth. The show refuses to reduce them to stereotypes or victims; instead, it presents them as fully realized individuals whose struggles are part of their humanity but not their entirety.

The lesson here for writers is the importance of **addressing social issues with honesty** while also imbuing characters with **empathy and nuance**. *Rent* doesn't shy away from the harsh realities of life, but it also celebrates the resilience of the human spirit. By tackling difficult subjects head-on, while still allowing space for love, joy, and connection, writers can create stories that resonate on a deeper, more emotional level and reflect the complexities of real life.

LOVE, LOSS, AND LIVING in the Moment

At the heart of *Rent* is its exploration of **love, loss, and the importance of living in the moment**. The show's iconic song, "Seasons of Love," asks the poignant question: "How do you measure a year in the life?" The answer, of course, is love—measuring time not by material success or achievements but by the connections we make and the love we give and receive.

Throughout *Rent*, characters grapple with the idea of **mortality**—whether through the lens of the AIDS crisis or personal loss—and come to realize that life is fleeting. The urgency of "No day but today," a line echoed throughout the musical, becomes a mantra for the characters as they navigate their relationships and hardships. This message resonates not only with the LGBTQ+ community of the 1990s, many of whom were directly affected by the AIDS crisis, but also with anyone who has faced loss and understands the importance of cherishing the present.

In addition to romantic love, *Rent* explores the idea of **chosen family**, showing that the bonds between friends can be just as important as those with biological family members. The group of artists at the center of the show form a tight-knit community, supporting each other through illness, financial struggles, and personal crises. The love they share, in its many forms—platonic, romantic, and communal—becomes a source of strength and resilience.

For storytellers, the lesson from *Rent* is the power of **focusing on the present moment** and the emotional weight of human connection. By emphasizing the idea that life is unpredictable and fleeting, writers can tap into a universal truth that resonates deeply with audiences. Stories that highlight the importance of love, in all its forms, and that encourage characters to live fully in the moment often create an emotional bond with the audience, as these themes reflect fundamental human experiences.

Diverse and Complex Characters

One of *Rent*'s greatest strengths is its ensemble of **diverse and complex characters**, each with their own struggles, dreams, and fears. The musical gives voice to characters who are often marginalized or overlooked in mainstream media, particularly the LGBTQ+ community, people of color, and those living with HIV/AIDS. Characters like Angel, a drag queen and street performer, and Collins, a Black professor, are given equal weight in the narrative alongside characters like Mark, Roger, and Maureen.

Each character in *Rent* is multidimensional, and the musical avoids reducing them to their struggles. Angel is living with AIDS, but they are also full of love, compassion, and generosity, becoming a guiding light for the other characters. Mimi is a struggling addict, but she is also fiercely independent, passionate, and determined to live life on her own terms. Even characters like Maureen, who can be seen as self-absorbed or dramatic, are given moments of vulnerability and depth that make them feel real and relatable.

The lesson here is that **diverse representation matters**, and creating characters with complexity and depth is key to crafting authentic, emotionally resonant stories. By giving voice to characters from different backgrounds and allowing them to be fully realized individuals with strengths, flaws, and unique personalities, *Rent* creates a rich, layered narrative that reflects the diversity of the world. Writers can take inspiration from *Rent* by ensuring that their characters, particularly those from marginalized communities, are portrayed with the same nuance and complexity as any other character.

Music as a Narrative and Emotional Tool

Rent is a **rock musical**, and its score, with its blend of rock, pop, and musical theater, serves as a powerful **narrative and emotional tool**. The music in *Rent* isn't just there to entertain; it drives the story forward, reveals character motivations, and heightens emotional stakes. Songs like "One Song Glory" give insight into Roger's desperation to leave behind a meaningful legacy, while "Take Me or Leave Me" showcases the fiery, passionate relationship between Maureen and Joanne.

One of the most effective uses of music in *Rent* is its ability to convey the **emotional landscape of the characters**. "Will I?" is a heart-wrenching number where characters living with HIV/AIDS express their fear and uncertainty about the future. The simple, repetitive structure of the song reflects the cyclical nature of their thoughts, capturing the deep anxiety of facing a life-threatening illness. On the other hand, songs like "La Vie Bohème" celebrate the rebellious, artistic spirit of the characters, using upbeat rhythms and playful lyrics to create a sense of community and joy amidst their struggles.

For writers, the lesson here is that **music (or its narrative equivalent in non-musical media)** can be used to enhance emotional storytelling. In *Rent*, the music serves as both a narrative device and an emotional anchor, allowing the audience to connect with the characters on a deeper level. Writers can achieve similar effects by carefully crafting moments that reveal characters' inner emotions, using dialogue, imagery, or symbolic actions to create emotional resonance.

The Power of Community

At its core, *Rent* is a story about **community**—the idea that, in the face of hardship, people find strength in each other. The group of friends at the center of the show—Mark, Roger, Mimi, Angel, Collins, Maureen, and Joanne—come from different backgrounds, but they are united by their shared experiences of poverty, illness, and love. Throughout the musical, they support each other in ways that biological families often can't, forming a chosen family that becomes their anchor in difficult times.

The community in *Rent* is not without its challenges. The characters argue, make mistakes, and sometimes hurt each other, but they always come back together, recognizing that their bond is what sustains them. This portrayal of community reflects the real-world struggles of many people living through the AIDS crisis, who relied on their friends and chosen families for support when traditional systems failed them.

The lesson for storytellers is the power of **depicting strong, supportive communities** in narratives. Stories that explore the dynamics of friendships and chosen families can resonate deeply with audiences, particularly those who find strength in their own communities. By showing characters who lift each other up in times of crisis, writers can create narratives that reflect the importance of human connection and the resilience that comes from standing together.

Authenticity and the Rawness of Life

One of the most striking qualities of *Rent* is its **authenticity**. Jonathan Larson wrote the musical with a deep understanding of the struggles faced by young artists in New York City, particularly those affected by poverty, addiction, and the AIDS crisis. His passion for telling their stories with honesty and integrity shines through in every aspect of the show. The rawness of *Rent*—its unapologetic portrayal of difficult subjects, its gritty setting, and its emotionally charged characters—gives it a sense of immediacy and truth that resonates with audiences.

The authenticity of *Rent* is perhaps most evident in its central message: **No day but today**. This idea, repeated throughout the show, reflects the urgency of living fully in the present, especially in the face of uncertain futures. The characters in *Rent* are flawed, struggling, and sometimes broken, but they are also vibrant, passionate, and alive. The show's refusal to shy away from the messiness of life—its triumphs and failures, its joy and pain—gives it an emotional depth that continues to resonate with audiences.

For writers, the lesson from *Rent* is the importance of **authentic storytelling**. Stories that embrace the rawness and complexity of life, that don't shy away from difficult emotions or messy situations, often feel the most real and impactful. Writers can draw from their own experiences or the experiences of those around them to create stories that reflect the truth of the human condition, capturing both its beauty and its challenges.

Lessons from *Rent* offer invaluable insights into how to tell authentic, emotionally charged stories that resonate across generations. Through its exploration of love, loss, community, and the struggles of marginalized individuals, *Rent* has become a timeless narrative that speaks to the human experience. Its unapologetic approach to addressing social issues, its diverse and complex characters, and its use of music to convey deep emotions make it a powerful example of how storytelling can both entertain and provoke thought.

Writers and creators can learn from *Rent*'s ability to tackle difficult subjects with compassion and honesty, its focus on community and chosen family, and its message of living fully in the moment. By embracing these storytelling techniques, creators can craft narratives that not only reflect the realities of life but also inspire empathy, connection, and hope in their audiences. Like *Rent*, the most impactful stories are those that capture the rawness of life and remind us of the importance of love, friendship, and resilience.

Good luck with your next great show and your career.

Andrew

Don't miss out!

Visit the website below and you can sign up to receive emails whenever Andrew Parry publishes a new book. There's no charge and no obligation.

https://books2read.com/r/B-A-FROLC-YWXCF

BOOKS 2 READ

Connecting independent readers to independent writers.

9 798227 509673